Race, Class, and Politics
in the Cappuccino City

Race, Class, and Politics in the Cappuccino City

DEREK HYRA

The University of Chicago Press
Chicago and London

The University of Chicago Press, Chicago 60637

The University of Chicago Press, Ltd., London

Published 2017

Printed in the United States of America

26 25 24 23 22 21 20 19 18 17   1 2 3 4 5

ISBN-13: 978-0-226-44936-4 (cloth)

ISBN-13: 978-0-226-44953-1 (paper)

ISBN-13: 978-0-226-44967-8 (e-book)

DOI: 10.7208/chicago/9780226449678.001.0001

Cover photo by Jim Stroup

Library of Congress Cataloging-in-Publication Data

Names: Hyra, Derek S., author.

Title: Race, class, and politics in the cappuccino city / Derek Hyra.

Description: Chicago ; London : The University of Chicago Press, 2017. |
    Includes bibliographical references and index.

Identifiers: LCCN 2016037402 | ISBN 9780226449364 (cloth : alk. paper) |
    ISBN 9780226449531 (pbk. : alk. paper) | ISBN 9780226449678 (e-book)

Subjects: LCSH: Gentrification—Social aspects—Washington (D.C.) |
    Gentrification—Political aspects—Washington (D.C.) | African American
    neighborhoods—Washington (D.C.) | Inner cities—Washington (D.C.) |
    Urban renewal—Washington (D.C.) | Washington (D.C.)—Social
    conditions—21st century. | Washington (D.C.)—Race relations—Economic
    aspects. | Equality—Washington (D.C.)

Classification: LCC HT177.W3 H97 2017 | DDC 307.3/41609753—dc23 LC
    record available at https://lccn.loc.gov/2016037402

♾ This paper meets the requirements of ANSI/NISO Z39.48–1992
(Permanence of Paper).

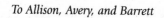

To Allison, Avery, and Barrett

CONTENTS

ACKNOWLEDGMENTS

This book would not have come to fruition without the support of several key institutions and organizations as well as many individuals. First, I would like to thank two academic institutions, Virginia Tech (VT) and American University (AU). I initially conceived this book in 2007 while working for the federal government in Washington, DC, and knew I needed to be in academia to pull it off. VT's College of Architecture and Urban Studies, its School of Public and International Affairs, and its Urban Affairs and Planning Program provided me an associate-level faculty position and a wonderful scholarly home for beginning this investigation. Jim Bohland (retired), Jack Davis, Casey Dawkins (University of Maryland), Sonia Hirt (University of Maryland), Gerry Kearns (National University of Ireland–Maynooth), Paul Knox, Robert Lang (University of Nevada–Las Vegas), John Randolph (retired), and Karen Till (National University of Ireland–Maynooth) all played critical roles in bringing me to VT, and I am very appreciative of their support.

During my first VT semester, I met Karen Roberto, Director of the Institute for Society, Culture, and Environment. Karen and I instantly connected, and she graciously provided funding for my Washington, DC, neighborhood research. A critical ingredient of a rich ethnographic study is time off from teaching, and Karen provided course release funds so I could conduct my fieldwork. I cannot thank Karen enough for her encouragement and financial support.

A number of VT colleagues also supported this book in a variety of ways. I would like to thank Ralph Buehler for his DC bike conversations, Margaret Cowell for her DC economy insights, and Shalini Misra for her thoughts on how the District has globalized. I also would like to thank Giselle Datz, Matthew Dull, Adam Eckerd, Anne Khademian, Ted Koebel, Patrick Roberts, Thomas Sanchez, and Kris Wernstedt for providing a thought-provoking, interdisciplinary academic learning environment, which helped to cultivate my ideas. I owe much gratitude as well to my outstanding VT graduate research assistants, Allison Heck, Priscila Izar, and Raksha Vasudevan, for their invaluable transcription, archival data collection, and editorial assistance.

In 2014, I was offered a faculty position at American University in the School of Public Affairs within the Department of Public Administration and Policy. The post came along with the opportunity to establish a research facility, the Metropolitan Policy Center. So I departed VT and started at AU as I wrapped up this book. My AU colleagues have provided an incredibly fertile academic environment in which to finish it. I thank Michael Bader, Scott Bass, Carolyn Gallaher, Sonya Grier, Bradley Hardy, Barbara Romzek, Meagan Snow, and Brett Williams. I also thank my AU students, including Meghan Doughty, Trevor Langan, Will Perkins, Statia Thomas, Carly Weted, Brandie Williams, and James Wright, for supporting the book's completion in a variety of ways. Lastly, I want to thank the VT and AU students who participated in my Washington, DC, Planning, Development, and Politics courses for deepening several of my thoughts on the District.

Many scholars outside VT and AU contributed immensely to these pages. Much appreciation goes to Scott Allard, Eli Anderson, Ryan Centner, Herb Gans, Howard Gillette, Ed Glaeser, Kathryn Howell, Amanda Huron, Jackelyn Hwang, Danilo Pelleteire, Sabiyha Prince, Jake Rugh, Clarence Stone, Tom Sugrue, Brandi Thompson Summers, Jeff Timberlake, Liza Weinstein, Bill Wilson, and Sharon Zukin. Each of these individuals provided important feedback that strengthened the book. I particularly would like to thank Blair Ruble, who read the entire manuscript. His insightful comments and suggestions, as well as timely words of inspiration, kept me focused on the project's completion. I owe another debt of gratitude to my undergraduate and graduate academic mentors, Michael Dawson, Jack Dovidio, Steve Fawcett, Rhonda Levine, the late Manning Marable, Omar McRoberts, Saskia Sassen, and Richard Taub, who provided the scholarly foundation on which this book stands.

In preparing this manuscript, I had the privilege of testing out preliminary ideas at different workshops, seminars, and conference venues. The American Sociological Association's 2015 Annual Meeting; American University's Center on Health, Risk and Society seminar series; George Mason University's Graduate Student Public Sociology Conference; University of Chicago's Workshop on City, Society, and Space; the University of Oxford's Ethnography, Diversity and Urban Space Conference; the Washington, DC, Studies Writing Group; and Yale University's Urban Ethnography Workshop all provided invaluable opportunities to share and receive feedback on different chapters. The critiques I received at these gatherings greatly refined my thoughts. At the University of Chicago Press, I thank the two anonymous reviewers, whose excellent comments and suggestions sharpened my conceptual and theoretical contributions.

No successful ethnographic investigation can be accomplished without the support of key community stakeholders and residents. To this end, I would like to thank foremost the Organizing Neighborhood Equity (ONE DC) staff. To Dominic Moulden, Rosemary Ndubuizu, Jessica Gordon Nembhard, Gloria Robinson, and Jessica Rucker: your organizing efforts at ONE DC are inspirational, and I truly appreciate your willingness to allow me to be part of your important work. I also owe a debt of gratitude to Tim Christensen, Alex Padro, and Scott Pomeroy for guiding me through various community niches within Shaw/U Street. A special shout-out goes to Curtis "C-Webb" Mozie and all the ballplayers at the Kennedy Recreation Center.

It is a privilege and a pleasure to publish with the University of Chicago Press. The press's tradition of printing pioneering urban ethnographies is unmatched. I thank Doug Mitchell for his unwavering manuscript support, and Kyle Wagner for seamlessly managing all the production details. I also would like to thank former staff member Mara Naselli and also Sandra Hazel for their wonderful editorial assistance in preparing this book for publication.

My friends and family are my primary motivators. Matthew Goodman, David Kirk, Percival Matthews, Robert Renner, and John Wedges have been important parts of my life, and their continued encouragement, advice, and friendship keep me focused on our collective social justice calling. I also want to thank Chris Ballard, Marie Johns, John Komoroske, Brett Libresco, Michael McManus, Chad Moutray, Mike Schaub, and Jeremy Sheridan for their friendship, and for helping me obtain a better understanding of Washington, DC's regional economy and political landscape.

It would have been almost inconceivable to write this book without my family's steadfast loving support. I want to thank deeply the Hyras, Deschamps, and Matthieus for all their love and encouragement. I especially want to acknowledge my wife, Allison. Her commitment to our family and my scholarly pursuits never ceases to amaze me. I am so happy and honored to be on life's journey with her. Since my last ethnographic book, two special people have entered my life: Avery and Barrett. Watching my children grow up is such a precious experience. Their joy and laughter constantly remind me that the world is a magical place. And the pixie dust I receive from them and my entire support network made this book possible.

PART ONE

The Setting

ONE

Making the Gilded Ghetto:
Welcome to 14th Street

Tim Christensen, the White, middle-aged president of the Logan Circle Community Association, enthusiastically describes the new farmers' market that opened at Washington, DC's 14th and U Streets intersection:

> Oh, it's really nice. There're produce stands. . . . They've really diversified, so they go way beyond produce. So you can get organic, grass-fed meat and all kinds of really interesting pastas and that sort of thing. There's a pasta guy, and he's Italian. . . . His pasta is unbelievable. He has this ravioli, duck-egg ravioli, where he puts a duck-egg yolk inside a ravioli package raw and refrigerates it, and he suggests having it for brunch with bacon and hash brown potatoes. It's unbelievable! . . . At 14th and U, who would have thought?

Not too long ago, this intersection was one of the city's most infamous drug markets, and was described as such by two African American, Pulitzer Prize–winning journalists. Leon Dash designated it the "heart of Washington's drug corridor" during the late 1980s, with its "clusters of drug dealers, addicts and jugglers standing on all four corners of the intersection."[1] Eugene Robinson explained that throughout that decade, "U Street and its environs had become one of the city's most notorious open-air illegal drug markets, offering mostly heroin . . . [and] quickly diversifying into cocaine."[2] Today, this once infamous drug market has been transformed into a thriving farmers' market.

Just a block north of the 14th and U Farmers' Market, Shaw/U Street's economic and racial transformation is starkly apparent. For years, the northwest side of the intersection housed the AM.PM Carry Out, an "old school" soul food breakfast and lunch takeout (fig. 1). Like New York City bodegas, the carryouts in DC serve moderately priced food to people on the go.

Figure 1. AM.PM Carry Out.

Most of AM.PM's customers were working-class African Americans. In 2010, however, it closed due to "lease issues," most likely escalating commercial rent.[3] In 2014, the former carryout location, under different management, became Provision No. 14 (P14), an upscale neo-American culinary experience where patrons can order a $28 burger of foie gras, truffles, goat cheese, and lobster.

Next to this posh eatery is Martha's Table, a nonprofit social services organization that distributes almost six hundred thousand meals yearly to homeless families and at-risk youth. Martha's has been on this block since 1982.[4] In the mornings, long lines of homeless people, mostly African American, wait to enter Martha's. After eating, many hang around—some even camp out with their belongings all day—to catch up with friends and pass the time until their next meal is served.[5]

Across the street from P14 and Martha's are two luxury condominium high-rises, Langston Lofts and Union Row (fig. 2), built in 2005 and 2007 respectively. Their contemporary urban design, with large exposed steel structures and iron patios, contrasts with the iron bars once covering the windows at the carryout. The condo units offer upscale urban loft living, with large floor-to-ceiling windows, wood floors, open floor plans, granite countertops, and stainless steel kitchen appliances. In 2015, one-bedroom units in the Union Row complex were listed between $350,000 and $500,000, two-bedrooms between $600,000 and $900,000.[6] The base of Union Row's commercial space houses Yes! Organic, a newly established natural grocery market, and Eatonville, an upscale, soul food–style restaurant where urban professionals enjoy pecan-crusted trout, fried chicken, and live jazz.

The first-floor commercial space of the Langston Lofts development is occupied by Busboys and Poets, a bookstore, coffeehouse, wine bar, performance venue, and restaurant all in one, which pays homage to the community's African American heritage.[7] At any given time, Black, White, and Hispanic students, professionals, and urban hipsters use their laptops at communal tables, peruse the bookshelves, or visit with friends seated at the long dark-granite bar, on fabric and faux-leather couches, or at dining tables. The private Langston Hughes Room at the back of the restaurant holds a stage for book launches, poetry readings, and other performances. In this presentation space, the likes of Cornel West, Ralph Nader, and Eve Ensler have spoken on race, politics, gender, and culture to people enjoying a cappuccino, beer, or glass of wine.

Figure 2. Union Row and Langston Lofts.

Those living in Union Row or Langston Lofts, dining at Eatonville and Busboys, or shopping at Yes! Organic stand in sharp contrast to some of those eating just across 14th Street. Eatonville, Busboys, Yes! Organic, and P14 cater to the more affluent new arrivals—the mainly White but also Black and Hispanic, gay and straight professionals; Martha's serves, and AM.PM once served, the longer-term, low- and moderate-income Black population that formerly was the majority in this community.

From the Dark to the Gilded Ghetto

In the 1960s, a leading Swedish anthropologist, Ulf Hannerz, and a prominent American anthropologist, Elliot Liebow, studied the impoverished Washington, DC's Shaw/U Street neighborhood. Their work resulted in two urban classics: Hannerz's *Soulside* and Liebow's *Tally's Corner*.[8] While each explored different sections of Shaw/U Street—Liebow studied a carryout much like AM.PM, and Hannerz a street near the community's geographic center—they both observed severe deprivation. As Liebow noted, the area at the time was nearly all Black and had the city's "highest rate of persons receiving public assistance; the highest rate of illegitimate live births; the highest rate of births not receiving prenatal care; the second highest rate of persons eligible for surplus food; and the third highest rate of applicants eligible for medical assistance."[9]

Despite their setting in a bleak neighborhood environment, these books changed how people across the globe viewed inner-city Black American life. Through their detailed ethnographic accounts, the authors showcased the human side of the ghetto and described the complex strategies people used to organize their lives as they struggled to survive amid concentrated poverty. For Hannerz and Liebow in the 1960s, Shaw/U Street represented, like New York City's Harlem and Chicago's Bronzeville, the quintessential Black American ghetto.[10]

From the 1960s until the 1990s, Shaw/U Street was a space for understanding what historian Arnold Hirsch coined the "second ghetto," and what Kenneth B. Clark labeled the "dark ghetto." Hirsch's *Making the Second Ghetto* and Clark's *Dark Ghetto* explained the powerful forces and detrimental outcomes arising from the formation of socially walled-off, impoverished, inner-city Black spaces during the mid-twentieth century.[11] The decisions of White-controlled city councils, planning commissions, and public housing authorities to concentrate high-rise public housing in certain neighborhoods; the decisions of White-controlled banks to redline and deny credit to African Americans; and the decisions of White-operated companies to leave inner-city areas were critical to the downward spiral of these neighborhoods into concentrated poverty pockets.[12] The harmful influence of concentrated poverty on individuals living in these neighborhoods was not labeled as neighborhood effects until years later by urban sociologist William Julius Wilson, but the influence these areas had on dysfunctional behaviors such as crime, drug use, poor school performance, and teen pregnancy, as well as poor health outcomes, were duly noted by Clark.[13]

Yet while Shaw/U Street once symbolized the dark ghetto, today it represents the *gilded ghetto*. In *Dark Ghetto*, Clark coined *gilded ghetto* to describe the similar pathologies of the affluent in the segregated White suburbs. "There is a tendency toward pathology in the gilded suburban ghetto," he wrote. "An emptiness reflecting a futile struggle to find substance and worth through the concretes of things and possessions. . . . The residents of the gilded ghetto may escape by an acceptance of conformity, by the deadly ritual of alcoholism, by absorption in work, or in the artificial and transitory excitement of illicit affairs."[14] Clark saw in the suburban ghetto ill behaviors comparable to those occurring in inner-city Black America.

This book, which analyzes the making of the gilded ghetto, uses the term not as a reference to suburban challenges or pathologies but rather to indicate the intricate social and economic redevelopment processes, and outcomes, associated with the twenty-first-century transformation of second ghettos. Once places where poverty, drugs, and violence proliferated, these areas have become spaces where farmers' markets, coffee shops, dog parks, wine bars, and luxury condominiums now concentrate. The transition of American urban "no-go" Black zones to hip, cool places filled with chic restaurants, trendy bars, and high-priced apartment buildings defines the gilded ghetto. My contemporary use and redefinition of the gilded ghetto both references and explains what happens when those who, in the past, would have settled in the suburbs instead choose to reside in the dark ghetto.[15]

This monumental redevelopment trend is occurring not just in Washington, DC, but elsewhere as part of a larger national pattern. The 2000s, compared with the 1980s and '90s, saw an increase in the percentage of low-income minority neighborhoods that were redeveloped. Urban sociologist Ann Owens, who assessed the redevelopment patterns of metropolitan neighborhoods between 1970 and 2010, predicted that persistent racial stereotyping of minority neighborhoods, especially those with a large African American presence, would make those areas least likely to redevelop.[16] While in the 1980s and '90s this hypothesis was true, her data surprisingly revealed that something changed in the 2000s. In the 1990s, only 11 percent of urban minority neighborhoods redeveloped, but this rose to 17 percent in the 2000s. Owens speculated that the increased rate of African American inner-city redevelopment was partly due to the unexpected influx of White residents to these areas. In a subsequent study, urban planners Lance Freeman and Tiancheng Cai provided evidence that supported Owens's hunch and showed that compared with the 1990s, the percentage of urban Black neighborhoods experiencing a significant White influx doubled in the 2000s. As more Whites were willing to move to once impoverished African American neighborhoods, gentrification rates skyrocketed.[17]

A 2015 *Governing Magazine* report revealed that in the fifty largest US cities, only 9 percent of low-income tracts gentrified in the 1990s, while in the 2000s the gentrification rate increased to nearly 20 percent.[18] Features of the gilded ghetto can be seen in Boston's Roxbury, New York City's Harlem, Atlanta's Sweet Auburn District, Miami's Overtown, New Orleans' Tremé, Pittsburgh's Hill District, Kansas City's 18th and Vine District, Chicago's Bronzeville, Houston's Freemen's Town, San Francisco's Fillmore District, and Portland's Albina community. These Black urban neighborhoods saw open-air, illicit drug markets replaced by gourmet food markets.[19] The "iconic ghettos" are becoming gilded ghettos.[20]

Shaw/U Street experienced tremendous demographic shifts as it redeveloped. In 1970, the community was 90 percent Black; however, by 2010, African Americans comprised only 30 percent of its population.[21] While the proportion of the community's Black population declined, the White percentage rose substantially, particularly in the 2000s. Whites represented 23 percent of the Shaw/U Street population in 2000, rising to 53 percent by 2010.[22] As the community received an influx of Whites, property values dramatically increased 145 percent between 2000 and 2010, well above the city's overall rate during the same time period.[23]

Atypical Gentrification

While this might seem similar to a typical White-led gentrification scenario, it is not. Shaw/U Street is not going through the gentrification experience we have become accustomed to in US cities, in which young artists, mainly White, move into a low-income minority area, the area becomes hip, and then professionals arrive.[24] Next, property values escalate, then the former residents are displaced, and a new neighborhood emerges.

Shaw/U Street's redevelopment processes are much more complicated and complex. For instance, several White newcomers proclaim that they sought this particular community because it represents an opportunity to experience and participate in an "authentic" Black space. Whereas aspects of

Black culture have been used to sell music for years, only recently have they been commoditized to market neighborhood redevelopment.[25] The general perception has been that when a neighborhood was coined or labeled Black, it stimulated White flight.[26] Nowadays, in some circumstances, such a designation stimulates a White influx. Inner-city real estate developers name their new luxury buildings after celebrated African Americans, such as Langston Hughes and Duke Ellington. Area restaurants mimic this African American naming game: Marvin, which acknowledges DC-born Motown sensation Marvin Gaye, is one of the most popular eateries along 14th Street. Thus, as the neighborhood redevelops it retains part of its African American identity, and this identity is critical to the making of the gilded ghetto. Rather than abandoning its Black history, Shaw/U Street's revitalization is closely tied to the community's African American past.

In addition, despite huge increases in property values, a sizable low-income African American population remains, living primarily in subsidized housing. Unlike several inner-city communities whose public housing stock is managed by local public housing authorities, a large proportion of Shaw/U Street's affordable housing is owned and managed by area churches, enabling thousands of low-income and working-class African Americans to stay.[27] In 2015, DC mayor Muriel Bowser and US Department of Housing and Urban Development secretary Julián Castro strolled through the neighborhood and touted it as a successful mixed-income model due to its ample stock of affordable housing.[28] Subsidized housing helps to maintain the community's racial diversity. As Novella, a longtime African American resident of one of the church-owned, subsidized developments, declares, "I will be the last fly in the milk bowl. I'm not leaving this community."

On the surface, Shaw/U Street, compared with many DC neighborhoods, appears integrated. Figure 3 displays the percentage of African American residents for census tracts throughout the city. Shaw/U Street clearly has a number of tracts that vary racially, while most other sections of the city contain a very high or low percentage of African Americans. The community contains the underclass—the gangbanger, the homeless, the poor; and the new (upper) middle class—the young Obama political appointee, the lobbyist, the lawyer, the high-tech programmer, and the professional same-sex couple.

Some commercial establishments and public spaces seemingly display racial and economic integration, but delving deeper into the neighborhood's social fabric uncovers more economic and racial segregation than at first glance—*diversity segregation*. Diversity segregation occurs when racially, ethnically, and economically disparate people live next to one another, but

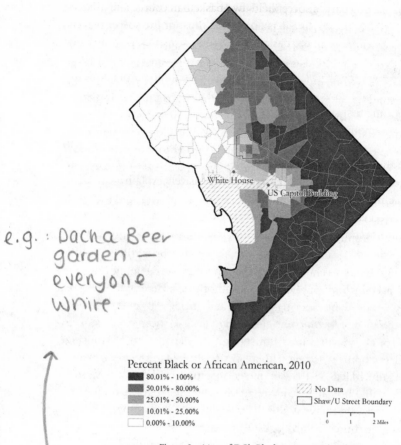

e.g. : Dacha Beer garden — everyone white.

Percent Black or African American, 2010
■ 80.01% - 100%
■ 50.01% - 80.00%
■ 25.01% - 50.00%
■ 10.01% - 25.00%
□ 0.00% - 10.00%

▨ No Data
□ Shaw/U Street Boundary

0   1   2 Miles

Figure 3. Map of DC's Black percentage in 2010.

not alongside one another. In other words, on the surface the community looks diverse, but in actuality is socially segregated.

The U Street Neighborhood Civic Association and the Logan Circle Community Association consist mainly of White residents organized to enhance the economic viability of the neighborhood, while Organizing Neighborhood Equity and the East Civic Association are predominately African American and serve the interests of the low-income minority populations fighting to remain there. Only a few associations have a mixed racial and class composition, such as the Convention Center Community Association, which tries to address multiple neighborhood preferences.

Public spaces, such as parks and recreation centers, also tend to be segregated. For instance, a park in the center of the community contains four distinct spaces: a dog park, a soccer field, two basketball courts, and a skate-board area. Most of the dog walkers are White, most of the soccer players are Hispanic, and almost all the basketball players are Black. The only truly integrated park space is the skateboard area, where teenagers of all races help one another with their latest tricks. Rather than a model of social in-tegration, Shaw/U Street is filled with pockets of micro-level segregation.

This is not the first study to highlight that redeveloping mixed-income, mixed-race neighborhoods contain micro-level segregation. There is an excel-lent investigation of micro segregation in Boston's South End by sociologist Laura Tach.[29] But while Tach's research deftly uncovered the phenomenon of micro-level segregation, this book more comprehensively explains why it oc-curs and what might be done to address it.

Shaw/U Street is a vibrant and inclusive neighborhood, at least compared with other more economically and racially homogeneous DC neighbor-hoods, yet it is still struggling with the legacy of racial segregation and dis-crimination. While this community once suffered from high rates of poverty, drugs, and crime, some of its White newcomers believe that elements of this past make it edgy and authentic. Some even talk about the occasional car-jackings, muggings, and shootings as if these things were cool, like a true-life version of the popular HBO series *The Wire*, while some low-income Black residents discuss crime as if they fear being victimized.[30] Social disconnects such as these lead to intense frictions and tensions.

yoga, cafés, wine, beer gardens. /

Additionally, the community has an African American identity that is be-ing used to entice newcomers, yet its African American population is losing its political power, which drives the proliferation of certain amenities that fit the preferences of newcomers over long-term residents. But the loss is not just political but also cultural, exacerbating resentment and public withdrawal among longtime residents. While some *New York Times* and *Washington Post* reporters and local political leaders claim that Shaw/U Street is a successful model of a mixed-income, mixed-race community, in reality it suffers from diversity segregation; and this, in part, explains why low-income people, who are able to stay in affordable housing, are not more fully benefiting from the economic changes that have taken place.[31]

Gentrification Theories and On-the-Ground Mixed-Income Living

In the 2000s, compared with the 1990s, gentrification was more present across urban America, generating much literature addressing its causes, particularly in African American inner-city neighborhoods.[32] Frequently,

the gentrification literature debates whether production or consumption explanations drive redevelopment.[33] Production scholars tend to assume that
public policies and economic circumstances encourage investments and attract newcomers to once economically neglected communities, while the
consumption camp argues that cultural tastes and preferences shape gentrification patterns.[34] We know a great deal from John Arena, Edward Goetz,
Jason Hackworth, and Lawrence Vale about how federal housing policies,
such as public housing reforms, are associated with inner-city gentrification.[35]
Moreover, we understand from scholars including Michelle Boyd, Lance
Freeman, and Mary Pattillo how changing Black middle-class consumption
patterns and preferences relate to the redevelopment of impoverished African American neighborhoods.[36] However, we know much less about how
global and federal forces interact to explain urban redevelopment patterns,
and why upper-income Whites are now attracted to formerly low-income
African American communities.[37]

I argue that both production and consumption processes are important
in explaining gentrification, and I do not try to resolve this gentrification
debate in the pages that follow. Rather, my investigation showcases how political, economic, and cultural circumstances set the context for gentrification,
and explains that both political decisions and new urban living preferences
and consumption patterns result in neighborhood change. This investigation, more than prior neighborhood change studies, explains how external
community political and economic circumstances and emerging White preferences for inner-city African American neighborhoods drive the transition
from the dark to the gilded ghetto.

Another core question within the literature is whether gentrification
leads to residential displacement. Quantitative studies by Lance Freeman
and Frank Braconi, and others, suggest that residential displacement is less
likely in gentrifying neighborhoods than in neighborhoods where property
values are stable.[38] In contrast, a host of qualitative investigations, including
my own, rigorously document forced residential displacement in communities experiencing gentrification.[39] However, these qualitative studies are
unable to systematically determine the scale of displacement, and whether
it can be linked solely to the process of gentrification.

While the gentrification literature importantly examines whether residential
displacement occurs alongside redevelopment, this book redirects the focus to
whether low-income people who are able to stay benefit in meaningful ways.[40]
Compared with other gentrification issues, this important topic receives much
less scholarly attention.[41] Shaw/U Street's long-term residents, newcomers, and
key community stakeholders debate whether the community's transformation

is benefiting low-income residents. Theresa, a civically active African American resident of a subsidized housing complex, speaks about the professional newcomers who believe that their neighborhood presence will improve opportunities for low-income residents:

> Just because you've a certain level of opportunity in your life does not mean that that has transferred to everybody in your community. Because you've had the ability to go to college. Because you've had the ability to get a job. Because you didn't have a problem with those things. No matter what color you are, doesn't mean that every other person has had that opportunity in this community. I mean, we have kids in this community whose parents were pimps, whose mothers were prostitutes, who . . . take care of their parents because their parents are drug addicts. I mean, these are the kids we're dealing with now. I mean . . . they [newcomers] think that they're improving the community 'cause they want to do things like have dog parks. In their eyes, that's improvement.

The social tensions are evident. Not all low-income residents are convinced that mixed-income living, and the community improvements it potentially brings, will improve their lives.

Other residents and Shaw/U Street stakeholders claim benefits for low-income people able to stay in the neighborhood. Alex Padro, a Hispanic civic leader who has lived in the community since 1994, remarks, "But the thing that is most compelling is that even folks that you know have some qualms about the changes are grateful for the fact that we don't have as many boarded-up houses . . . and it's not just 'those people' or 'the newcomers' that are the beneficiaries. Everybody is, whether they're seniors and they're Black or they're new arrivals and they're White or Asian or Hispanic and gay."[42] So whose perspective is more accurate: Theresa's or Alex's?

This book sets out to answer four questions. First, what broader political and economic dynamics relate to the transformation of the dark ghetto into the gilded ghetto? Second, what attracts some White residents to historic yet low-income urban African American neighborhoods? Third, what happens when people who have been segregated for so long come together in a diverse neighborhood? Lastly, how are low-income people benefiting when more affluent people move near them?

My Research Approach

Neighborhoods are best understood by interacting with the people who live in them. To detect the change dynamics influencing Shaw/U Street and the redevelopment outcomes, I situated myself in this community. The ethnographic case study method, where the researcher observes and participates in neighborhood life, allows for a deep understanding of social phenomena not easily quantified or understood apart from their context.[43] The technique "involves both being with other people to see how they respond to events as they happen and experiencing for oneself these events and the circumstances that give rise to them."[44] This research approach is indispensable for discovering, detailing, and explaining complicated social processes. From 2009 to 2014, I spent considerable time speaking with and observing a diverse set of neighborhood residents and key community stakeholders.

In this book, I focus on macro political and economic circumstances, as well as assess more micro-level neighborhood change processes and outcomes.[45] I build upon sociologist Robert Sampson's keen insight that "neighborhoods are not merely settings in which individuals act out the dramas produced by autonomous and preset scripts, or empty vessels determined by 'bigger' external forces, but are important determinants of the quantity and quality of human behavior in their own right."[46] To capture macro dynamics, neighborhood structures, and micro-level interactions, I apply the vertical ethnographic approach to gauge the importance of, and connection between, distant and more proximate neighborhood change processes.[47] I assume that neighborhood circumstances are influenced by political and economic contexts at multiple levels—the global, the national, and the local—and that these contexts are interconnected and matter for understanding neighborhood change processes, outcomes, and meanings.

I strategically chose to investigate the Shaw/U Street neighborhood because of its racial diversity. In my prior ethnographic work during the late 1990s and early 2000s, I studied the redevelopment of Harlem in New York City and Bronzeville on the South Side of Chicago.[48] During that period, these historic African American neighborhoods experienced Black gentrification, and intraracial class conflict was a critical element of the revitalization processes unfolding within them. In contrast, as Shaw/U Street redeveloped, it received a much greater proportion of Whites and offered an intriguing opportunity to investigate interracial relations in the context of urban community transformation.[49] I presumed that due to the nation's history of segregation, racial and class conflict would be an important part of the community change process.[50] However, I was also interested in discovering the extent that, and the circumstances under which, distinct racial and economic groups collaborated and interacted with one another.

My original aims were to understand conditions related to the creation of this mixed-race, mixed-income community, how race and class explained community-level debates and conflicts, and how low-income people benefited from living in close proximity to upper- and middle-income individuals. However, I quickly learned that sexual orientation, beyond race and class, was critical to the changes taking place in Shaw/U Street. Some of the community's initial gentrifiers in the 1990s consisted of gay men purchasing and rehabilitating the Victorian-style homes and row houses near its Logan Circle section. With an influx of this population, several gay-oriented clubs, restaurants, and stores opened, and Shaw/U Street became one of the centers of DC gay life.[51] Consequently, a central community tension involved long-standing Black Baptist churches trying to prevent the establishment of gay clubs in the area. Thus, while I was initially focused on particular research questions, I let the research site tell me what else was important, and so remained flexible to the possibility that new and important topics, questions, and social categories would emerge as I experienced community life.[52]

To learn about Shaw/U Street's inner workings, I deployed an array of strategies. Foremost, I spent nearly a year volunteering with Organizing Neighborhood Equity (ONE DC), one of the community's grassroots organizations.[53] ONE DC allowed me to connect with many low-income residents living in the community's subsidized housing. It also provided a unique opportunity to participate in organizing efforts to combat both commercial and residential displacement.

While working as an organizer, I embedded myself in the community's social fabric. I frequented area parks, recreation centers, libraries, coffee shops, restaurants, and nightclubs. I also attended hundreds of community meetings at block clubs, civic associations, and Advisory Neighborhood Commissions. Sometimes I would just listen at these meetings, but other times I represented the equitable development viewpoints of ONE DC. Although I worked for that organization, and developed meaningful and lasting relationships with its staff, I intensively explored neighborhood change for more than three years after leaving it. Both my social distance from ONE DC and my being guided by multiple "Docs" allowed me to investigate neighborhood change processes from different perspectives.

By multiple "Docs" I am referring to the key informant in William F. Whyte's (1943) *Street Corner Society*. Initially, ONE DC's Dominic Moulden, a nearly twenty-year DC community organizer, was my key informant, my "Doc." Dominic and other ONE DC staff were critical in connecting me with low-income residents. However, to understand a diverse community, one needs multiple key informants, so I was fortunate to have two residents,

Tim Christensen and Alex Padro, guide me as well. These individuals helped me gain access to newcomer networks and institutions important to the neighborhood's gay population.

I met many people in various community settings, and formally interviewed a diverse set of over sixty residents and community stakeholders.[54] I spoke with people of different races and ethnicities (White, Black, and Hispanic), sexual orientations (straight and gay), and tenure of residency (new and longtime). I also talked with real estate developers and political leaders as well as local business owners. By speaking with members of diverse community segments, I obtained a comprehensive understanding of neighborhood change.

Making the Case for Washington, DC

The nation's capital both motivates and deters scholars who hope to comprehend its complexities. Many academics avoid studying DC because they believe that its unique relationship with the federal government prevents generalizing DC-based findings to other cities. However, if we carry out this logic to other US cities, few would study New York City, because of either its distinct relationship with world finance or its atypical density. Few would study Chicago, because of its exceptional machinelike political structure. And few would study Los Angeles, because of its unmatched patterns of sprawl and connection to the entertainment industry. Yet ample studies on all three have greatly informed our knowledge of cities and urban life.[55]

A Washington, DC, study can tell us much about the future of urban America, particularly as cities increasingly become dominated by an advanced service-sector economy. The federal government's impact on DC is still important, yet how it influences the city and metropolitan region has changed. In the 1980s and 1990s, the federal government began outsourcing many of its functions. Just as multinational firms outsourced their legal, human resources, and marketing departments, the federal government, too, has farmed out its previously internal functions to private companies. The outsourcing of these functions changed the nature of the DC economy. By the 1990s, DC more closely resembled other US cities, because its economy, while still dependent on the federal government, had diversified with private service-sector employment opportunities.[56] With this economic diversification, DC in the 2000s more closely resembles "an ecological unit with many of the same social, racial, economic, and geographic forces that one finds in nearly all large American cities."[57]

However, it is important to note that DC has some unique aspects. First, and most important, it's our nation's capital. Tied to this is a particular history of racial discrimination and civic representational repression.[58] Since its founding in 1802, DC has never had congressional representation; and for nearly one hundred years, between 1874 and 1973, it did not even have locally elected municipal officials. The lack of federal and local electoral representation for DC residents is deeply connected to racial discord and to congressional leaders who did not want African Americans to have substantial control over the nation's seat of government.[59] Then in 1973, citizens of the District achieved the right to elect their own municipal representatives. For the last thirty years, most elected officials have been African American, but recently the political power has shifted toward Whites. This historical political context is critical to understanding Shaw/U Street's contemporary revitalization processes, redevelopment outcomes, and their meanings, and somewhat limits the generalization of these findings to other cities and African American communities. Yet although DC is unique in some regards, the Shaw/U Street case will help scholars better understand other redeveloping low-income, urban African American neighborhoods across the country, especially those experiencing a White influx.

The Shaw/U Street Neighborhood: An Iconic Black Community

No community better illustrates the shift from the dark to the gilded ghetto than the Shaw/U Street neighborhood.[60] It was once known as the "Harlem of DC," and its main thoroughfare, U Street, was known in the 1920s, '30s, and '40s as "Black Broadway."[61] In the early part of the twentieth century, Shaw/U Street was the center of Black business, entertainment, education, and religion in DC.[62] Some of the city's long-standing Black churches originated within this community. By 1910, the area boasted over two hundred Black-run businesses, including one of the few luxury Black-owned hotels in DC.[63] Between 1910 and 1950, numerous African American luminaries, such as Alain Locke, Mary McCloud Bethune, Carter G. Woodson, Sterling Brown, E. Franklin Frazer, Charles Hamilton Huston, Langston Hughes, Jean Toomer, and Duke Ellington, had lived in or frequented the neighborhood. Many of these prominent figures were faculty of Howard University, which sits at the northeastern edge of the neighborhood.

Following this era of self-reliance and racial isolation, the community severely declined between the 1960s and 1980s.[64] When subsidized housing was built there following the 1968 riots, the Black middle class fled to emerging Black suburbs in Maryland's Prince George's County.[65] By the late 1960s, this once vibrant area was known as "Shameful Shaw," because drugs, crime, and poverty had taken over.[66]

During the 1960s, as poverty became increasingly entrenched, the area became the center of DC's Black grassroots political protest movements. In or near the neighborhood, civil rights leaders such as Walter Fauntroy, Marion Barry, and Stokely Carmichael led organizations that included the Model Inner City Community Organization, Community Pride, Inc., and DC's chapter of the Student Nonviolent Coordinating Committee.[67] Although these civic leaders influenced national and citywide politics in the 1970s and '80s, Shaw/U Street continued to decline, and had some of the highest concentrations of poverty, subsidized housing, and crime in DC.[68]

However, beginning in the mid-1980s and 1990s, the neighborhood began to revitalize. Initially, it saw an influx of a diverse set of upper- and middle-income newcomers. In the 1990s, the percentage of households earning over $75,000 increased 55 percent, 71 percent, and 233 percent for Whites, Hispanics, and Blacks respectively.[69] Also during this period, the community lost over one thousand low- and moderate-income Black households (earning below $25,000). Despite some loss of poor people, Shaw/U Street retained a sizable amount of low-income households, as nearly 40 percent of the community's remaining African American members earned below $15,000.

Although Shaw/U Street started to gentrify in the 1990s, its redevelopment greatly accelerated in the 2000s once Whites became the primary set of newcomers. During that decade, with an increased influx of young White professionals, property values skyrocketed and large luxury condominium and apartment complexes popped up like dandelions, including the Ellington in 2004, Langston Lofts in 2005, Union Row in 2007, Progression Place in 2013, City Market at O in 2014, and the Louis in 2015.[70] Upscale furniture stores, such as Room and Board and West Elm, and chain grocery stories, like Whole Foods and Trader Joe's, also staked claims in the community. 14th Street, once DC's vice corridor, is now the city's foodie restaurant row, and many of the city's hippest bars, restaurants, and coffee shops have recently opened in the neighborhood.[71]

The Contributions of This Book

Race, Class, and Politics in the Cappuccino City contributes to, and extends, understandings of urban and community change in at least four important ways. First, this book demonstrates that neighborhood change and inner-city economic development are related to global, national, and local dynamics. It also explains how aspects of the global economy, federal government spending patterns, and local government decisions in the mid-1990s and early 2000s influenced DC's central business district expansion, which is an important part of Shaw/U Street's redevelopment story. Inner-city redevelopment cannot be fully understood without accounting for complex political and economic dynamics occurring beyond the neighborhood.

Second, the text presents a nuanced narrative of contemporary race relations. While some scholars claim race has become less significant, I reveal that desires to either minimize or reinforce iconic Black ghetto stereotypes influence Black branding and neighborhood redevelopment processes.[72] I coin the term *living the wire*: choosing to reside in an "authentic" urban community whose energy and edge are based on preexisting stereotypes of the iconic Black ghetto, where Blackness, poverty, and crime are associated with one another. The concept helps to explain what attracts some White newcomers to live in a Black-branded neighborhood, and illuminates how racial stereotypes remain embedded in America's urban environment as it presumably becomes less segregated.[73] While the marketing of aspects of Black culture as an attractable community asset may signify some improvements in American race relations, it also reproduces and maintains traditional iconic ghetto racial stereotypes, and reinforces existing social tensions.

Third, this book elucidates the challenges and intricacies of mixed-income, mixed-race living environments. While there are signs that we are becoming a more tolerant society, preexisting social categories, such as race, class, and sexual orientation, help to explain intense neighborhood conflicts. Whereas traditional social categories may not explain individual behavior, they nonetheless remain critical to understanding the organizational infrastructure and political battles that emerge in a racially and economically diverse neighborhood.

Fourth, *Race, Class, and Politics in the Cappuccino City* deepens the gentrification debate by detailing and explaining some of the political and cultural consequences associated with mixed-income neighborhoods. This research demonstrates that neighborhood poverty alleviation advocates need to understand these important after effects of mixed-income living. Processes of political and cultural displacement breed resentment among long-term residents, further exacerbating diversity segregation and limiting meaningful social interactions across preexisting social divides. Addressing political and cultural loss and micro-level segregation is critical to creating equitable and sustainable mixed-income, mixed-race communities that more effectively offer greater opportunity for low-income families and individuals.

Over the last fifty years, some insightful DC studies on poverty, Black life, race, and redevelopment politics have been completed.[74] This study enhances DC scholarship by focusing on how the city's changing political economy relates to the gentrification of a historic Black community. While much history has been written about Shaw/U Street, such as Blair Ruble's fascinating *Washington's U Street* and Sabiyha Prince's *African Americans and Gentrification in Washington, D.C.*, this book more fully explains the critical link between contemporary urban political and economic circumstances and neighborhood change as well as demonstrates how current changing community conditions affect long-term residents' political power.

Not only does this study contribute to our understanding of the nation's capital—it also advances a new urban paradigm. In the 2000s, Washington, DC, became the *Cappuccino City*.[75] I describe DC as such because in some ways, its redevelopment processes and outcomes reflect this relatively expensive caffeinated drink. In the early 2010s, the city lost its Black majority, and Chocolate City, as DC was once known, converted into the Cappuccino City as it became more White, educated, and expensive. Between 2000 and 2010, the city experienced a 5.2 percent population increase, and nearly fifty thousand Whites entered the city.[76] The procedure of adding white steamed milk foam to dark espresso, the ingredients of a cappuccino, mirrors the influx of young mainly White professionals into DC's Black urban neighborhoods near the central business district. While some original African American residents are able to stay in these redeveloping neighborhoods, they are losing political power, and poverty and people of color are migrating and increasing in the DC suburbs, mimicking the dark outer edges of a cappuccino.[77]

This pattern of central city redevelopment, driven largely by a White influx, and increasing minority and poverty presence in the inner suburbs is not unique to DC.[78] The cappuccino lens provides an urban account that not only helps to understand Washington, DC, and its Shaw/U Street neighborhood but highlights community processes and outcomes likely occurring in other advanced service-sector cities, such as New York City, Atlanta, New Orleans, and Houston.[79]

A Map of the Book

Chapters 2 and 3 set the context for investigating neighborhood change in the nation's capital. These chapters outline DC's complex, evolving political and economic landscape and explain the primary factors that influence it as well as some of its effects on neighborhood development. Chapter 2 assesses DC's local political landscape, both its structure and its norms. One factor that makes DC politics so multifaceted, compared with other US cities, is its unique "District" status and strong relationship with the federal government. Since 1978, with the election of Marion Barry, DC has been a political machine. Its hierarchical political structure resembles a typical urban machine, but is distinctive in that it is a Black machine. In the 2000s, as the proportion of the city's White population increased, the Black machine declined. The weakening of this machine helps to explain, and give deeper meaning to, the redevelopment circumstances in Shaw/U Street.

Chapter 3 shifts from politics to DC's economic circumstances, focusing on the city's transition to a postindustrial economic powerhouse. For nearly two centuries, DC was a federal town of "great intentions." In the early twenty-first century, however, its metropolitan region became a prominent global metropolis. While many US cities' communities were inundated with foreclosed properties during the Great Recession of the late 2000s, several DC neighborhoods were filled with enormous cranes constructing major high-end commercial and residential developments.[80] Chapter 3 explains how and why Washington appeared on the international scene as a premier global city in the 2000s. I assess how multiple forces originating at different levels of society are associated with the expansion of downtown DC in the late 1990s, and demonstrate that this central business district boom partly explains Shaw/U Street's gilded ghetto transformation in the 2000s.

From DC's downtown, chapter 4 interrogates the Black branding processes in Shaw/U Street. This community is an interesting case, because its African American brand became institutionalized as the community experienced a significant influx of Whites and lost much of its Black population. In this chapter, I advance our understandings of how urban African American stereotypes shape the Black branding processes and associated neighborhood redevelopment outcomes, and advance important insights on the evolving relationship between race and gentrification.[81]

Chapter 5 explores Shaw/U Street's civic society to understand the local politics of this diverse mixed-income, mixed-race community. I explain the processes by which race, class, and sexual orientation interests become embedded in the community's organizational structure and influence community-level debates and decisions that affect neighborhood conditions. I argue that Elijah Anderson's concept of the cosmopolitan canopy, which stresses ethnic and racial civility in public spaces, does not easily generalize to gentrifying urban neighborhoods, and in so doing I demonstrate that conflict, based on preexisting social inequalities, better characterizes political interactions in economically transitioning racially diverse areas.[82]

Chapter 6 investigates some of the political consequences as the neighborhood moves from the dark to the gilded ghetto. While some residential displacement has occurred, certain affordable housing policies have kept a sizable proportion of long-term, low-income residents in place. Despite these efforts, political and cultural displacement has occurred as upper-income newcomers flocked to this historic African American neighborhood and became civically engaged. This chapter highlights and explains important political and cultural implications of neighborhood revitalization that are often overlooked by urban policy makers and scholars.

Chapter 7 presents a new urban framework, *the cappuccino city*, and chapter 8 points to multiple policy solutions to ensure greater equitable development in the gilded ghetto. While DC was once known as Chocolate City, demographic and political shifts and new preferences for urban living have meant that the city is now better characterized as the Cappuccino City. Chapter 7 outlines DC's cappuccino city elements, and describes what we might expect in similar cities and corresponding suburban regions. In chapter 8, I focus on ways to mitigate *diversity segregation* through the development of *third spaces* as a potential mechanism to bring about greater political and social equity as neighborhoods transition from low- to diverse-income communities.[83] Third spaces and bridge makers might be important ingredients in facilitating more inclusive and equitable mixed-income urban living environments that ultimately benefit the poor.

A Cautionary Note

Before continuing, it is important to note my biases and assumptions. My perspective is that when the political will is there, we accomplish place-based development, even in what appears to be dire economic situations. Under certain circumstances, it is not too difficult to promote place-based inner-city development. However, it is challenging to ensure that revitalization benefits the existing residents. In my analysis of both the dynamics influencing and the meaning of the emergence of the gilded ghetto, I constantly interrogate how this development can benefit low-income minorities struggling with the legacies of discrimination and the ill conditions of the dark ghetto. For me, the interesting puzzle is how to avoid the mistakes of the old urban renewal program and promote contemporary urban development that is just, fair, and equitable. My hope is that this book offers knowledge that contributes to this objective.

TWO

The Rise and Fall of DC's Black Political Machine

It's a mass of irony for all the world to see.
It's the nation's capital, it's Washington DC.

—Gil Scott-Heron

To fully comprehend Shaw/U Street's contemporary redevelopment, Washington, DC's evolving political landscape must be understood. For one thing, few cities have had a complex political history as profoundly influenced by race and racism as Washington, DC. An investigation of the city's political history demonstrates the importance of race in the nation's capital, which in turn is critical to understanding the revitalization of the city's most historic African American community. Second, Washington and Shaw/U Street's political histories are closely intertwined. For almost one hundred years, DC had no locally elected officials.[1] However, the landmark Home Rule Act of 1973 reinstated local elections, and Shaw/U Street's African American leadership was critical in advancing the city's democracy. Lastly, DC's changing political landscape is important for explaining those city- and neighborhood-level political decisions (explored in subsequent chapters) driving Shaw/U Street's recent redevelopment trajectory.

The city's current political system is difficult to describe. While some scholars, such as political scientist Stephen McGovern, view Washington, DC, as a growth machine, others, including urban planning scholar Scott Campbell, argue that it lacks a viable public-private growth coalition.[2] Still other DC writers claim that the city operates as a Black political machine.[3]

One factor making the DC political landscape so tough to explain as opposed to its counterparts in other US cities is its unique and evolving relationship with the federal government. Because of the city's special non-state status, its political system's relationship to the federal government is complicated. Michael Fauntroy, a political scientist and expert on District affairs, says that the federal government's power, even after the establishment of home rule, makes it hard for the city "to control its destiny."[4]

The federal government exercises much more influence over DC than it does in other US cities. For instance, it has veto power over any DC law.[5] Additionally, it does not allow the DC government to tax commuters.[6] Moreover, the national government has established federally dominated local planning agencies, such as the National Capital Planning Commission, which influence important DC development decisions.[7] Through a variety of mechanisms, federal oversight makes it challenging for scholars to situate the District's political structure within a traditional urban politics framework such as elitism, pluralism, or one of the growth or politically leaning regimes.[8]

DC's political norms and values are also hard to identify.[9] The city was formed from two southern states, but has always attracted people from around the country. President Kennedy once joked, "Washington is a city of Southern efficiency and Northern charm," and Carl Abbott described the city as "an intellectual switchboard for information originating elsewhere."[10] In short, DC is a hybrid, even today. A variety of regional and cultural norms come together to inform and shape its unique local political culture.[11]

Shortly after the implementation of the 1973 Home Rule Act, DC became a growth-oriented political machine embedded within an overarching national political structure. Its political machine, with its hierarchical structure, resembled a typical machine. However, it was a Black machine, unified and solidified by inter- and intraracial tensions. Then in the 2000s, as the proportion of the city's White population increased, the Black machine declined. Its demise is connected with DC's transformation from a Chocolate City to a Cappuccino City, and with important political decisions and economic circumstances that influenced Shaw/U Street's transition from the dark to the gilded ghetto.

DC's Changing Political Structure

The District's government structure has changed throughout the late eighteenth, nineteenth, and twentieth centuries. In the late eighteenth century, our nation's founders selected a new capital city. The Residence Act of 1790 established a federal district carved from the southern slave states of Maryland and Virginia.[12] Ten years later, with a few elements of French architect

Pierre Charles L'Enfant's grand city blueprint in place, the federal government moved from Philadelphia to DC. In 1801, the Organic Act put the entire ten-square-mile territory under the control of Congress. Congress feared that local partisan politics might interfere with national issues, and so did not give the District congressional representation, though some local governing powers were initially given to District residents.[13]

The city of Washington was established in 1802, with a presidentially appointed mayor and a resident-elected city council. In 1812, Congress expanded local government powers and allowed the city council members to appoint the mayor. Then in 1820, Congress established a new city charter permitting an elected mayor. This locally controlled government form persisted for over fifty years until 1871, when Congress established a territorial government for which the president appointed a territorial governor.[14] Three years later, the territorial government was abolished, and a three-member Board of Commissioners, composed of two presidential appointees and one representative from the Army Corps of Engineers, was created to manage city affairs. This arrangement lasted until 1967.

Starting in 1961, DC began to regain its own electoral political power. That year, the Twenty-Third Amendment to the US Constitution granted residents of the District of Columbia the right to vote in presidential elections. Then in 1967, President Johnson persuaded Congress, under Reorganization Plan No. 3, to abolish the Board of Commissioners and grant him the authority to appoint a mayor-commissioner and nine-member city council.[15] Additionally, in 1970, Congress enacted a law establishing a city-elected nonvoting delegate in the US House of Representatives. These decisions to give DC more political representation culminated in the breakthrough 1973 Congressional Home Rule Act, which reestablished a locally elected DC government, composed of a mayor and a thirteen-member city council.[16]

While the Home Rule Act greatly increased the city's autonomy over its own affairs, it had several limitations. Congress maintains a line-item veto power on DC's annual budget, DC is not allowed to tax commuters, its judges are appointed by the president and approved by Congress, and Congress has a thirty-day review period for new DC laws, during which it can veto any that are newly approved. Additionally, DC remains without a state government or formal congressional representation, and has to negotiate directly with Congress for additional federal revenue.[17]

Several factors, then, explain DC's changing political structure—but none are as important as racial sentiments. The District of Columbia was built by commandeering portions of two states that had high concentrations of slaves. In 1800, the population of DC was 8,144, 30 percent of

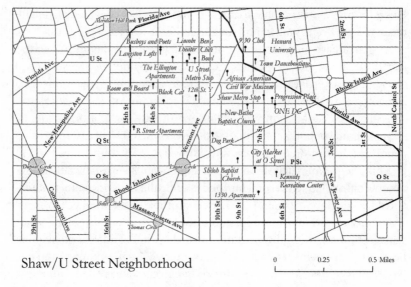

Shaw/U Street Neighborhood

0   0.25   0.5 Miles

Figure 4. Map of Shaw/U Street.

which was Black, and mostly slaves.[18] Over time, tolerance for slavery began to wane. In the 1840s, many residents of and visitors to the nation's capital were disturbed by the visible slave trading that occurred near the Capitol and White House, and there was a push to outlaw DC slave sales. The fear that the slave trade would be banned in the District (it eventually was, in 1850) led the city of Alexandria, originally a section of DC, to secede back to Virginia.[19]

Compared with other southern cities, DC was perceived as progressive on racial issues, and many Blacks who could buy their freedom migrated there.[20] By 1860, the city's population had grown substantially to 75,080, and the number of free Blacks was 11,131.[21] During the Civil War, approximately 40,000 Blacks entered the District, and by 1870 DC's population had reached 131,700, 30 percent of which was Black.[22]

The area that eventually became Shaw/U Street (fig. 4) was one of the main entry points for Blacks in DC. The northern tip of L'Enfant's original city plan housed Camp Barker, among the many Civil War–era camps in DC established to hold Confederate contraband, that is, runaway or captured slaves.[23] After the war, the camp was closed, and many former slaves settled in the area, establishing homes, businesses, and churches. The US Freedmen's Bureau, charged with helping former slaves, opened a hospital nearby. The location of Camp Barker and the Freemen's Hospital (and later Howard

University and its hospital) was critical to the Shaw/U Street area eventually becoming DC's center for African American life.[24]

As more Blacks entered the city, both during and just after the Civil War, they began to play a critical role in local political affairs. The African American population had the right to vote, and in the 1868 mayoral election, it contributed a substantial number of votes. In an extremely close election, the White Republican candidate, Sayles Bowen, an early supporter of emancipation, won. Out of a total 18,000 votes, 8,200 were cast by African Americans.[25]

As Blacks' political power increased along with their population in the nation's capital, Congress contemplated altering the city's government structure. It considered revamping the elected structure of the local government to a territorial government that would be politically appointed by the president. Some viewed the proposed territorial government as a mechanism by which the White-dominated federal government could limit African American influence in local affairs.[26] Historian Howard Gillette notes, "Democrats, including financier William W. Corcoran, had supported the new government as a means of eliminating . . . the influence of blacks that they believed had beset local affairs since the war."[27] In 1871, Congress created the territorial government, eradicating the ability of both African American and White DC residents to vote for their local public officials.

A key component of the new territorial government was the Board of Public Works, created to stimulate the city's development. Since its establishment, the nation's capital had not lived up to Pierre Charles L'Enfant's grand plan. Many of its roads remained unpaved, and its physical infrastructure lagged behind other US cities and world capitals. The hope was that the Board of Public Works, with federal government backing, would facilitate city growth and fulfill L'Enfant's vision.

No person was better positioned to exploit the new territorial government than Alexander Shepherd. Shepherd, founder of the DC Board of Trade, was a White entrepreneur who viewed the new territorial government and the Board of Public Works as an opportunity to enhance his business dealings.[28] He wanted to benefit financially from the federal government's interest in developing the city. Initially appointed the vice president of the Board of Public Works, in 1873 he was selected the territorial governor.[29]

Shepherd used his political positions to distribute development contracts for sewers, street paving, and tree planting to his business allies. According to urban historian and political scientist Blair Ruble, "[He] was the local version of a new type of urban American—the businessman politician who parlayed municipal power into a machine for providing the public infrastructure necessary for economic growth."[30] Shepherd would accomplish an incredible amount of city development, but his particular machine system of rule would not last long.

Under "Boss" Shepherd, the territorial government spent at a rapid pace and fell into arrears. An 1872 federal law mandated that the territorial government could not have debt exceeding $10 million, but by 1874 that amount was estimated at $18 million.[31] This debt and the poor performance of some Shepherd-endorsed development contracts led to the federal government abolishing the territorial government in 1874. Four years later, the restructuring of the local government was officially legislated into a three-person, presidentially appointed Board of Commissioners.[32]

The short-lived, unsuccessful territorial government had a major impact on the future of DC politics. First, it led to a nearly century-long period in which DC residents, though federal and local taxpayers, had little formal influence over the politics of their territory. Second, it signaled to some that the federal government would control DC as long as there was a threat that African Americans might influence local government.[33] Lastly, the Shepherd era, with its machine-like politics and associated city debt, foreshadowed what was to come once DC residents took back their local political power.

From 1874 until 1967, DC's local political environment burrowed itself into informal civil society through citywide and neighborhood associations and churches. In these racially segregated social spaces, residents attempted to influence decisions affecting the city. Blair Ruble, in *Washington's U Street*, explains;

> Thick networks of businesses and civic and religious institutions became one way in which African Americans could exert influence over the broader community. In the pernicious and supercharged world of Washington race relations, these African American organizations often would be distinguished from their white counterparts by assuming the title of "civic associations." White organizations, by contrast, frequently were called "citizens associations."[34]

In these civic and citizen associations and churches, African Americans and Whites maintained their political skills until circumstances allowed them to regain the city's formal political structure.[35]

During this period, Shaw/U Street, known at the time as Mid-City, nurtured much of the city's Black political leadership.[36] In prominent African American churches, such as Fifteenth Street Presbyterian Church, Metropolitan Baptist Church, New Bethel Baptist Church, Shiloh Baptist Church, and Saint Luke's Episcopal, DC's Black power elite was cultivated. Furthermore, the community's 12th Street YMCA "was a major meeting place in which African Americans of varied economic levels gathered, and where young people found role models among people of achievement."[37] Additionally, because of Howard University's close proximity to Shaw/U Street, residents had the opportunity to learn from prominent Black intellectual figures like Alain Locke, Carter G. Woodson, E. Franklin Frazier, and Ralph Bunche, through seminars held at the Y and other neighborhood institutions. Shaw/U Street, like Harlem in New York City and Bronzeville in Chicago, was the epicenter of DC's Black political life, and soon this community's leadership would help restore local democracy to the nation's capital.

The Rise of Chocolate City

Following World War II, White middle-class families left many American cities, including DC, to move into the suburbs.[38] During this period, DC became known as Chocolate City. In 1950, its population was just over 800,000; by 1960 it had declined to 760,000. What was more striking, nearly 170,000 Whites had left the city. This middle-class White flight, along with a nearly equivalent African American influx, made DC the first major US city that was predominantly Black.[39]

It also became increasingly poor. And the poorer DC became, the more the middle class—both Blacks and Whites—fled to the suburbs.[40] Many middle-income African Americans moved to Prince George's County, Maryland, while much of the White population moved to Fairfax County, Virginia, and Montgomery County, Maryland.[41] As White and Black middle classes left, DC's poverty increased and became more geographically concentrated in places like Shaw/U Street.

Shifting demographics and poverty concentration in some US cities were associated with political instability. In the 1950s and '60s, sections of American cities burned to the ground as police brutality triggered protest and civil unrest within impoverished Black communities.[42] During this period, racial tensions were arguably at an all-time high, and Black incorporation into the ruling governing apparatuses of cities was seen as a possible mechanism to ease social conflict.[43]

By the mid-1960s, DC had avoided major rioting.[44] Some felt that the military presence in and surrounding the city had deterred it.[45] However, some national leaders recognized that without a locally elected government there, an urban riot might be on the horizon.[46] Additionally, civil rights demonstrations were elevating the hypocrisy of a capital city denying voting rights in a nation claiming to be the world's promoter of democratic principles.[47]

In 1967, President Johnson persuaded Congress to allow him to restructure the DC government. Through appointments, he quickly incorporated local Black leadership. Johnson appointed DC's first Black mayor, Walter Washington, as well as a majority Black city council.[48] Washington was perceived as a conservative leader respected by the city's Black and White elites. He had earned his BA and JD from Howard University, and was among DC's Black bourgeoisie. Washington worked most of his career in the District's Alley Dwelling Authority, later renamed the National Capital Housing Authority, and was eventually its executive director. He served as DC's appointed mayor from 1967 to 1974.

Black incorporation into the reemerging DC political structure in 1967 was not sufficient to stem the outcry and backlash from African Americans after the assassination of Martin Luther King, Jr. in 1968. Hours after King had been killed, people took to Shaw/U Street's 14th and U Streets intersection. Initially the crowd, led by Black activist Stokely Carmichael, requested that businesses along U Street close to mourn the loss of the national civil rights leader, but eventually the mob grew out of control.[49] The riots lasted five days and were mainly contained in 14th, U, and 7th Streets, NW and H Street, NE by 3,100 local police augmented by 13,000 federal troops ordered in by President Johnson. When the smoke cleared, 12 people had been killed, 1,097 injured, and 6,100 arrested; 1,200 buildings had burned, and damages were estimated at $27 million.[50] Shaw/U Street's main business corridors, 14th, U, and 7th Streets, had been burned to the ground (fig. 5), and in the ensuing years the community became more impoverished and racially isolated.

After the riots, certain national leaders were convinced that DC's population needed greater political control and Black incorporation; however, some congressional representatives did not want DC's majority African American population to obtain such power and autonomy.[51] For instance, Congressman William Natcher, the White southern Democratic chairman of the House Subcommittee on District of Columbia Appropriations, felt "uneasy" about the prospects of increased African American power over the District. "Our Capital City is under the jurisdiction of the Congress of the United States and not under the jurisdiction of the looters and the burners who have no respect for this city," he said to local leaders.[52] Congressman John McMillan, another long-term White southern Democrat and chairman of the House District Committee, was openly hostile to home rule.

However, in 1972 McMillan surprisingly lost his bid for reelection. Rev. Walter Fauntroy (fig. 6), a civil rights activist and DC's first African

Figure 5. Aftermath of the 1968 DC riot on 7th Street
(©George Tames/The New York Times/Redux).

Figure 6. Walter Fauntroy (*left*) and Marion Barry
(Reprinted by permission of D.C. Public Library).

American nonvoting congressional delegate in 1970, was instrumental in McMillan's defeat. He helped to mobilize the Black vote in McMillan's South Carolina political district, contributing to his loss.[53]

Fauntroy had deep Shaw/U Street roots. He grew up in the community at the tail end of its "Black Broadway" heyday.[54] He graduated from Paul Lawrence Dunbar High School, originally established by Fifteenth Street Presbyterian Church in 1870 and the first Black high school in America.[55] From Dunbar, he attended Virginia Union University and then went on to receive a divinity degree from Yale University.

After earning his educational credentials, Fauntroy returned to Shaw/U Street. He took over leadership at New Bethel Baptist Church, his childhood place of worship. While at New Bethel, he founded the Model Inner City Community Organization, a coalition of DC churches instrumental in redeveloping sections of Shaw/U Street following the DC riots. He worked with area churches and the US Department of Housing and Urban Development to build subsidized housing to replace the community's burned-out structures.[56] Maybe even more significantly, he also prevented major urban renewal efforts from leveling the community's remaining historic housing stock, which would have resulted in significant residential displacement. Lastly, he ensured that the Metro, DC's subway system, would eventually develop two stations in the community.[57] Fauntroy not only helped to rebuild Shaw/U Street after the riots, but aided in fundamentally altering the course of DC's political system when he spearheaded the movement to defeat McMillan.

Once McMillan was defeated, Congressman Charles Diggs, an African American from Michigan, became the head of the House District Committee in 1973. Diggs helped push through DC's Home Rule Act. This historic national legislation restored the right of DC residents to elect their own local government.

The Home Rule Act and a subsequent amendment structured DC's contemporary political system. DC residents elect a mayor, eight city council ward representatives, four citywide council members, and a city council chair to four-year terms.[58] The act also constructed 37 political subdistricts, known as Advisory Neighborhood Commissions (ANCs). These commissions, a formal layer of civil society just beneath the city council, promote public participation in decisions affecting neighborhoods. ANC commissioners are locally elected by their subdistrict residents and make recommendations to the city council and city agencies on matters such as zoning, liquor licensing, and small grant making in their areas. Shaw/U Street's ANCs, which will be examined in chapters 5 and 6, are important public spaces where residents voice their community preferences.

While the newly minted DC political system in the 1970s was heading down a somewhat uncontroversial path with the election of mayor Walter Washington, the mayoral election in 1978 would greatly alter the city's political destiny. Marion Barry (fig. 6), an African American Washington outsider yet civil rights movement insider, took over DC's local politics. Barry, "mayor for life," would remarkably be elected mayor four times, thereby solidifying DC's Chocolate City political narrative.

Boss Barry

Marion Barry was a central figure in both the national civil rights and the DC protest movements. The son of a Tennessee sharecropper, he was a founding member and first chair of the Student Non-Violent Coordinating Committee (SNCC). After dropping out of a PhD program in chemistry at the University of Tennessee, he moved to DC to open SNCC's local office. He also organized a successful transit strike and the Free DC campaign, a boycott of businesses opposing home rule. However, what positioned him best to embark on his DC political career was his involvement in Pride, Inc.[59] A private company established in 1967 by Barry and his second wife, Pride, Inc. provided jobs for African American DC youth and adults living in concentrated poverty.[60]

The Pride headquarters was located near the U Street corridor, and so Barry spent much of his time hanging out in the community.[61] In the impoverished Shaw/U Street area, he would learn the "code of the street."[62] Barry partnered with Rufus "Catfish" Mayfield, a hustler with an arrest record, to learn the codes and norms of the DC streets, and together they recruited and organized struggling African American men like those Elliot Liebow met in Shaw/U Street, and wrote about in *Tally's Corner*.[63]

A charismatic leader, Barry moved with confidence and comfort in the city's boardrooms, bureaucratic offices, back alleys, and nightclubs, and became an attractive mayoral candidate garnering the respect of several disparate and equally critical factions. Some of DC's White community saw him as capable of managing and controlling the city's low-income Black population, and his inspiring rise from a childhood in public housing to mayoral candidate helped mitigate White guilt from the legacy of slavery and Jim Crow.[64] Moreover, progressive Whites and African Americans viewed Barry as someone who cared deeply about the plight of low-income people.

Finally, the mainly White business community could work with him. They understood that Barry would use the race card to rail against the White-controlled federal government in order to rally his African American voting base, but in private he would cut mutually beneficial deals.

With Mayor Barry, the national capital city was "an example of black nationalism in power."[65] He pursued political and economic Black empowerment and "became a symbol of racial pride."[66] He insisted that companies conducting business with the city hire minorities, and increased the percentage of city minority contracts from 10 to 35.[67] Lastly, he insisted on real estate developers having minority partners in their deals to secure rezoning permits and city development subsidies. DC reporters Harry Jaffe and Tom Sherwood note that "some [business leaders] may not have liked it, but they knew the new rules of the game."[68] Barry was representative of the cadre of "civil rights" mayors, which included Detroit's Coleman Young, Gary's Richard Hatcher, and Atlanta's Maynard Jackson, who commandeered their cities' formal political establishments.[69] He and his trusted and talented advisors, many of whom were African American, attempted to demonstrate to the city, the federal government, and the world that Blacks could effectively run the nation's capital.

However, the Barry administration soon realized that managing DC was extremely difficult. It inherited debt left by the former mayor, the city's economic base was deteriorating as more affluent Whites and Blacks moved to the suburbs, and raising sufficient revenue was hampered by federal constraints. The city could not tax incoming commuters as many other cities did to raise funds, and over 50 percent of DC land was appropriated to non-taxpaying entities: domestic and international government agencies, universities, and nonprofits.[70] These circumstances made it difficult for the city government to collect sufficient revenue for effectively managing and maintaining city services.

During Barry's first term, he reduced the city's budget by cutting nearly four thousand jobs and limiting services.[71] These tactics ran counter to his campaign pledges to low-income African Americans. In fact, most of the promises he had made to these constituents, particularly those in public housing, had to be deferred.

During his second term, Barry turned his budget-trimming, Black empowerment agenda into a Black political machine focused on downtown growth. Under his administration, downtown DC revitalized as he "enthusiastically endorsed the policy of aggressive downtown development as the city's primary urban revitalization plan."[72] During Barry's first and second terms, downtown office construction boomed, and between 1978 and 1983, 13.7 million square feet of space was added, mainly to the western section of the city's central business district.[73] "In return for financing his campaigns, for withholding most criticism of his government, and for including Barry's friends in their deals, Barry would give the businessmen almost a free hand in developing Washington's downtown business district," Jaffe and Sherwood note.[74]

Barry was a pragmatic machine boss. He understood DC's tax revenue shortfall and strategically formed relationships with elite downtown business leaders to redevelop parts of the city's central business district. This tactic provided him with two types of patronage resources: subcontracts for minority firms from larger White real estate developers and, more important, increased revenue from commercial real estate property taxes, which he used to augment the city's payroll.[75] That payroll rose from 39,000 in 1982 to 48,000 in 1990, and personnel became half the city's budget.[76] In 1988, DC had one city worker for every 13 residents, which at the time was the highest ratio of its kind in the country, and the city budget ballooned from $1.2 billion to $3.2 billion.[77]

When Barry increased the city's payroll, he solidified his power. "Mayor Barry used the city government to . . . provid[e] thousands of Blacks with well paying jobs," Michael Fauntroy notes.[78] Government workers made up the "cadre of precinct captains and 'coordinators' in each of the city's eight wards."[79] Furthermore, Barry controlled the city council, known as the "Marionettes" since many were "dependent on him for constituent services."[80] In all, as DC author Jonetta Barras claims, "during his 16 years in office, Barry built an organization that . . . rivaled Chicago's Richard Daley."[81]

Race, Class, and Neighborhood Norms

DC's history of interracial group tensions helped Barry maintain control of his machine. He used DC's poor race relationship with Congress to maintain his power base among low- and moderate-income Blacks, many of whom viewed the city as America's "last colony." Michael Fauntroy explains, "The Black majority in the Nation's Capital has operated within a larger framework of minority status, in part because of the subordinate position of the city relative to the majority White-dominated Congress."[82] This White-Black power struggle between the federal and the local government kept Barry and his Black machine in power despite overall deplorable city service performance. Barry understood the anger, frustration, and resentment many

Black residents of DC had "with Congress . . . despite the presence of home rule," and he used these sentiments to his political advantage.[83]

Barry also used intraracial class tensions in election campaigns.[84] He did not garner much respect from DC's African American elites; to them, he was merely an opportunist without long-standing DC roots. While these elites strongly supported home rule and a Black-controlled DC government, they "loathed Barry's lifestyle and unacceptable pronunciation."[85] Barry was a known womanizer, and he spoke the language of the street.[86] At Pride, Inc., for instance, he referred to his workers as "cats" and "dudes" and the police as "pigs," and he was unafraid to call someone a "motherfucker."[87] For these reasons, DC's African American aristocracy preferred the likes of Walter Washington, for he had distinguished roots in the city "as a member of the old [Black] guard," and he symbolized "black privilege."[88]

Black middle- and upper-income households were an important political faction; however, their numbers were relatively small. The migration of the Black middle class to the DC suburbs in Prince George's County provided the opportunity for a charismatic leader to corral the city's Black urban underclass as a political base. Barry successfully mobilized the low-income Black population in communities like Shaw/U Street by exploiting racial mistrust between Blacks and Whites, but he highlighted his nonacceptance by elite African Americans as well.

In 1980, Barry faced mayoral primary challenger Patricia Harris, an African-American graduate of Howard and George Washington Universities who had served in the Carter administration. Barry cast her as an out-of-touch elite who did not understand the struggles of everyday Black Washingtonians.[89] He won the primary, with nearly 60 percent of the vote.[90] Barry knew how to leverage racial as well as class tensions to bolster his power over the city.[91]

Barry also knew DC neighborhood norms. While the city is a mix of southern and northern political cultures, southern political values predominate, particularly in DC's African American neighborhoods.[92] Social interactions within neighborhoods are influenced by the "culture of the Carolinas," where people build dense, deep relationships based on intersections of "family and friendship, history and place."[93] A larger percentage of Black Washingtonians migrated from the South, and they maintain their southern connections with one another.[94] These relationships are formed and reinforced in the civic associations, in the alleys, in the streets, and at the carryouts.

Barry personified DC southern norms. He was constantly on the street and connected with people in a family-like way. According to DC author Sam Smith, "Marion Barry could speak to, and would listen to, more people [in the city] than most."[95] Despite his personal shortcomings, to low-income Black Washingtonians he was "the man who helped so many of them get jobs, who helped their grandchildren secure summer employment."[96] One Shaw/U Street resident I interviewed, an elderly African American woman, said that "[Barry] took care of his people, his problems were personal. . . . He was a great mayor, and what he did off the clock was his own personal problems." He touched the southern core of many DC residents, who desired a deep kin-like connection to their political leader. As one African American mother put it, "I felt Marion could have been my son."[97]

The Demise of the Political Machine

While Barry's political machine ensured him electoral victories, the city "was on the verge of financial meltdown."[98] City service delivery in the housing, education, and health care sectors was perceived as awful. Some claimed that DC was composed of many "impoverished neighborhoods struggling with drug infestation, teenage pregnancies, violent crime, and diminishing economic opportunity."[99] Others described certain city sections as urban wastelands, where "drugs, murder, and poverty" persisted just out of sight of the national monuments.[100] Shaw/U Street was regarded by many as one of the communities falling into the "urban wasteland" category, as drugs, crime, poverty, and prostitution were major neighborhood issues during the Barry years.[101]

Exacerbating matters, the Barry machine, like many others, was filled with political corruption. Several close advisors to Barry went to jail for the misuse of public funds or accepting bribes.[102] For years, federal prosecutors unsuccessfully tried to link these illegal acts to Barry himself. Also, numerous DC residents knew that their mayor was making poor personal choices that hurt the city's national image. He was often seen late at night in strip clubs, and his reputation as a womanizer and drug user became widely known throughout the nation's capital.[103]

In 1990, local and federal law enforcement officers brought Barry down on drug charges. In what has now become one of the most well-known sting operations in US history, Barry was enticed by a former girlfriend to a DC hotel room, where he was videotaped smoking crack. After federal and local law authorities rushed the room and handcuffed Barry, he infamously said, "The bitch set me up!"[104]

Although most politicians would have been finished after such a blunder, Marion Barry made an incredible comeback. After serving six months in prison, he was elected in 1992 to the Ward 8 DC City Council seat. In 1994, he was reelected to a fourth term as mayor, defeating the incumbent African American, Sharon Pratt Dixon. In the primary race against Dixon, Barry again used intraracial tensions to beat his opponent, who some perceived as aloof and elite.[105]

The federal government could not tolerate Barry's reelection. In 1995, Congress and President Clinton stepped in almost immediately after Barry's fourth mayoral election victory and began stripping him of his power, using the rationale that the city was on verge of bankruptcy.[106] Under the District of Columbia Financial Responsibility and Management Assistance Act of 1995, the federal government instituted a Control Board to oversee the city's finances, and it took away almost all of Barry's and the city council's formal authority.[107]

The presence of the Control Board signaled the demise of the Black machine. The legislation instituting the board also mandated the appointment of a chief financial officer (CFO), who would work mostly independently of the city council and mayor.[108] Barry recommended Anthony Williams, an African American with degrees from Yale and Harvard, who was CFO of the US Department of Agriculture.[109] As DC's CFO, Williams balanced the city's budget. He was eventually elected mayor for two consecutive terms once the power of the local government was restored under the District of Columbia Management Restoration Act of 1999.[110]

While Marion Barry represented Black empowerment, Mayor Williams was a technocrat.[111] Williams, who often sported a bow tie, was a skilled accountant, the "ultimate bean-counter," whose main interest was putting DC back on sound financial footing rather than promoting African American advancement.[112] As Howard University political scientist Daryl Harris noted, "Williams was not cut from a race-conscious mold."[113] To some, he was "the antithesis to Barry."[114]

Williams's success in balancing the city's budget changed how people saw the DC government and the city. Once corrupt, DC was now corporate, and investors took notice of the city's improved credit rating.[115] Williams advocated for financial incentives to construct a particular type of downtown, one that was both residential and commercial.[116] While Barry focused on commercial downtown development, Williams wanted a District of living, shopping, and entertainment that would "attract people back to DC's downtown."[117] In 2003, at the beginning of his second mayoral term, Williams declared his goal to attract one hundred thousand DC newcomers.[118] To that end, he incentivized amenities, such as a new major league baseball stadium and high-end condominium buildings. To entice newcomers, he also made it a priority to establish neighborhood redevelopment plans and bike lanes in some of the low-income minority neighborhoods near the downtown.[119]

The infrastructural improvements he instituted began to attract Whites back to the city and subsequently stimulated gentrification in several low-income Black neighborhoods, including Shaw/U Street. "Consequently," Daryl Harris observes, "many black Washingtonians came to view him as efficient in matters having to do with the budget but insensitive in matters having to do with the day-to-day realities of black life in the District."[120] While Barry had the pulse of the city's low- and moderate-income African Americans, Williams kept his distance, and was perceived as having greater concern for improving government efficiencies "rather than the larger issues of social and racial justice"; some viewed him as "practically estranged from the black community."[121] After serving two terms, in 2006 Williams decided not to run for a third.

DC's next mayor, Adrian Fenty, was cut from political cloth similar to Williams. Fenty, a native Black Washingtonian and graduate of Oberlin College and Howard University Law School, was a technocrat interested in effective government and "race-neutral" politics.[122] His rise in DC politics came through the ANC structure. After serving as an ANC commissioner, he was elected to the city council in 2000. Then, in the 2006 mayoral primary election, Fenty soundly defeated the city council chair, Linda Cropp, winning every city ward.

When Fenty was elected DC's mayor, he appointed few African Americans to prominent political posts, and took "Williams's reforms and ratcheted them up to warp speed."[123] Like Williams, Fenty, who was an avid amateur triathlete, favored infrastructural developments, such as new schools, bike lanes, and dog parks, that were perceived to primarily attract young, educated White newcomers to transitioning low-income African American neighborhoods.[124]

Some DC residents felt that Fenty was more concerned about overall economic development than the plight of long-term, low-income Black residents; however, many initially thought his reelection was secure.[125] Crime rates went down under his leadership, and DC continued to shake off its reputation as a mismanaged urban wasteland.[126] Poor neighborhoods, like Shaw/U Street, were beginning to turn into high-priced condoland.[127]

But in the fall of 2009, Fenty began to lose support among many Black DC voters. Some thought his leadership style was too distant and racially neutral. He did not spend much time in the streets talking with people, as Barry had done.[128] He also developed a reputation for carrying multiple Blackberries and for "rapidly returning e-mails," preferring e-mail over personal conversation.[129] This approach did not resonate with many low-income African American voters, and it bucked the city's southern culture. Bernard Demczuk, a DC historian and longtime Shaw/U Street resident, claimed that Fenty "simply does not understand nor does he know the culture of Washington, D.C."[130] As Richard "Rick" Lee, a longtime African American Shaw/U Street business owner, stated, "I mean, Fenty could have been a hell of a guy because he had all the tools, but didn't have any social skill(s)."

Though the city has always struggled with its racial divide, Fenty "rarely talk[ed] about race."[131] Some viewed his neutrality on the subject as problematic. In addition, there was a growing perception that Fenty's improvements to schools and transportation "favor[ed] wealthier and predominately white neighborhoods."[132] Furthermore, some African Americans felt that he was "more aligned with the wave of gentrifiers," many of whom were White, at the expense of long-standing African American residents.[133]

There was also speculation that the growing discontent among Black voters mainly stemmed from Fenty's choice of Michelle Rhee for school chancellor. He appointed Rhee, the Asian American founder of the nationally recognized New Teacher Project, to improve the city's school system. During her tenure, she restructured the city's contract with the DC teachers' union, which made it easier for her to fire nearly a thousand school administrators and teachers deemed ineffective.[134]

The firings shook the political patronage foundation that had been in place since the Barry days. A *Washington Post* article reported that Fenty "lost the support of vast numbers of Black voters who derided him for ignoring their communities and slashing government jobs. Many of those jobs were held by African Americans, who since the advent of D.C. home rule have used city employment as a steppingstone to the middle class."[135] This understanding that the city government was a key economic means of advancement was created by Barry's patronage machine. When Rhee "laid off hundreds of teachers, many blacks saw something more than a simple purge of poorly performing educators. They saw an assault on economic opportunity," and the disappearance of the lingering machine system.[136]

As Fenty's support from African Americans began to wane, Vincent Gray, the city council's chair, decided to run against him. Gray was a native-born Black Washingtonian who attended Shaw/U Street's Dunbar High School and received a degree from George Washington University. He began working in DC's government in 1991, when he was appointed to direct the city's Department of Human Services, a long-standing political patronage hotbed. Gray, who was now in his late sixties, had been friends with Barry for a number of years.[137]

Barry, after being stripped of his mayoral power in 1995, returns to represent DC's African American Ward 8 in the city council in 2004. He supported Fenty in his 2006 election; however, he backed Gray in the 2010 mayoral primary. Kojo Nnamdi, one of the city's leading public radio voices, commented during the 2010 Fenty-Gray primary election that Barry "assigned himself a central role in the Gray campaign."[138] As the election neared, Barry appeared at several Gray events to publicly support him.[139] Both men lived in low-income, African American DC wards, spoke directly about racial inequity, and approached political outreach with grassroots, personal touches that resonated with the city's southern cultural traditions.[140] Some feared that a Gray win might signal a return to the Marion Barry era, while others celebrated that possibility. Shaw/U Street was divided in this election, with the majority of Whites supporting Fenty and African Americans backing Gray.[141]

Even though both mayoral candidates were Black, the election outcome was heavily skewed along racial lines. Most White wards overwhelmingly voted for Fenty, and the Black wards voted for Gray. In the White-dominated Wards 1, 2, and 3, Fenty received 60 percent, 70 percent, and 80 percent of the vote respectively. With Marion Barry's backing, Gray received 80 percent of the vote in the Black Wards 7 and 8.[142] With an overwhelming majority of votes coming from the city's low-income African American communities, Gray won. This racial voting pattern, some of which was prompted by government actions that destabilized the old Black patronage system, suggests that Fenty did not lose so much to Gray as to the machine legacy of Marion Barry and the persistence of the city's racial, class, and cultural dynamics.

However, Gray's win would become steeped in controversy. During the election, a little-known primary candidate, Sulaimon Brown, trashed Fenty on the campaign trail. At times he made Fenty sweat and look uncomfortable during debates.[143] After the election, Brown landed a six-figure job in Gray's administration, but was quickly fired. He did not go quietly, however, and alleged to the media that he had been paid by Gray supporters to attack Fenty during the primary. While no formal charges were directly brought against Gray, the prospect of a Gray shadow campaign that propped up Brown made Gray's mayoral tenure a single term. He was defeated by challenger Muriel Bowser in the 2014 mayoral primary. Bowser, who holds a Master's of Public Administration from American University, won with the overwhelming support of the White-dominated areas of the city.[144]

While Bowser is African American, DC's Black machine has faded. In 2014, Marion Barry passed away at the age of seventy-eight. At the time, he was representing Ward 8 on the city council. His death marked the symbolic end of the Black political component of Chocolate City, but in actuality the transition started in 1995, when the Control Board seized his power. After control was taken from Barry, the subsequent mayors Williams and Fenty implemented policies that resonated more with White DC newcomers than with many long-term Black Washingtonians. Additionally, with the city's demographic racial transition of Whites entering the city and Blacks exiting, African Americans barely held on to their majority status. In 2000, African Americans comprised 60 percent of the city's population; by 2010 that figure declined to 51 percent.[145] As Chocolate City waned from a demographic standpoint, it also diminished from a political perspective. Not only did DC's recent African American mayors align their policies to attract newcomers, but more White political leaders were elected. By 2015, the city council was ruled by a White majority. This citywide racial demographic and political shift symbolized DC's transformation from Chocolate to Cappuccino City and, as we will see, influenced Shaw/U Street's redevelopment trajectory in critical ways.

Summing Up

Understanding DC's political history is important for several reasons. First, DC, and its changing political landscape, cannot be separated from race and racism. While federal interests understandably trump local interests in a capital city, race concerns were behind federal decisions to reform DC's political structure. Some scholars suggest that the territorial government of 1871 was set up in part to prevent African Americans from harnessing increased political power, and others claim that DC's lack of home rule was prolonged by racist White southern Democrats in key congressional DC oversight positions.[146]

In this context of White-Black antagonism, Shaw/U Street became DC's iconic African American community. The neighborhood housed many noteworthy Black churches and civil rights organizations, and cultivated leaders that would help restore and govern the locally elected democratic structure in the nation's capital. Shaw/U Street fostered the development of both Walter Fauntroy and, to a lesser extent, Marion Barry, arguably the most important DC Black leaders of the twentieth century. While Fauntroy spent his formative years in Shaw/U Street, for Barry the area was where he initially cut his DC political teeth, learned the codes of the DC streets, and began to understand how to bring together a wining mayoral coalition shortly after home rule was implemented.

Poor interracial relations in the nation's capital help to explain why Barry could maintain a Black political machine even amid scandal. Some DC residents viewed his arrest in 1990 as another instance of White America taking power from Black leaders.[147] The reelection of Barry as mayor became a powerful message: White America could not take out another Black politician.[148] The support he received even after his arrest has to be understood within the context of DC's contentious racial history. Historian Howard Gillette states, "It is hard to believe [Barry] could have survived so long and exerted such influence had full political representation been guaranteed to Washington's residents."[149] Barry's political career would be baffling outside the context of America's and DC's racial divide.

Furthermore, race remains important for understanding DC's contemporary political circumstances. As the racial makeup of the city was changing, many of the policies during Williams's and Fenty's administrations were perceived to be favoring incoming Whites over existing African Americans. Gray's defeat of Fenty and Bowser's defeat of Gray were clearly determined along racial voting lines. White neighborhoods supported Fenty and Bowser, and African American areas backed Gray. As one DC journalist succinctly put it, "Race constantly sits in the front seat, resolute and virulent, demanding attention. It is the District's primary way of looking at things, the prism through which civic life is most accurately viewed."[150]

While race and racism are important parts of the DC political narrative, the city's changing political landscape must also be understood through the lens of class antagonism within Black America. First, upper-income African Americans wanted to distance themselves from lower-income African Americans just as much as upper- and middle-income Whites did. Both of these groups left DC for the suburbs.[151] The movement of the Black middle class left a high concentration of lower-income African American DC residents and hence a fertile ground for the formation of a political machine. If middle-income residents, both Black and White, had stayed in the city, it is unlikely that DC would have adopted a machine system of government, since there would have been a greater voting bloc for candidates that connected with middle-class voters. With a large low-income population, elite Black candidates often did not resonate well with the majority of DC voters. Barry understood the class tensions within Black America, and exploited them for his political gain. As will be highlighted later in the book, intraracial conflict is key to the contemporary circumstances of the Shaw/U Street community.

Political culture is another important aspect of DC's political landscape. Southern culture, with its association with deep familial ties, continues to persist within the neighborhoods. Certain constituents' consequent desire to identify with political leaders helps us to understand why Barry was so successful; he was constantly on the street. Even with his strong DC roots, Fenty struggled to maintain deep ties with the majority of DC's population, in part because of his "technical" strategy for governing.[152]

While race, class, and culture are important elements in explaining the changing DC political landscape, the federal government, beyond racial considerations, remains a dominant institution. Whereas political historian Steven Erie explains that in other cities political machines typically decline due to local reform efforts, changing city demographics, or diminished federal resources, in DC the federal government's direct oversight largely explains the fall of Barry's machine.[153] Once DC's political machine focused too heavily on maintaining control rather than on the overall fiscal health of the city, the federal government stepped in to wrest control from Barry, as it had done under Boss Shepherd.

After the federal government seized DC's local government in 1995, two technocrat Black mayors were elected, and the city began its movement away from the political machine model and toward a growth-oriented regime. These mayors implemented policies aimed at attracting newcomers to the city. However, once low-income Black neighborhoods started to gentrify and the base of the former patronage system was being dismantled, the legacy of the machine struck back. Fenty, a technocrat, was ousted; Gray, a candidate perceived to have machine ties, was in. But with the accusation of political corruption, the passing of Marion Barry, and the continued movement of Whites to the city, DC's Black political machine and notions of Chocolate City have, for the most part, disappeared. The politics of DC has become the politics of attracting newcomers, and in DC most of those newcomers are White.

The changing political context is important for understanding decisions that influenced Shaw/U Street. As noted, the Williams administration focused on turning sections of downtown into a thriving living and entertainment center, and the expansion of downtown helps to drive up housing demand in nearby African American neighborhoods, like Shaw/U Street. Furthermore, both the Williams and the Fenty administrations made it a priority to deploy neighborhood economic development policies, such as bike lanes, that specifically attracted newcomers to established minority communities.

But politics alone does not explain the rise of DC's downtown or the redevelopment of minority neighborhoods. The next chapter unpacks how the city's contemporary political circumstances and its economic environment intersect, to explain first the redevelopment of downtown DC in the late 1990s and early 2000s, and then the subsequent gentrification of Shaw/U Street in the middle and latter parts of the decade. We will then return to the dynamics of race and class to understand how they collectively shape Shaw/U Street's redevelopment processes and the neighborhood's transformation into the gilded ghetto.

THREE

From Company Town to Postindustrial Powerhouse

The overall shift of the U.S. economy toward information and services drove the explosive growth [of] . . . Washington.

—Carl Abbott

In the nineteenth and twentieth centuries, Washington, DC, compared with other major US cities like New York, Chicago, and Los Angeles, remained a relatively sleepy government enclave that did not rise to the level of other national capital cities, such as London or Paris. It largely lingered as a city of "great intentions." However, in the latter part of the twentieth and into the early twenty-first centuries, the greater DC metropolitan region became a postindustrial powerhouse.[1]

Today, the DC metropolitan area is one of the country's most affluent. In 2010, ten of the twenty wealthiest US counties were located there, up from six in 1990.[2] Moreover, in 2012 it had the nation's third-highest concentration of households earning $191,500 or above, behind only the New York and San Jose metro regions.[3] Whereas for most of the twentieth century DC was largely ignored as a global city, by the early twenty-first century it was assessed by some as being among the ten strongest metropolitan economies in the world.[4] As a *Washington Post* reporter succinctly puts it, "The nation's capital has become a moneyed metropolis."[5]

DC's economy was so strong, in fact, that the Great Recession of 2007–9 had little impact. While many US cities' minority low- and moderate-income communities were overwhelmed by foreclosed properties during that period, several of DC's low-income African American neighborhoods were filled with construction crews building major high-end commercial and residential developments. The redevelopment of Shaw/U Street, in the 2000s and beyond, is connected with the rise of the DC region and the city as a principal postindustrial powerhouse.

How and why did Washington become a premier global city over the last fifteen years? Why did its economy remain level during one of the country's most severe recessions? And how is this economic boom connected with Shaw/U Street's redevelopment?

Multiscale development dynamics at the global, federal, and local levels drive DC's recent financial success. The proliferation of the global service-sector economy is linked with the city's economic development.[6] However, its postindustrial explosion was not due solely to its advanced service-sector economy; federal and local government actions also played a role.[7] Federal government outsourcing and procurements as well as the DC government's focus on downtown development jointly contribute to the city's economic progress and its development trajectory at the dawn of the twenty-first century. Thus, an array of forces, at multiple levels—global, federal, and local— are important for understanding the rise of DC, the renaissance of its downtown in the 1990s, and the subsequent redevelopment of Shaw/U Street in the 2000s.

The Global Economy and the Rise of the Postindustrial City

Any assessment of twenty-first-century urban America must contend with the increased importance of the global economy. The interconnection of national economies is deeper and more prevalent than any time in modern history. Increased global connectivity among nations is associated with technological advancements, integrated financial markets, multinational corporations, international trade associations and agreements, and foreign direct investments.[8] Foreign direct investments, one global connectivity and interdependence indicator, grew from $638 billion in the late 1980s to $4.1 trillion in the early 2000s.[9]

The increased global connectivity among nations has also been associated with the emergence of a network of world/global cities.[10] The dominant function of global cities, as noted by prominent scholar Saskia Sassen, is to control, coordinate, and manage an intricate set of international transactions. Global cities do not necessarily produce material products, but instead synthesize, analyze, and assess worldwide production, assemblage, and distribution processes. They are critical information processors, becoming "space(s) of flows."[11] In these cities, high-wage white-collar managers in the private and public sectors run the decentralized global economy.

Global cities typically develop a bifurcated labor market. As middle-income manufacturing jobs leave a city, high- and low-wage service-sector jobs increase or become larger proportions of the overall municipal economy. High-wage service workers manage and coordinate international flows and transactions. Low-wage service workers, including nannies, maids, food service employees, and taxi drivers, cater to the lifestyles of high-wage global managers.[12] The bifurcated labor market leads to the formation of a dual city, where expanded income inequality becomes visible in both the social and the built environments.[13]

One common development trend in global cities is the growth of the central business district and the correlated gentrification of adjacent low-income neighborhoods.[14] This pattern of development relates to high wage earners' preferences for being located near dense employment clusters, maximizing business and social interactions with like-minded peers.[15] The global city then turns into the "consumer city" or the "entertainment city" as it tries to align its downtown social and physical infrastructure with the tastes and preferences of high-wage service workers and international tourists.[16]

Global Washington

DC, and the federal government within it, influenced the world through international military actions, diplomacy, trade, and aid during the nineteenth and twentieth centuries. Yet it was not until the emergence of the contemporary global economy and the United States' transition from an industrial to a postindustrial economy that DC began to be truly recognized as an important economic global city.[17] While political scientist Stephen McGovern suggests that the proliferation of the global economy was "fortuitous for Washington," the mechanisms underlying this change are still unclear.[18] The following sections detail how the changing global economy is associated with DC's emergence as a postindustrial powerhouse.

DC's important international institutions and characteristics make it a key twenty-first-century global city. It is a satellite home for 187 foreign governments through their DC embassies and offices.[19] Correspondingly, the United States has nearly three hundred embassies, consulates, and diplomatic missions worldwide, which are coordinated in DC by the US Department of State.[20] DC is also an international tourist destination, served by three major airports. In 2011, it had approximately 1.7 million international visitors, ranking it seventh among US cities for the number of foreign tourists.[21] Yet although embassies and tourism are important, well-known DC international connections, many other worldwide linkages are cumulatively more important.[22]

Defense

The DC metropolitan region is the US military's global headquarters. Key institutions, such as the Pentagon (the Department of Defense), the Department of State, the Central Intelligence Agency, the National Security Agency, and the Department of Homeland Security, are in or just outside the city. While several scholars, such as John Chambers and Noam Chomsky, have written about the United States' global connections through its military, much less is known about DC's private, multinational defense sector, its relationship to federal government spending, and its growing impact on the economic landscape of the city and its region.[23]

DC's emergence as a major global hub relates to the growth of large, multinational private defense firms within the city and its nearby suburbs.[24] Table 1 lists the top five US-based government defense contractors in 2011. In that year, these major defense firms received over $113 billion in government contracts—a $22.2 billion increase from 2006. The companies include Lockheed Martin, with its headquarters in Bethesda, Maryland; Boeing, with its government operations office in Arlington, Virginia; General Dynamics, with various locations throughout Northern Virginia; Northrop Grumman, headquartered in Fairfax, Virginia; and Raytheon, with its numerous sites in Northern Virginia. They all develop missile-guided defense systems, cutting-edge aerospace technologies, radar systems, commercial and military aircraft, and nuclear-powered submarines.

The expansion of the private defense industry enhances DC's global connections. The firms noted in table 1 do not just conduct US government business; they provide military support for nations worldwide. In 2013, these firms collectively had over 292 international offices. Their worldwide impact through defense technologies and other military services is immeasurable.

The DC-based private defense contract industry is an important part of the regional economy. For instance, in 2008 the federal government spent nearly $2.8 trillion on needs such as retirement benefits, Medicare expenses, unemployment insurance, nutritional assistance, municipal grants, salaries to federal workers, and procurements to private firms.[25] Almost $135 billion of this was doled out directly to the DC metropolitan region in either federal salaries or procurements to private firms. Of this $135 billion, the largest share, over $30 billion, was US Department of Defense procurements,

Table 1. Top Five US Defense Contract Firms.

Firms	2006 Federal contracts (in billions)*	2011 Federal contracts (in billions)*	DC metro locations	Worldwide locations
Lockheed Martin	32.0	42.4	Bethesda, MD	75
Boeing	20.4	21.6	Fairfax, VA	70
General Dynamics	12.0	19.4	Northern VA	40
Northrop Grumman	16.9	15.0	Bethesda, MD	27
Raytheon	9.6	14.8	Falls Church, VA	80
Total	91.0	113.2		292

Source: https://www.fpds.gov/fpdsng_cms/index.php/reports.
*Information gathered from company websites: http://www.lockheedmartin.com/us/who-we
-are.html; http://www.boeing.com/aboutus/international/about.html; http://www.generaldynamics
.com/about/gdworldwide.cfm; http://careers.northropgrumman.com/locations.html;http://www
.raytheon.com/ourcompany/history/.

awarded to private, multinational defense contract companies with extensive DC footprints. Clearly, the expansion of the defense sector in and
around DC in the 2000s has increased the importance of the city, and its
region, as a global business hub.

Finance

DC is not an international economic powerhouse like New York, London,
or Paris, but it is an extremely important global financial actor and regulator.[26] Two components make the city critical to global capital markets. First,
over $9 trillion in private and public financial assets is managed there. DC's
estimated 2008 worldwide financial value was around $600 trillion, mak-
ing its global finance share approximately 1.5 percent.[27] Second, and perhaps more important, the US capital market's regulatory framework is based
in DC; it sets the parameters for US capital flows, which in turn influence
worldwide capital markets.

DC is home to key private and public financial regulatory institutions
that oversee and monitor domestic and world capital markets.[28] A collection
of DC-based regulatory agencies, authorities, and commissions are charged
with providing safety and soundness for the entire US financial system. They
regulate everything, from particular loan products, to a firm's capital-to-asset
ratio and lending reserve balance, to standards for brokers and securities
dealers. Entities such as the US Security and Exchange Commission, the US
Financial Industry Regulatory Authority, the Office of the Comptroller of the
Currency, the Federal Deposit and Insurance Company, the Federal Reserve,
and the relatively new US Consumer Financial Protection Bureau shape the

Table 2. Select Key DC Metro Financial Institutions.

Institution	≈ 2012 Financial assets/figures	Location
Fannie Mae and Freddie Mac	$5 trillion, assets 2008	DC/McLean, VA
US Dept. of the Treasury	$2.45 trillion, tax revenue in FY2012	DC
Federal Reserve Board	$808 billion, assets 2004	DC
Thrift Saving Plan	$289 billion, assets 2011	DC
International Monetary Fund	$223 billion, loans as of 2012	DC
The World Bank Group	$53 billion, loans in FY2012	DC
Inter-American Dev. Bank	$10.9 billion, loans in FY2011	DC
Capital One	$312.9 billion, assets in 2012	McLean, VA
The Carlyle Group	$157 billion, assets in 2013	DC
Total	$9.3 trillion	

regulatory framework for commercial banks, investment banks, private equity firms, and hedge funds. Thus, DC institutions regulate global capital flows through New York's Wall Street and Chicago's commodities markets.

DC metro-based financial institutions also collectively manage a substantial share of global public and private assets (table 2).[29] They include the US Federal Reserve Board, which controls the Federal Reserve System (i.e., the US Central Bank) and sets Federal Reserve interest rates; the US Department of the Treasury, which collects and manages with congressional oversight an annual budget of $2.45 trillion; Fannie Mae and Freddie Mac, which together manage about $5 trillion in mortgage assets; the Thrift Saving Plan, which manages the federal workforce's $289 billion retirement fund; the International Monetary Fund; the World Bank Group; the Inter-American Development Bank; Capital One, among the nation's major commercial banks; and the Carlyle Group, one of the largest private equity firms in the United States.

The decisions and actions of the DC-based financial management and regulatory entities can have a great impact on world capital markets. This is illustrated by the events and actions leading up to and during the Great Recession of 2007–9. This recession had its underpinnings in the US housing finance system, particularly the increase in the origination and securitization of subprime mortgage products.[30] A substantial increase in unsustainable subprime mortgage lending occurred during the 2000s, which was associated with the relaxed financial regulatory environment supported by agencies such as the Federal Reserve and the Office of the Comptroller of the Currency.[31]

These and other DC financial regulatory institutions had the authority to limit risky subprime mortgage products, but instead allowed them to proliferate. These products were bundled into securities that provided the foundation for highly leveraged derivatives. The subprime-backed securities and derivatives were bought by leading DC financial institutions such as Fannie Mae and Freddie Mac, as well as Wall Street and international investment firms. The DC-based US Security and Exchange Commission and the US Financial Industry Regulatory Authority, tasked with regulating the secondary mortgage and derivatives markets, chose not to limit these risky investment products and patterns.

In 2007, US real estate prices began to drop; this, coupled with a substantial default rate for the subprime mortgages and the devaluing of highly leveraged subprime-related derivatives, led to severe financial losses and an overall freeze in the US credit markets.[32] A two-year national recession eventually resulted, with unemployment rates doubling from 5 percent to 10 percent.[33] This domestic economic downturn later had negative global consequences, since many major international investors had gambled on the subprime-related products.[34]

In 2008, the recession forced DC-based regulatory financial institutions to act to preserve the collapsing US financial system. To lubricate the financial credit markets and save several large US financial firms, the Treasury Department structured and oversaw a $700 billion bank bailout, known as the Troubled Asset Relief Program. In total, nearly $13 trillion (including the relief program) in loans, loan guarantees, and other financial instruments was deployed by the federal government, mainly through the Treasury Department, the Federal Reserve Board System, and the Federal Deposit and Insurance Company, to provide critical support and liquidity to the US financial system.[35] Moreover, the federal government took over Fannie Mae and Freddie Mac, private companies that controlled trillions in mortgage assets. These unprecedented actions perhaps prevented a financial collapse equivalent to the Great Depression.

The actions of DC's regulatory financial institutions are associated with both the buildup to and the escape from the Great Recession. The decision to allow subprime loans to proliferate and the response once these risky subprime-backed secondary mortgage and derivative investment products devalued are deeply related to the arc of one of the worst economic recessions in US history. Consequently, while DC does not have a stock market, decisions originating in that city can greatly affect US and international capital flows, making it a vital global financial center.

Federal Outsourcing

The city's global connections are mainly related to its function as a federal government hub, but the distinction between its public and private sectors

Table 3. Federal Spending in Washington Metro Areas, FY2000–2010 (in Billions).

Area	2000	2007	2008	2010	Δ 2000–2010	% Δ 2000–2010
DC	$28.2	$43.48	$47.20	$61.9	$33.7	120
Suburban MD	-	$30.90	$33.15	-	-	-
Suburban VA	-	$50.61	$54.46	-	-	-
DC Metro	-	$124.99	$134.81	-	-	-
US	$1,637.2	$2,556.21	$2,792.61	$3,276.4	$1,639.2	100
DC/US (%)	1.7	1.7	1.7	1.9		

Source: Fuller 2009, 2012.

is becoming increasingly blurred.[36] As the US economy has moved from industrial to postindustrial, a shift in the structure of federal government spending has occurred. Since the 1970s, the federal government has increasingly outsourced its functions to private multinational firms, many with a DC footprint, leading to the rise of a global DC.[37]

In the past, the bulk of federal government direct spending in the DC area was on government worker salaries and wages; today, however, the government's outsourced spending on private contractors dwarfs its public-sector employment expenditures.[38] In 1983, civil servant salaries and wages accounted for 44.4 percent of the total US government spending in the Washington metropolitan area, while private-sector procurements accounted for 24.7 percent.[39] By 2008, this spending pattern reversed itself, so that 49.3 percent of total federal spending was on private-sector procurements and 24.6 percent was on government salaries and wages.[40] The reversal expanded local private-sector employment and profits, and is associated with the expansion of multinational firms, beyond the defense industry, that have a major DC presence.[41]

In addition to the shifting structure of federal government spending, the government's overall spending increased, with monies disproportionately going to the DC region (table 3). In 1983, total federal spending in the Washington metropolitan area amounted to $27.2 billion, and by 2008 it had jumped to $134.8 billion.[42] Journalists Deborah Nelson and Himanshu Ojha note, "The outsourcing boom has been particularly dramatic in the Washington region. Direct spending by the federal government accounts for 40 percent of the area's $425 billion-a-year economy."[43]

The geographic deployment pattern of the US Department of Homeland Security's (DHS) procurement funds exemplifies the disproportionate concentration of federal funds in the DC region. Between 2005 and 2010, the Washington, DC, region, compared with other US metros, received the largest share of these funds, $37 billion, and the next-highest metro amount was $2.7 billion—more than ten times less.[44]

DHS's procurement within the national capital metro area went disproportionately to DC. Between 2005 and 2010, the department spent $15.5 billion out of $37 billion there—the largest amount of any funding received in other DC-region municipalities.[45] Furthermore, according to urban planner Margaret Cowell and her colleagues, "the District's share of total homeland security procurement . . . increased from 30% in 2005 to almost 42% in 2010, indicating an increased concentration of homeland security activity in the nation's capital."[46]

As the federal government spent more money in DC and the region via private procurement, revenues of locally based multinational consulting firms skyrocketed.[47] Table 4 displays the revenues of several major consulting firms with a major DC presence. In 2012, these firms had combined revenues totaling approximately $49 billion, a $19-billion increase from 2005.

Table 4. Select DC Metro Consulting Firms.

Firm	≈2005 Revenue (in billions)	≈2012 Revenue (in billions)	DC metro locations	Worldwide locations*
PriceWaterhouseCooper	$20.3[a]	31.5 (12)	VA, DC	149
McKinsey & Company	3.8[b]	7.0 (11)	DC	102
Booz Allen Hamilton	3.6[c]	6.2[h]	McLean, VA	47
SRA International	0.882[d]	1.7 (10)	Fairfax, VA	1
FTI Consulting, Inc.	0.427[e]	1.6 (11)	McLean, VA	24
ICF International	0.331[f] (06)	0.937[i] (12)	Fairfax, VA	17
Gallup Consulting	0.220[g]	0.300 (08)	DC	40
Total	29.6	49.2		380

Sources: [a]http://www.nndb.com/company/637/000119280/; [b]http://www.studymode.com/essays/Case-Analysis-Mckinsey-Company-Managing-1073815.html; [c]http://washingtontechnology.com/toplists/top-100-lists/2006/9.aspx; [d]http://www.answers.com/topic/sra-international-inc; [e]http://www.washingtonpost.com/wp-srv/business/post200/2005/FCN.html; [f]http://www.icfi.com/news/2007/icf-reports-fourth-quarter-and-2006-full-year-results; [g]http://www.inc.com/profile/gallup; [h]figure calculated from revenues from Booz Allen Hamilton (5.9 in 2012) and Booz and Company (1.3 in 2011).
*Information gathered in 2013 from company websites: http://www.pwc.com/gx/en/site-index.jhtml (international business, not office locations); http://www.mckinsey.com/global_locations; http://www.booz.com/global/home/who_we_are/worldwide_offices_html; http://www.fticonsulting.com/our-firm/global-reach/index.aspx; http://www.icfi.com/contact-us/offices; http://www.gallup.com/strategicconsulting/en-us/main.aspx; "Public Companies," *Capital Business*, December 16–23, 2014.

PriceWaterhouseCooper, McKinsey and Company, Booz Allen Hamilton, and others aid in strategic planning, implement policy evaluations, and provide accounting services for US and foreign government agencies as well as troubleshoot for other multinational firms.

While these consulting firms might not greatly alter the global economy, their DC footprints enhance the city's economic standing by simultaneously providing high-wage service-sector jobs and increasing the city's global connectivity.[48] As these companies expanded locally, they also increased their worldwide connections. Collectively, they have over 380 offices worldwide.

High-Wage Labor Market Growth

As the Washington, DC, economy boomed in the 2000s, the labor market has to some extent followed the patterns predicted by global city theorists. As table 5 indicates, the city's already small manufacturing sector decreased by 29 percent between 2005 and 2010. During that same period, the overall number of DC employment opportunities increased by 6 percent, adding over 46,000 jobs. DC is increasingly gaining government-related (i.e., government enterprises) and government (i.e., federal, civilian) jobs. These top two private- and public-sector employment categories comprise 58 percent of DC's jobs, and increased 6 percent and 9 percent respectively between 2005 and 2010. Many of the jobs in these categories command salaries well above $75,000.

Table 5. Employment in Select DC Industry Sectors, 2010.

Sector	Number of jobs	Percentage	% Change 2005–10
Government enterprises	268,587	33	6
Federal, civilian	208,814	25	9
Professional	124,633	15	4
Health care	64,651	8	14
Education	52,453	6	10
Administrative	47,794	6	<1
Local government	40,017	5	1
Retail trade	21,745	3	5
Information	21,091	3	−16
Military	19,756	2	−13
Construction	13,295	2	–
Manufacturing	1,769	<1	−29
Total	825,469	100	6

Source: Cowell et al. 2012.

Growing Inequality

However, the growing DC economy did not spread itself equitably, owing to the city's changing dual labor structure in the 2000s among other factors. A 2012 report notes, "The top 5 percent of households in Washington, D.C., made more than $500,000 on average last year, while the bottom 20 percent earned less than $9,500—a ratio of 54 to 1."[49] In 1990, DC's ratio was 39 to 1. The current gap between the top and bottom earners is wider in DC than in any other state, and third of all the major US cities.[50]

The changing distribution of household income in the 2000s also indicates other growing disparities. In 2000, 63,158 households earned over $75,000; in 2009, that number skyrocketed to over 102,790 households, a 63 percent increase.[51] At the same time, the number of households making less than $50,000 declined from 145,879 to 108,278, a 26 percent decrease. While it might appear, then, that the rising tide was lifting all boats, this likely was not the case. During the same period, the number of households earning between $50,000 and $75,000 remained unchanged. Thus, the decreased number of poor people was probably not occurring because they were earning more; rather, it is more likely that low-income people were moving out of the District due to affordable housing concerns. Consequently, the last decade brought growth in the number of affluent households and middle-wage household stability, and a decline in the number of lower income households, changes correlated with growing income disparity.[52]

DC's growing inequalities are deeply associated with race. For instance, the gap between Black and White unemployment rates has substantially widened in recent years. In the 2000s, White households gained income, while African American household income remained stagnant. American Community Survey results between 2000 and 2008 show the Black median household income in DC rising slightly, from $38,400 to $39,200, while White median household income increased from $89,600 to $107,600 (in 2008 constant dollars).[53] Similarly, in 2007 the unemployment rate was 9.4 percent and 1.9 percent for Blacks and Whites respectively, a gap of 7.5 percentage points. By 2011, the Black unemployment rate was 19.4 percent and the White unemployment rate was 3.3 percent, a gap of 16.1 percentage points.[54] Furthermore, in 2010 the African American poverty rate was 27 percent, compared with 8.5 percent for Whites.[55]

During the Great Recession, DC's unemployment rate remained relatively low compared with the national average, and its property values were stable.

Some scholars attributed this stability to increased federal spending in the DC region.[56] It seemed that the federal government was "a substantial buffer against the pitch and yaw of national economic trends."[57] Its spending created jobs, which attracted people, particularly Millennials (the generation born between about 1980 and about 2000), to DC at an astonishing rate.[58] This population movement to the city sets the context for the expansion of the downtown area and the redevelopment of nearby low-income minority neighborhoods.

The Back-to-the-City Movement and the "March of the Millennials"[59]

In the 1990s and 2000s, the pattern of urban flight and disinvestment, witnessed in many US cities in the 1960s, '70s, and '80s, reversed itself, and population and capital investments arrived in certain urban cores at unprecedented rates.[60] This trend received various names, including the back-to-the-city movement, the urban turnaround, the fifth migration, the great inversion, and the new urban renewal.[61]

A number of US cities, including DC, have been experiencing a back-to-the-city movement in which people are moving to certain central-city areas. Table 6 displays the changing downtown population patterns from 1970 to 2000 for several US cities. Between 1990 and 2000, downtown DC experienced a 4 percent population increase, a huge reversal from the prior ten years, when it lost nearly 19 percent of its downtown population.

Although DC was experiencing an increased downtown population in the 1990s, the city as a whole was still losing residents; however, in the 2000s this citywide depopulation trend reversed itself. Between 2000 and 2010, the population increased from 572,059 to 601,723, a 5.2 percent gain.[62] In addition, whereas the population of many cities during the 2000s rose with an influx of Asians and Hispanics, DC was one of the few cities experiencing an increased population primarily of Whites.[63] Between 2000 and 2010, the number of Whites in DC increased by nearly 50,000, and the city lost nearly 39,000 African Americans.[64] By 2010, the once solidly majority Black Chocolate City was only slightly more than 50 percent African American.[65]

The white foam of the Cappuccino City was pouring into the District between 2000 and 2010. A disproportionate number of these new residents were young, educated Millennials.[66] According to a *Washington Post* analysis, "Almost all of the District's population growth between 2000 and 2010 was due to young adults age 20 to 34, whose numbers swelled 23 percent."[67]

Table 6. Population Change in the Downtown of Select Cities, 1970–2000.

City	1970	1980	1990	2000	% Δ 1970–80	% Δ 1990–2000
Washington	30,796	25,047	26,597	27,667	−18.7	+4.0
Baltimore	34,667	29,831	28,597	30,067	−13.9	+5.1
Philadelphia	79,882	72,833	74,686	78,349	−8.8	+4.9
Pittsburgh	9,468	6,904	6,517	8,216	−27.1	+26.1
Atlanta	23,985	18,734	19,763	24,931	−21.9	+26.1
Chicago	52,248	50,630	56,048	72,843	−3.1	+30.0

Source: Birch 2005.

Table 7. DC's Employment Change by Geography, 1996–2012.

	1996	2006	2010	2012	Δ 1996–2012	% Δ 1996–2012
Greater downtown	308,000	366,000	379,000	384,000	76,000	25
Rest of DC	315,000	322,000	333,000	348,000	33,000	10
Total	623,000	688,000	712,000	732,000	109,000	17

Source: Downtown DC Business Improvement District 2013.

Moreover, between 2009 and 2012, DC had the highest increase of Millennials—nearly 12,000—compared with any other US city.[68]

Many Millennials were moving in or near the downtown to be close to where the city's jobs were being created and concentrated. Table 7 shows the employment patterns in downtown DC compared with the rest of the city between 1996 and 2012. While the city's overall employment increased 17 percent, downtown's increased 25 percent. The downtown location of these jobs is important, because Millennials typically want to live near their workplace—but first DC had to upgrade its downtown.[69]

The Emergence of the Downtown and Its Entertainment District

DC's downtown has been slowly redeveloping since the 1970s, but its revitalization, particularly in the eastern half, accelerated substantially during the 1990s and 2000s. The eastern part, known as old downtown, was sparsely populated in the 1980s and '90s, housing primarily low-income African Americans.[70] In 1990, the old downtown area's population was 64 percent African American, and the median household income was around $18,500.[71]

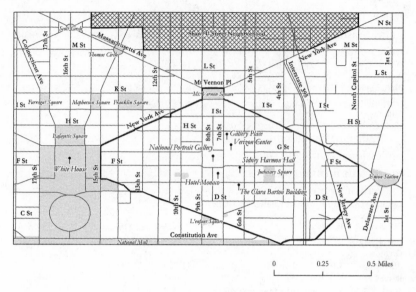

Figure 7. Old downtown DC.

In the late 1990s, a concerted effort was made to redevelop old downtown (fig. 7). From 1997 to 2010, over $10 billion was invested in construction projects in its business improvement district.[72] These investments, supported with federal and local government funding, increased property values and attracted high-wage residents. Between 1990 and 2000, it is estimated that old downtown median property values rose from $225,000 to $400,000.[73]

During the early 1990s, many complained that DC's downtown lacked a major sports entertainment complex like New York's Madison Square Garden, and that only a few of its cultural amenities remained opened past 5 p.m. Furthermore, old downtown DC was dilapidated and downtrodden.[74] This area received much less development attention in the 1970s and '80s than the mainly White western part of downtown, known to most as "K Street" or "lobbyist row."[75] According to one high-end real estate lender, old downtown was "virtually a no-man's land."[76] José Andrés, a world-renowned DC chef who eventually opened several trendy, upscale restaurants in the east downtown district, recalled that in the early 1990s, "after business hours, the streets were deserted and almost no one lived down here."[77] However, in the late 1990s and early 2000s the area, once noted only for its humdrum 9-to-5 federal office buildings, was transformed into a thriving 24–7 entertainment center.[78]

The late Abe Pollin, a longtime DC real estate developer and former owner of the Washington Wizards professional basketball team and the Washington Capitals professional hockey team, hoped to transform old downtown into a hip nighttime entertainment hub. His goal went beyond a single sports arena: he and his DC real estate development colleagues were attempting to transform the rough and underused eastern section of DC's downtown into a desirable, upscale living destination.[79]

Pollin envisioned a downtown entertainment anchor that could host his professional teams and stimulate the old downtown area's redevelopment. In 1997, he financed the construction of the MCI Center (in 2006 renamed the Verizon Center), a $200-million, twenty-thousand-seat sports entertainment development. Originally, municipal bonds were to finance the arena's construction, but the city's financial woes and its impaired bond rating, partly caused by Marion Barry's machine, made this strategy very costly. Instead, Pollin acquired private capital for the arena, an extremely risky gamble. He doubled down on his life's work and "pledged his two teams, US Airways Arena [which housed his teams in the DC suburbs], nearly all of his real estate properties and his arena-management business to get the [arena construction] loans."[80]

While DC newspaper columnists and political leaders credited Pollin with singlehandedly building the MCI center, he did have nearly $70 million in federal and local public-sector financial support. The federal government deployed nearly $19 million to the Washington Metropolitan Area Transportation Authority, and the city itself, to relocate a Metro stop underneath the arena.[81] Moreover, the DC government, under the auspices of the Control Board, spent $50 million to prepare, clear, and assemble the massive redevelopment site.[82]

Construction of the MCI Center stimulated nearby development. In 1999, two major DC firms, Akridge and Western Development, run by commercial real estate heavyweights John "Chip" Akridge III and Herbert Miller, partnered to redevelop the 2.4-acre adjacent plot (fig. 8).[83] In 2004, Gallery Place, a $274-million, 660,000-square-foot, mixed-use transit-oriented development, opened. It stands next to the MCI Center, and shares the Metro stop. Gallery Place is what geographer Paul Knox labeled a "festival" development, with entertainment as one of its central functions.[84] The residents of its nearly two hundred luxury condominiums have access to not only the Verizon Center but the Regal Movie Theater complex; Lucky Strike bowling; Washington Sports Club; Urban Outfitters and Loft clothing stores; Bed, Bath and Beyond; Aveda; and numerous restaurants, such as Clyde's, as part of the Gallery Place development.[85]

Figure 8. Galley Place.

As with the Verizon Center, Gallery Place benefited from substantial local government aid. The mixed-use, luxury development was among the
first DC real estate projects to be financed in part through a tax increment
financing district.[86] In 1998, the DC City Council passed legislation that
allowed the city to issue bonds that would be paid for by the increased tax
revenue generated from the development project once it was completed.
Nearly $74 million of Gallery Place's $274-million price tag was paid for
by the city through tax increment bond financing.[87] The city also provided
$9 million in subsidies by waiving certain real estate development fees and
road and sidewalk infrastructure improvements. Thus, DC paid $83 million,
or 30 percent, of the project's construction costs. The city also aided the
Gallery Place development by assisting in the land acquisition and assem-
bly process: the city and the Washington Metropolitan Area Transportation
Authority, the largest landowners within the redevelopment site, sold their
holdings to the development partnership.[88]

In addition to DC-government and private-sector investments, the federal government contributed to the area's redevelopment boom. The Smithsonian's American Art Museum/National Portrait Gallery is directly across
the street from the Verizon Center. The museum is housed in a unique,

historic Greek revival architectural landmark. Constructed in 1836, it has housed the US Patent Office as well as the National Gallery.[89] The building, and its subsequent additions, has served multiple purposes, such as a temporary hospital during the Civil War and the home of several national government offices, including the General Land Office, the Bureau of Indian Affairs, the Civil Service Commission, and the Government Accounting Office. In 1953, the federal government transferred the building completely to the Smithsonian, which has operated the American Art Museum and the National Portrait Gallery in a section of the building since 1868. In 2000, the museum closed for an extensive $283-million, six-year renovation, almost exclusively paid for with federal funds. In 2006, when the museum reopened, it was in the heart of an area that had rapidly redeveloped into DC's nighttime entertainment and tourist hub.[90]

The federal government did not just reinvest in its own properties in the area, it also helped to convert some landholdings into private market amenities. The Hotel Monaco is just a block south of the American Art Museum/National Portrait Gallery. This palatial, all-marble building was constructed between 1839 and 1866, and once served as the US General Post Office. The Kimpton Group, which owns the luxury Monaco hotel chain, obtained a sixty-year ground lease on the property from the US General Services Administration and converted it into an upscale hotel. The renovations were completed in 2002 at a cost of $32 million.[91]

A block east of the Hotel Monaco is the luxury Clara Barton/Lafayette development. The US General Services Administration owned the 1.7 acre plot, and in 1999 JPI, a development company, won its development proposal to construct the massive luxury Clara Barton/Lafayette building.[92] Completed in 2005, the development is mixed-use, with 428 plush condominiums, several posh restaurants, a Starbucks, and a 250-seat performance theater. The building has incredible amenities, including a roof deck with pool, large patio grills, and granite countertops; a media center with a large projector screen and stadium-style seating; a common party room with a pool table; and workout facilities, with TV screens mounted on treadmills and elliptical training equipment.[93]

The development of the Verizon Center, Gallery Place, the American Art Museum/National Portrait Galley, the Hotel Monaco, and the Clara Barton/Lafayette building, along with other attractions, such as the Sidney Harman Hall for the Shakespeare Theatre Company, changed the east downtown DC landscape.[94] This area, once described as rundown, now boasts some of the most sought-after downtown living, dining, and entertainment spaces. For instance, in 2016 two- and three-bedroom condos in the Clara

Table 8. Select Old Downtown Redevelopment Projects, 1997–2006.

Development	Private $ (in millions)	Govt. $ (in millions)	Development type	Year completed
Verizon Center	$200	$70	Sports	1997
Gallery Place	274	83	Mixed use	1998
Hotel Monaco	32	-	Luxury hotel	2002
Clara Barton	102	-	Mixed use	2005
Art Museum	283	283	Museum	2006
Total	$891	$436		

Barton/Lafayette building were selling at around $600,000 and $850,000 respectively.[95]

Today, the old downtown DC entertainment enclave houses a bourgeoning population of high-wage employees in the advanced service sector who can be viewed as international economy managers. While globalization (along with federal outsourcing) might help to explain the proliferation of high-wage service jobs, global dynamics alone do not explain the real estate development pattern that has taken place in east downtown DC over the last fifteen years. As shown in table 8, the old downtown development was completed by an informal private-public partnership, where nearly 49 percent ($436 million) of the total development costs were borne by federal and local governments. Consequently, the redevelopment and revitalization of old downtown can be attributed to an accumulation of global, federal, and local forces. Global and federal forces created an increased number of high-wage service jobs in the city, and national and local government funds have been used by the DC real estate development community to assist in building infrastructure seen as critical to attracting high-wage service-sector workers to the downtown area.

Connecting Downtown Growth to Shaw/U Street's Redevelopment

The demand for and resulting development of high-cost living and entertainment options in old downtown during the late 1990s and early 2000s are related to the increased market pressures on low- and moderate-income neighborhoods near the central business district.[96] Between 1990 and 2000, median home values in old downtown jumped 79 percent.[97] The downtown development in the 1990s priced both real estate developers and prospective residents out of the central business district, so they needed to look just beyond its borders for relatively cheaper development deals and housing.[98] Jim Abdo, a well-known DC real estate developer, "could not afford to play in the downtown-development arena" at that time, so in the 2000s he began buying and rehabbing rundown Victorian homes in Shaw/U Street.[99] He headquartered his real estate office in the gritty neighborhood, and built condos and lofts that catered to young professionals, many of whom wanted a relatively affordable neighborhood within walking distance from downtown. In the 2000s, luxury condominium and apartment projects, some built by Abdo, popped up all over Shaw/U Street and were filled by people who could not afford downtown or the DC neighborhoods further west. As political scientist Stephen McGovern explains, "The downtown building boom had helped to rejuvenate nearby residential neighborhoods by encouraging an influx of young white collar workers who wanted to be a pleasant walk or short Metro ride away from their downtown jobs."[100] One *Washington Post* blogger snarkily noted, "In the new D.C., the rich take a stroll. The poor take a hike," due to gentrification pressures.[101]

In the 2000s, more people moved to the downtown and nearby central business district neighborhoods than to other areas of the city. Figure 9 shows the population increase between 2000 and 2010 for Washington, DC. Most of the dark areas, which had a 50 percent or higher population increase, are concentrated downtown. Clearly the greatest population gains in the city were in and near the downtown neighborhoods. While the city in the 2000s had an overall 5 percent population increase, the inner-core neighborhoods experienced a 9 percent increase, and the periphery city neighborhoods increased by only 3 percent.[102] These data suggest that the neighborhoods in and near downtown were in greater demand than city areas further from it. And this demand to live near downtown put redevelopment pressures on the inner-core, low-income minority communities, such as Shaw/U Street.[103]

The expansion of downtown in the late 1990s and early 2000s accelerated Shaw/U Street gentrification, but prior redevelopment had been taking place in the neighborhood before this period. In the late 1980s and early 1990s, Shaw/U Street started to revitalize after some significant city investments and neighborhood efforts. In the mid-1980s, mayor Marion Barry decided to build the Frank D. Reeves Municipal Center at the northwest corner of the 14th and U Streets intersection, where the drug trade had persisted for years. This, along with the completion in 1991 of the U Street Metro stop, aided by the advocacy of civil rights activist Walter Fauntroy, helped to stimulate interest by real estate developers in the community. Moreover, several "pioneer" residents at this time were members of DC's gay community. DuPont Circle, an area just west of Shaw/U Street that was the center of DC's

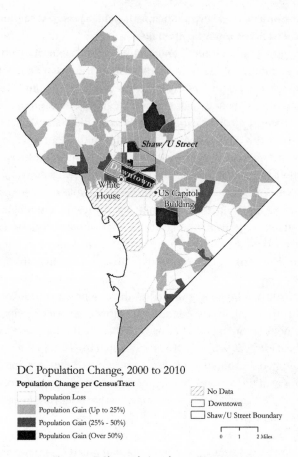

DC Population Change, 2000 to 2010

Population Change per Census Tract

Population Loss

Population Gain (Up to 25%)

Population Gain (25% - 50%)

Population Gain (Over 50%)

No Data

Downtown

Shaw/U Street Boundary

0   1   2 Miles

Figure 9. DC's population change, 2000–2010.

gay life at the time, was becoming expensive; many people were moving east to rehabilitate the community's beautiful housing stock of row houses and Victorian three-story homes.[104]

Tim Christensen, who opened the book with his description of the 14th and U Farmers' Market, represents a cohort of gay men who moved into the Logan Circle area of the Shaw/U Street neighborhood in the 1990s. He says, "I love beautiful architecture, and I love beautiful interior design. And I love communities that . . . have a lot of curb appeal. And so speaking for myself, I get all of those things in Logan Circle. And was able to get them as a relatively young guy at a price that I could afford." Alex Padro, a Shaw/U Street neighborhood advisory commissioner, explains, "This neighborhood . . . has a significant GLBT population because GLBT people tend to be among the pioneers that will go into a neighborhood and take those [houses] that are in bad shape and renovate them."

Despite some redevelopment and an influx of gay newcomers through the '90s, the community's redevelopment was slow at first, and so the area remained an up-and-coming neighborhood. During this time, some popular theaters and musical venues opened or greatly expanded, such as the Studio Theater, the Black Cat, and the 9:30 Club.[105] Additionally, a nonprofit housing developer, Manna, spearheaded an affordable-housing redevelopment effort.[106] With funding from the Local Initiative Support Corporation, Manna rehabilitated several commercial and residential projects. During the 1990s, Shaw/U Street property values increased by 39 percent.[107] However, in the 2000s the redevelopment shifted from nonprofits to the private-market, for-profit real estate developers, like Abdo and JBG, whose capital investors had deep pockets.[108]

With the back-to-the-city movement, the rise of the downtown, and the movement of Millennials to the community in full swing during the 2000s, Shaw/U Street became one of the city's hottest neighborhoods. Between 2000 and 2010, its population increased 17 percent, compared with the city's 5 percent increase.[109] Also during this period, Shaw/U Street property values increased well beyond their 1990s rate (35 percent vs. 145 percent), and at a rate faster than for old downtown and DC as a whole.[110] Furthermore, Shaw/U Street also had the third-highest percentage change in Millennial residents: the number of people aged twenty to thirty-four years increased in the community by over five thousand.[111]

Many of the new young professionals that I interviewed said they moved to the neighborhood in the 2000s, as Tim did, to get more space than they otherwise would have in downtown or in the already redeveloped Northwest DC neighborhoods, like Foggy Bottom/West End, Georgetown, and DuPont. Ralph, a newcomer and an openly gay White man in his thirties, is a lawyer and a Shaw/U Street blogger. He says, "There are a lot of great things about the neighborhood . . . that drew me to Shaw. I love our diversity and rich history, I love the architecture in Shaw, and I find convenient Shaw's proximity to a lot of things, including Logan Circle, 14th Street, U Street, and downtown."[112] He also explains that he and his partner chose Shaw/U Street over Georgetown, Dupont, and downtown because "we found a house that we just loved. And we could afford it."

Other newcomers, even ones employed in the DC suburbs, chose Shaw/U Street. David, a twenty-something African American who grew up in Northern Virginia and works for a high-tech, federal contract security firm, explains to me at a coffee shop why he decided to live in the community. He first says it's because the area has "restaurants, bars, and a Metro" close by. I ask why he didn't move closer to where he works, and he replies, "When anyone wants to do something, they go to the city. It seems like a place for a young person to be, not in the suburbs. It's boring." Then he declares, "I can't stand the suburbs! I couldn't imagine being in the suburbs." David is an anomaly because he is an African American newcomer, but he represents those who came of age in the suburbs, work in the suburbs, and still prefer inner-city living.

With young professionals like Ralph and David moving to the neighborhood in the 2000s, the real estate market boomed. Large luxury apartment and condominium buildings started popping up as well as numerous hip bars. Moreover, the 14th Street corridor became the city's high-end furniture and restaurant row.[113] The closing of a thrift furniture shop and the opening of Room and Board, a national luxury furniture store, on 14th Street symbolizes the changes taking place in the neighborhood. In some of the newer high-end, mixed-use apartment buildings, boutique-clothing stores now sell washable cashmere t-shirts for $88, signaling that the neighborhood's transformation from the dark ghetto to the gilded ghetto is fully complete.[114]

Summing Up

Twenty-first-century urban development theories highlight several dynamics as contributing to city growth. These theories are categorized into three main paradigms: Manuel Castells's information city, Saskia Sassen's global city, and Terry Clark's entertainment-consumer city.[115] All these theories are grounded in the US economy's transition from an industrial to a postindustrial society.[116] While they are illuminating, none by itself fully explains how a sleepy federal town morphed into a major global economic player.

While DC's reputation as a global city has been debated over the years, the District, and it metropolitan region, has increasingly become global. Deindustrialization and increased international interconnectivity advanced the importance of DC's already established role as a worldwide command and control center for defense and finance. Additionally, increased federal government outlays relate to the expansion of DC-area private multinational companies, which grew both locally and internationally. Lastly, the federal and the local governments aided and incentivized the "DC growth machine" to construct downtown commercial and residential infrastructure that catered to the city's expanding set of high-wage earners.[117] Thus, the DC boardrooms and bureaus and their interconnected relationships are important for understanding the city's enhanced standing as a global city. While DC was well positioned to reap the benefits of a more global postindustrial economy, federal and local government investments as well as private real estate actions were critical to its twenty-first-century boom.

By playing a key advanced "command and control" function in the global economy, DC has recently transformed in a way that supports many aspects of the world cities thesis.[118] Its service-focused labor market has become even more dominant, and this advanced service economy correlates with widening income inequality, exacerbating the city's preexisting racial disparities. In turn, the city's widening income inequality is intricately linked with the revitalization and centralization of the urban core. This redeveloped core both houses and caters to high-wage service-sector professionals, and the now upscale and expanded downtown is associated with increased housing market pressures on nearby low-income communities of color, such as Shaw/U Street.[119]

Although authors such as Carl Abbott and Paul Knox have highlighted the importance of international dynamics in DC, my global argument is distinct for two reasons.[120] First, DC's global role is more important than most global city theorists have purported. In particular, its function as a regulator of capital markets is significant, because it sets the framework that guides domestic and global financial markets. This finding is relevant for the world cities literature, which has focused more on global financial flows than the regulation of these flows.[121] My DC analysis suggests that global city theorists, such as Manuel Castells, Saskia Sassen, and Peter Taylor, need to better incorporate the place-based nature of financial regulatory frameworks in their analysis of world cities and their importance to the global economy.[122] Second, the DC case highlights the importance of the intersection of global and local dynamics as well as public- and private-sector actors. Some scholars argue that the DC metropolis "has built its increasingly rich, numerous, and complex international roles and connections on its concentration of public sector rather than private sector activities, on bureaus rather than boardrooms."[123] In contrast, my analysis suggests that in fact, many DC boardrooms and bureaus are interconnected through the federal procurement process. Global DC and its command and control center function, more than any other US world city, comprises interrelated decisions among federal government agencies and multinational firms. Whereas "Washington's principal competitive advantage is that it is the site of the federal government," because "numerous businesses, particularly law firms, trade associations, and other lobbyists, find it essential to be based close to the nation's center of political power," we must also understand that with increased federal outsourcing, large, private multinational firms also drive DC's economy.[124]

DC's recent boom is a result of the intersection of global, federal, and local dynamics. However, some reports suggest that recentralization in certain cities is related not to global forces but rather to a domestic back-to-the-city movement. For instance, as baby boomers age, some cities are experiencing an influx of older empty-nester couples and retirees.[125] Between 2000 and 2010, DC's population share of residents between the ages of fifty and sixty-nine did increase, but showed smaller gains than the city's younger adult population growth.[126] This evidence suggests that more working-age people than retirees are coming to DC.

Are the jobs being created in DC and held by people in their twenties and thirties connected to the global economy? This question is not easily answered in the case of this city. Multinational firms have created many of its recent "global" service-sector jobs; however, these companies have expanded, in part, with increased federal procurement funds. Thus, the line between global and federal job creation dynamics is somewhat blurred. We do know that high-wage service jobs have been created in DC, and that people are disproportionately settling in and around the city center. "The Washington DC metropolitan area was the epicenter of domestic migration through the Great Recession," and its back-to-the-city movement, at least among young adults, was—like its boom more generally—the result of intersections of global, federal, and local dynamics.[127]

Just as the line between private- and public-sector forces is blurry, so too is the theoretical distinction between the entertainment city and the global city. Clearly, DC is making its downtown an entertainment as well as an international and domestic political center. The development of the MCI Center in 1997 and the Nationals baseball stadium in 2008 speaks to this notion. But DC's entertainment industry can also be seen as providing urban amenities necessary for attracting the young, global information-age worker. Furthermore, the salaries of the entertainment consumers are being paid by expanding defense, finance, and consulting business sectors that continue to deepen their international connections. Thus, DC is both a global and an entertainment city, and the two dynamics feed off each other.

There is some question as to the generalizability of the contemporary development patterns detected in our nation's capital, mostly due to the unique and powerful role of the federal government in structuring DC's economy. While there is no doubt that the federal government exerts more influence in DC than in any other American city, some trends, including deindustrialization, central business district revitalization, widening income inequality, and inner-city gentrification, are relevant for certain large US cities. These development patterns have recently been detected in Boston, New York, Philadelphia, Pittsburgh, Durham, Atlanta, Miami, New Orleans, Chicago, Minneapolis, Houston, Los Angeles, and Portland.[128] However, the intensity of global, federal, and local forces is surely different in each city. Furthermore, the outcomes of these dynamics have different implications, depending on each city's particular historic, social, economic, and political context.[129]

In DC, the presence of the federal government, the history of racial discord, and the lack of a vibrant manufacturing base from the early twentieth century are unique features that might relate to the stark and intense racial inequalities witnessed there in the 2000s. Nonetheless, the contemporary development patterns experienced in the nation's capital might predict and illuminate what will happen in several cities across the United States as the national economy becomes more internationally integrated and service-sector dominated.

Thus far, I have outlined DC's changing political economy, and partly explained its connection with the redevelopment of the Shaw/U Street neighborhood; however, to more fully understand why this particular community is revitalizing, I turn to a more in-depth examination of important internal community circumstances. The next chapter focuses on understanding how both Black branding and the distinct context of Shaw/U Street as an iconic ghetto attract some newcomers to the neighborhood. Up until this point, most of the explanations about Shaw/U Street's changes mainly support production gentrification causes, as I have primarily focused on the importance of the complex political and economic contexts surrounding the community. Now I turn to investigating the equally critical internal factors drawing Whites to this particular community, and whether the transformation of the dark ghetto into the gilded ghetto signifies and symbolizes racial progress.

PART TWO

What's Going On?

FOUR

Black Branding

While DC's changing political economy and the associated back-to-the-city movement accelerated the revitalization of Shaw/U Street, Black branding is also important for understanding that community's redevelopment. Black branding occurs when versions of Black identity are expressed and institutionalized in a community's social and built environments. Examples include a National Register of Historic Places designation, a comprehensive Black-themed redevelopment plan, the establishment of Black history walking tours, or historically significant African American–labeled signage, artwork, buildings, restaurants, and entertainment venues.[1] Typically, a combination of these items occurs within a Black-branded district. This definition of Black branding coincides with several components of what Michelle Boyd calls a "racial tourist district," where "organizations create and display cultural symbols that assert the identity of the neighborhood."[2]

blight

The use of Black historic preservation as a community redevelopment approach represents a significant change in US neighborhood revitalization strategies. Not long ago, an urban community's association with Blackness was mostly perceived as detrimental to its economic development. During the early twentieth century, those living in majority Black communities were unlikely to obtain mainstream home mortgage or small-business loans.[3] Furthermore, real estate brokers and speculators, through blockbusting, used the fear of an African American influx to provoke White homeowners to sell their properties below market value.[4] African Americans were perceived to cause neighborhood decline. As Boyd states, "Whites often avoided neighborhoods with black residents because of racist assumptions linking African Americans to crime, drugs, and lowered property values."[5] But nowadays in certain urban African American communities, neighborhood-based organizations, real estate developers, restaurant owners, and urban planners commodify and appropriate aspects of Blackness to promote tourism, homeownership, and community redevelopment.

Scholars suggest that urban ethnic-cultural districts can provide at least four types of potential benefits to low-income people and communities of color. First, cultural heritage efforts can stimulate economic development for low-income communities, which might benefit local residents if they are able to capture tourist dollars.[6] Second, the branding of racial/ethnic areas might make it more difficult for outside groups to claim these spaces through gentrification.[7] Third, culturally rich spaces can institutionalize memory in the nation's urban fabric of the struggles and triumphs of minority group members.[8] Lastly, ethnic groups that culturally brand their neighborhoods can "manage the stigma" by showcasing the fact that stereotypical portrayals in mainstream media outlets do not accurately characterize minority populations and the spaces they inhabit.[9]

While several studies document the use of, and influences on, racial branding in African American communities, few if any have investigated how Black stereotypes influence the Black branding process in a context of neighborhood racial transition.[10] For instance, in Michelle Boyd's investigation of Chicago's South Side, she argues that "Jim Crow nostalgia" by Black elite actors shaped the "uplift" narrative formed to stimulate the redevelopment of Bronzeville. She suggests that these elites structured that narrative, neglecting the community's poor, to entice the return of the Black middle class.[11] Further, as urban sociologist Mary Pattillo highlights, Black branding and gentrification can be "part of a racial uplift project," where "black middle and upper classes act as brokers, well-connected to the centers of elite power but grounded by their upbringings and socialization in more humble black surroundings."[12] Lastly, in a study of the Black branding of Atlanta's "Sweet" Auburn district, urban geographer Joshua Inwood details how an African American–led, government preservation effort conflicted with the desires of the district's Black business leaders. These studies are insightful, because they elevate class disagreements and tensions among African Americans in community contexts of redevelopment with little racial demographic transition. However, they tell us relatively little about interracial dynamics, and how Black stereotypes influence the Black branding process.

It is important to study the interracial dynamics associated with Black branding. Even in predominately Black communities, White capital is needed to stimulate redevelopment.[13] In addition, there is evidence that Whites, more than ever, are willing to move to urban African American communities.[14] For instance, some Black branded communities that previously experienced Black gentrification in the 1990s, such as New York's Central

Harlem and Bedford-Stuyvesant, have seen a significant influx of Whites in the 2000s.[15] Moreover, historically Black districts in Houston and Portland have redeveloped and become increasingly White.[16] Thus, White perceptions of Black communities are critical to the community change process. This chapter fills a gap in the existing Black branding and gentrification literature by detailing and explaining the role of racial stereotypes in the process of Black branding. Investigating Black branding and community change within a racially diversifying community can deepen our understandings of twenty-first-century race relations, gentrification, and Black urban experiences.[17]

Shaw/U Street's redevelopment provides an interesting case for understanding race relations and community change through the lens of cultural preservation and Black branding. During the 1990s and 2000s, local real estate industry representatives, restaurant and bar owners, and civic leaders, many of whom were White, promoted the community's Black history. The development of Shaw/U Street's Black brand coincided with significant property value escalation and the decline in the proportion of the area's Black population. The neighborhood, which was 90 percent African American in 1970, was just 30 percent Black in 2010, and yet much of its African American history has been institutionalized and preserved in a variety of ways. This chapter assesses how racial stereotypes influence Black cultural preservation branding in a community becoming less Black.

In this chapter, I tackle two questions. First, how are racial stereotypes related to Black branding? Second, what attracts outsiders, mainly Whites, to low-income Black spaces once negatively characterized as iconic ghettos? By investigating these questions, I attempt to advance our understanding of the relationship between race and redevelopment in a racially and economically transitioning, low-income African American community. I argue that desires to both minimize and reinforce iconic Black ghetto stereotypes influence the Black branding process. I use the term *living the wire* to help explain what attracts some White newcomers to live in an "authentic" Black branded neighborhood. *Living the wire* refers to newcomers' preferences for moving into an inner-city neighborhood because it has been branded as hip or cool, which, to a certain extent, is associated with danger, excitement, poverty, and Blackness: iconic ghetto stereotypes. While the marketing of aspects of Black culture as an attractable community asset may signify some improvements in American race relations, it also reproduces and maintains some traditional racial stereotypes, indicating that race remains a very powerful and complex dynamic in shaping contemporary urban environments. This chapter suggests that consumption explanations of gentrification have some merit, as the cultural tastes and preferences of its newcomers have shaped Shaw/U Street's redevelopment patterns.

Connecting the Dots: Race, the New Economy, and the Search for Authenticity

The past two decades have provided some signs that Americans are becoming more comfortable with people of other races and ethnicities. The elections of President Barack Obama provide one indicator of this; additionally, survey research suggests a great affinity for those of other races and ethnicities. In 2007, nearly 80 percent of all ethnic/racial groups had favorable ratings of one another.[18] Interracial and interethnic marriage rates have also increased. The interracial marriage rate more than doubled, from 6.7 percent to 15 percent, between 1980 and 2010.[19] Moreover, metropolitan neighborhoods are more racially integrated than any time in the past eighty years.[20] Some scholars argue that this accumulation of evidence suggests we are moving toward a postracial society in which skin color is increasingly less important.[21]

Other scholars, despite evidence of improved race relations, suggest that discrimination and negative stereotypes of African Americans have not greatly diminished.[22] Social psychologists such as Adam Person, John Dovido, and Samuel Gaertner note that White racism has fundamentally shifted from blatant to aversive racism, where prejudices "get expressed in subtle, indirect and often rationalizable ways."[23] Furthermore, sociologist Elijah Anderson claims that while race relations have improved, there is a persistent stigma placed on African Americans because of stereotypical connotations of the iconic Black ghetto. He argues that the common image of the Black ghetto is of an "impoverished, chaotic, lawless, [and] drug-infested" area. Due to this powerful and persistent stereotype, Anderson maintains that African Americans striving to attain middle- and upper-class status in American society must work extremely hard to "distanc[e] themselves from the ghetto and its image."[24]

US race relations have shifted within the context of a changing national economic structure. As noted in chapter 3, the nation and to some extent Washington, DC, have moved from a Fordist to a postindustrial economic system, where knowledge production and services dominate and income inequality has grown.[25] At the high end of the wage distribution sits an increased percentage of the highly educated, high-wage, mobile labor force.[26] Urban scholars including Japonica Brown-Saracino, Richard Florida, Kevin Gotham, David Grazian, Richard Lloyd, Christopher Mele, Richard Ocejo,

Frederick Wherry, and Sharon Zukin argue that mobile, high-wage knowledge producers crave a variety of "authentic" urban experiences.[27]

In some domains, stereotypical images of Blackness are strongly associated with such experiences. For instance, David Grazian explains how race is central for those individuals, primarily Whites, seeking the ideal blues club.[28] Grazian suggests that the relationship between authenticity and Blackness is based on persistent stereotypes. He notes that blues club locations and the race of their musicians are critical; those located in "slightly dangerous black urban neighborhoods" and featuring African American musicians are seen as most authentic. In the realm of the blues, "blackness connotes an extreme sense of authenticity."[29] He concludes that many White blues fans "often draw on very traditional stereotypical images of black men and women in their search for authenticity."[30] Grazian's research begs a consideration of whether persistent Black urban stereotypes and the search for authenticity influence the Black branding process in African American neighborhoods experiencing racial transition.

Whereas cities once focused their resources primarily on attracting jobs, by giving tax breaks to companies, for example, some scholars now suggest that cities are implementing policies to attract mobile middle- and upper-income populations with entertainment amenities rather than employment opportunities.[31] Terry Clark's entertainment machine paradigm claims that city politics are shaped more by consumer preferences than traditional growth machine actors: "Urban public officials, businesses, and non-profit leaders are using culture, entertainment, and urban amenities to . . . enhance their locations—for present and future residents, tourists, conventioneers, and shoppers."[32] As was seen in chapter 3, DC's politics in the 2000s heavily focused on creating an entertainment district downtown to attract newcomers.

Clark's entertainment-, amenity-, and consumer-based machine perspective also identifies "new rules of the game for consumption and politics" in a postindustrial city. He suggests that traditional social categories such as "class, region and ethnic background" are becoming less significant in predicting individual behaviors and policy preferences.[33] Clark proposes that entertainment machine–focused governments now implement consumer-oriented policies, which suffer much less from race, class, and gender biases compared with past policies executed by traditional growth machine cities.

One new consumer-oriented preference is for cities with racially diverse neighborhoods.[34] In response, many US cities are scrambling to signal diversity to potential urban consumers by constructing cultural tourist districts in Asian, Latino, and Black communities as places of middle- and upper-class

The 'creative' city

residence, entertainment, and shopping.[35] This chapter investigates aspects
of Clark's entertainment machine perspective by exploring whether racial
considerations, in particular racial stereotypes, influence the primary developers, sellers, and consumers of Black branded neighborhoods. However,
rather than coining DC an "entertainment machine," it is a "Cappuccino
City," where race, in the sense of both minimizing and reproducing Black
stereotypes, is critical to understanding why the formerly dark ghetto now
entices some upper-income White residents.

Constructing Black Narratives and
Fighting Racial Stereotypes

While some Black cultural branding initiatives are spearheaded mainly by
African Americans, much of Shaw/U Street's Black historic preservation can
be traced to one of DC's premier preservationists: Kathryn (Kathy) Schnei-
der Smith, a middle-aged White woman.[36] Smith, a District resident since
1965, is the founding editor of the journal *Washington History* and former
president of the Historical Society of Washington, DC. She also founded
the DC Heritage and Tourism Coalition, an alliance of over 230 arts, heritage, and community organizations, which in 2003 became Cultural Tourism, DC.[37] Through these institutions during the 1990s and 2000s, Smith
vigorously worked to preserve certain aspects of the capital's history in an
attempt to draw millions of DC tourists from the national monuments to
the city's diverse neighborhoods.[38]

Smith strove to educate DC visitors on essential city history apart from
the monuments on the National Mall. She wanted people to know that DC
and its neighborhoods have a distinct and worthy past. She believed that to
fully understand the city's history, one had to know its Black history. For
most of the twentieth century, Shaw/U Street had been Black Washingtonians' cultural and economic hub; thus, one had to become familiar with
this community's past in order to fully understand DC's Black history.

For over fifteen years, Kathy Smith was intimately involved in a number
of Shaw/U Street historic preservation projects. In 1994, she collaborated
with the African American–directed Thurgood Marshall 12th Street YMCA
and Marya McQuirter, an emerging African American scholar of American
history, to document both the Y's and the broader community's history.[39]
These efforts helped earn the Y a place on the National Register of Historic
Places.[40] This history project eventually expanded, becoming *Remembering
U Street*, a temporary public art installation of community history.[41] Along
with that exhibit, in 1997 Smith created the Duke Ellington's DC bus tour,

Figure 10. Black Heritage Trail sign.

which eventually morphed into a guided walking tour, Before Harlem, There Was U Street.[42]

Kathy Smith's cultural preservation work garnered her and the community local and national recognition. In 1999, she was a lead consultant on a Public Broadcasting Service documentary special, *Duke Ellington's Washington*, which prominently featured Shaw/U Street's Black history. In 2001, the detailed Black history Smith presented on her guided bus and walking tours was permanently institutionalized in the community's street infrastructure through Cultural Tourism, DC's work. The coalition obtained federal and city funding to install a series of large, permanent, billboard-like sidewalk posts displaying information about the area's Black past (fig. 10).[43] These posts, scattered throughout the neighborhood, make up two city-endorsed, self-guided walking tours: City within a City: Greater U Street Heritage Trail and Midcity at the Crossroads: Shaw Heritage Trail. In 2003, Cultural Tourism, DC collaborated with the 14th Street Main Street Initiative to further showcase the community's past by having selected commercial establishments display historic photos of prominent local Black institutions.[44] A year later, the preservation of the community's Black history gained further momentum when the DC Office of Planning released the "Duke [Ellington]

Plan," which laid out the city's comprehensive effort to fully transform much of Shaw/U Street into an African American cultural district.[45] The plan designated Cultural Tourism, DC the lead implementer of the cultural district. In all, thanks to Smith's steadfast efforts, it is nearly impossible to walk through Shaw/U Street without gaining some understanding of the community's connection to Black history.

Smith recalls in a conversation with me that when she began her Shaw/U Street cultural preservation work in the 1990s, she believed that "Shaw had one of the city's richest histories, but that the history was just unknown" to most people. She explains that part of the reason for the obscurity of the community's history was its insufficient documentation, but also that in the 1990s the community "felt dangerous"; thus, few outsiders ventured into the neighborhood to learn about it. To attract people to the community, she had to convince outsiders that the neighborhood was more than its short-sighted association with blight, drugs, crime, and prostitution. So her mission, in part, was to change the negative iconic ghetto stereotype associated with the community's more recent past.

The Creation of Iconic Black Ghettos:
A Complicated History

Reconstructing the narratives of African American ghettos can be difficult because of their multifaceted histories. In the late nineteenth and early twentieth centuries, as part of the Great Migration, many African Americans fled the Deep South in search of a better life in northern cities.[46] They sought employment opportunities and the promise of fewer racial restrictions. However, in many receiving cities, restrictive covenants legally barred individuals from selling their homes to African Americans.[47] As a result, few urban communities were open to Blacks, leading to the emergence of racially segregated but economically integrated Black Belts, "cities within cities."[48] In these Black ghettos, lawyers, doctors, and other professionals lived near those who were unemployed and receiving assistance from social welfare programs.[49] These segregated, mixed-income neighborhoods raised and nurtured some of the nation's greatest musicians, artists, architects, academics, medical experts, and political leaders.

In 1948, restrictive covenants were made legally unenforceable, and in the 1950s and '60s, many Black professionals left the Black Belts. Consequently, these Black ghettos became even more segregated and impoverished, because those with the least resources were unable to leave. Furthermore, federal and local policies steered massive public housing projects to these communities, institutionalizing concentrated poverty.[50] The extremely destitute and segregated conditions of the dark ghettos demonstrated that "America's Dilemma" continued in the 1950s and '60s.[51]

The deprived conditions of the dark ghettos created the nation's worst urban riots.[52] In the aftermath of these riots, between 1970 and 1990, circumstances in many Black ghettos grew even worse. Deindustrialization, disinvestment, Black middle-class flight, government cutbacks in social welfare spending, crime, and the rise of single-parent households are some of the explanations for this decline.[53] As businesses pulled out of these ghettos, they were replaced to some extent by an informal economy, most noticeably the drug trade.[54]

In the 1980s and '90s, the drug and gang activity in Black ghettos contributed to the stereotypical images of the iconic ghetto. Dangerous urban wastelands of abandoned buildings; uncontrollable, dangerous Black men; "thugs"; lazy, undeserving welfare queens who were unable to look after their children; and crackheads were among the images that went mainstream. In the late 1980s and early '90s, popular Hollywood movies, such as *New Jack City* and *Boyz n the Hood*, and rap groups, like the Geto Boys and N.W.A., exemplified the iconic ghetto and brought its inner-city images to suburban America.

While the images of drugs, despair, joblessness, and organizational deprivation are part of the Black ghetto's history, it is an exaggerated negative narrative.[55] Some residents of these neighborhoods during this more troubled time were middle class, and the majority of residents were not involved in the drug trade. Most were low- and moderate-income people struggling to survive and cope with concentrated poverty.[56] Yet because of persistent segregation and discrimination, the exaggerated negative ghetto narrative helps to maintain an association between Blackness and poverty. According to Elijah Anderson, the stereotypical iconic ghetto image is so strong that it implicates all African Americans. He suggests that African Americans who are not poor and do not live in the urban ghettos must go through great lengths to shed the piercing misperception of their being associated with a stereotypical image of Black inner-city life.[57]

Creating a Black Brand and Distancing from the Recent Past

For cultural historians, it can be challenging to accurately describe the complicated trajectory of segregated, African American communities that have produced both inspiring and terrifying outcomes. In Shaw/U Street, the "Black Broadway" entertainment narrative, with Duke Ellington as the celebrated centerpiece, dominates the reconstructed Black brand. This narrative embellishes the community's heyday, roughly between 1920 and 1940, when it was a segregated, mixed-income space.

The Greater U Street walking tour's written guide, coauthored by Kathy Smith, opens with the following:

> Until 1920, when New York's Harlem overtook it, Washington, D.C. could claim the largest urban African American population in the United States. The U Street area provided the heartbeat. It inspired and nurtured the elegance and the musical genius of Duke Ellington. In the 1930s and 1940s, the likes of Cab Calloway, Pearl Bailey, Sarah Vaughn, Jelly Roll Morton, and native son Duke Ellington played on and around U Street, and hung out at after-hours clubs in a scene so full of magic that it was dubbed Washington's "Black Broadway."[58]

This Black branding material largely ignores the neighborhood's more recent past.[59] In the late 1970s and '80s, the Shaw/U Street reputation coincided with notions of the iconic ghetto, as it was known for containing "the heart of Washington's drug corridor."[60] Not only were drugs a major concern, but prostitution was as well. One of the community's earliest White "pioneers," Jackie Reed, in describing the community's Logan Circle area in the late 1970s, says, "In 1978, it was hell here. We had the house down the corner, Kingman Place, was an active house of prostitution. The house right next door to us became a house of prostitution. . . . I never saw much drugs. I just saw women and men going in and out. . . . It was just awful! Twenty-four hours a day! Cars coming down the street honking. 'Hey, baby!' you know. It was just awful!"

The creation of the Black Broadway narrative was largely shaped by the desire of internal and external community actors to fight certain negative iconic Black ghetto stereotypes. Kathy Smith insists that the Black Broadway narrative came "from the community." During her cultural preservation research, she held several community forums and heard stories about the neighborhood from seventy-five mainly long-term residents. According to Smith, most community meeting/focus group participants were in their seventies and eighties; they told "how they made it" despite persistent segregation and discrimination. Smith explained that the residents did not speak about the crime and the drugs of the 1970s and '80s; rather, they shared their stories of "achievement" and "uplift." In this way, internal community forces were distancing the neighborhood's newly created brand from the stereotypical image of the ghetto.

The Black Broadway and racial uplift themes in the Shaw/U Street branding are similar to what Michele Boyd found in the Bronzeville neighborhood on Chicago's South Side.[61] Boyd highlights that one of the main goals of constructing Bronzeville as a Black racial cultural district was to change outsiders' negative perceptions of the area. She claims that Bronzeville's "neighborhood leaders were acutely aware that achieving their economic and political goals would require them to transform prevailing ideas about people as well as place."[62] She argues that to fight negative neighborhood perceptions, "supporters deliberately reconstructed the neighborhood's black history" into a rise-and-fall narrative.[63] As in Shaw/U Street, Bronzeville's reconstructed Black narrative is one of uplift and achievement in the 1920s, '30s, and '40s, followed by a prolonged period of decline. Boyd states, "This narrative of achievement and decline helps sell the neighborhood by imbuing its residents with heroism and historical significance."[64] The heroism motif partly distances the neighborhood's association with its poor and iconic ghetto images by "obscur[ing] the existence and contributions of average black citizens [and] attribut[ing] racial accomplishments to the miniscule black middle class."[65]

Although internal Black preferences to fight racial stereotypes helped shape Shaw/U Street's Black Broadway narrative, Cultural Tourism, DC staff also played a critical role. The organization wanted to market the community to outsiders. To do this, it presented a safe, simplified, noncontroversial community narrative. Smith notes that Cultural Tourism, DC was trying to tell and sell the neighborhood's history to outsiders that "didn't appreciate African American culture."

Because the neighborhood's history as presented by Cultural Tourism, DC was so sanitized, some critics said, "Where're the prostitutes? They were here during the 70s and 80s."[66] Others would ask about the absence of the 1960s history of protest politics, through which civil rights leaders such as Walter Fauntroy, Stokely Carmichael, and Marion Barry organized the neighborhood. Smith lived in DC's Capitol Hill neighborhood during the 1960s and knew of the protest politics stemming from Shaw/U Street, but says it was difficult to tell that story, as well as the more recent story of the proliferation of drugs and prostitution in the neighborhood. She rhetorically asks, "How do you talk about tough things? This wasn't the way to start a public history of Shaw." She speaks about how challenging it was to get funding to communicate a politically charged neighborhood story, noting that her major Cultural Tourism, DC sponsors were the DC Chamber of Commerce, the Humanities Council of Washington, DC, and the National Trust for Historic Preservation. She realized that some of these funders were not interested in communicating a comprehensive history; they wanted a public narrative that would attract development.

The selection of particular parts of Black history to fight stereotypes, market a community to outsiders who might not appreciate Black culture, and receive funding for neighborhood development can be problematic. One of Smith's African American preservation partners, Marya McQuirter, who helped with the research for the 12th Street Y, the public mural installation, and Greater U Street Heritage Trail, says that the rise-and-fall narrative of the walking trail was something that "I totally disagreed with." She explains, "So I was attempting to insert more poor and working class and tensions around gender and all these different things, but that's not the thrust that folks were interested in."[67] She mentions that intraracial class tensions and the presence of poor people were downplayed along with interracial relations and sexual orientation.[68] As she explains, "You could have narrated U Street as a place of cross-racial, cross-gender, cross-sexual interaction . . . cross-class interaction. . . . And then if you do that, then what does that do for the whole rise and fall narrative?"[69] By excluding references to the poor, Cultural Tourism, DC helped to distance the community from iconic ghetto stereotypes.

Often, historic preservation initiatives choose what is perceived as the high point of the area's development. As cultural preservation expert Andrew Hurley states, "Highlighting a golden age helped legitimize a neighborhood's historic status. . . . Privileging the distant past at the expense of the recent past, however, robbed people of the ability to make connections to the present. . . . Those who possessed local roots were usually those whose own history was most closely intertwined with the era of decline, precisely the period that booster-oriented preservationists wanted to forget."[70]

Both internal and external preservationists wanted to minimize the decline period because it reproduced a stereotypical ghetto image they were trying to diminish. The desires of both some local residents and Cultural Tourism, DC staff to tell a marketable uplift story help explain Shaw/U Street's constructed Black Broadway narrative. In this narrative, entertainment is highlighted, while other community themes like interracial relations, intraracial class conflict, protest politics, prostitution, drugs, and poverty are minimized.

Some who have intensely studied Cultural Tourism, DC and its actions in the Shaw/U Street area claim that its work greatly contributed to the community's redevelopment and White takeover. Stephanie Frank, in her master's thesis on tourism and gentrification in that neighborhood, argues that the "role of historic preservation and cultural heritage activities in the

[handwritten in margin: But as such, not actually authentic?]

Greater U Street neighborhood is a revanchist one. The efforts guised as those meant to preserve the neighborhood have instead put into motion the refashioning of the former 'heart of black Washington' into a white middle-class neighborhood." She maintains, "The white middle-class claiming of the Greater U Street neighborhood is aided by CT/DC's [Cultural Tourism, DC] efforts."[71] Kathy Smith remarks that some residents said to her, "You told our history and made the community look good"—which led to its gentrification.

While some scholars might claim that Smith's cultural preservation efforts contributed to a White takeover of Shaw/U Street, others point out that Black branding should protect a race district from gentrification.[72] According to Michelle Boyd, "As entertainment and culture industries rely increasingly on images of racial difference and urban culture, the populations that supply those images are included, rather than excluded, from those economies. By the same token, racial tourism offers the opportunity for marginalized populations to remain in their communities, to cultivate community pride, and to participate in the benefits of economic regeneration."[73] In Chicago's Bronzeville, the neighborhood Boyd studied, the Black branded community stayed, for the most part, Black—but this did not happen in Shaw/U Street.

Shaw/U Street's Black branding work occurred as the community was transitioning from Black to White, a context complicating the Black history preservation effort. Smith reached out to the community grassroots organization Organizing Neighborhood Equity (ONE DC), which has relationships with many in the neighborhood's lower-income African American population, to partner on the Black history tours. The idea was to have low-income, long-term residents actually give the tours. ONE DC's outreach coordinator and community organizer, Gloria Robinson, helped train the U Street tour guides for Cultural Tourism, DC. Robinson, who is African American, has had it rough at times. Maybe because of her life struggles or the fact the she grew up in the neighborhood, she, much like Dominic Moulden, ONE DC's lead organizer, is extremely committed to helping the neighborhood's low-income residents.

Robinson and I chat in ONE DC's conference room, where the motto "Gentrification Is a White Collar Crime" is written on a whiteboard. Gloria insists that the tours got to be uncomfortable, because most of the people taking part "looked like you, Derek." She recalls that the "tourists," instead of asking questions about the community's Black history, were more interested in learning about its crime rates, its transportation routes, and the quality of its public schools: "These are people looking to find a home! These aren't tourists." She says it felt awkward helping to support Black history tours to mainly White participants who clearly wanted to redevelop the area. Robinson began to resent these "tourists," and decided that it was best for ONE DC to stop sponsoring the tours.

Smith's Black history preservation effort was a strategy to reduce Shaw/U Street's iconic Black ghetto stereotype and to build an appreciation for its important history. The effort marketed the community to outsiders who craved an authentic neighborhood experience and appreciated the area's inspirational Black narrative. However, some newcomers were attracted to Shaw/U Street because of its recent past and authentic association with the iconic ghetto.

Living the Wire and Reinforcing Traditional Stereotypes

While aspects of Shaw/U Street's Black history and culture have been woven into the community's fabric and linked with the area's redevelopment, some newcomers are not convinced that its historic Black brand is directly tied to its current economic revitalization. Ben, a White newcomer and avid neighborhood blogger, says, "My observation is a lot of the newer residents particularly of younger . . . people, 30 and under, who are coming here, it's more commercial attraction than it is any value of . . . the cultural. . . . They may see some [of the community's] murals. They might know who people like Thurgood Marshall [are] but not what he did." Ben's comments reflect an understanding that not everyone is moving to Shaw/U Street because of its African American history.

The neighborhood has unquestionably become one of DC's hippest. The headline of a *New York Times* article on the community emphatically states, "U Street: The Corridor Is Cool Again." A *Washington Post* piece claims that along 14th Street, one of the community's principal commercial arteries, "hipster shops, edgy theater and eclectic eateries form Washington's new Main Street."[74]

The area's hipness is connected to its popular alternative performance venues, such as the Studio Theater, Black Cat, 9:30 Club, Bohemian Caverns, and Jazz Twin's, but it is also associated with the marketing of the community's Black history.[75] Catherine, a White newcomer in her early twenties, enthusiastically describes Shaw/U Street:

U Street has almost always had a cool reputation, back to, like, in the 1930s and '40s. It was where, you know, the musicians came to play. I've been here for three years, and the difference between what it is now and what it was three years ago is so different, even between what it was a year and a half ago.

So many different businesses [with a meaningful connection to the community's Black history] are opening. . . . There's Busboys and Poets to remember Langston Hughes, there's Eatonville that's named after Zora Neale Hurston. Um, there's Marvin [named for Marvin Gaye].

Catherine's remarks suggest that the commodification of certain aspects of the community's "heyday" Black history is tied to its redevelopment and reputation. She recounts the neighborhood's "cool reputation," based on its reconstructed Black Broadway era. She then speaks about some of the new trendy restaurants, Busboys and Poets, Eatonville, and Marvin, that pay symbolic homage to aspects of the community's Black history. She explains that this history and coolness attracted her to the neighborhood over other, "boring," sections of the city.

American society is more integrated than ever, and for some scholars this is a signal of increasing racial and ethnic tolerance.[76] Today, when some people select a city in which to live, one critical criterion is its racial and ethnic diversity.[77] Some inner-city African American communities have now become hip to White America; whereas Whites once fled from Black communities, now the twenty- and thirty-somethings, like Catherine, flock to them to experience what they perceive as cool, hip living.[78]

Other newcomers are drawn to these areas to *live the wire*—a term that both references David Simon's successful HBO series *The Wire*, and describes a bundle of dynamics that draw young people to gentrifying inner-city Black neighborhoods. *The Wire* offers a compelling and complex structural analysis of urban inequality and inner-city Black life in Baltimore.[79] However, much like ethnographic inner-city accounts of the drug trade, such as sociologist Sudhir Venkatesh's *Gang Leader for a Day*, the series clearly sensationalizes drugs and urban violence.[80] I chose the term *living the wire* to reference and symbolize the association among entertainment, urban poverty, violence, and Blackness: all iconic ghetto stereotypes.

Living the wire also refers to newcomer preferences to move into an inner-city neighborhood because it has been branded as hip or cool, which, to a certain extent, is associated with poverty and the violent past of inner-city Black neighborhoods. For some, the hip and cool notions of the neighborhood relate to its heyday history, as Catherine notes, but for others it relates to its status as an "edge" neighborhood once avoided by the city's mainstreamers.

Living the wire is a new form of urban slumming in which newcomers experience aspects of low-income neighborhoods, not by exploring them on bus tours or visiting them at night in blues clubs, but by actually moving into these neighborhoods for the ultimate "authentic" experience.[81] While living the wire has the potential to expose outsiders to the complex conditions of America ghetto life and may reduce stereotypes, racially diverse, mixed-income living environments can also reinforce traditional stereotypes of the iconic ghetto.[82] Hence, the concept of living the wire relates to the dual notion of desiring to experience firsthand the complex nature of the inner-city life but also wanting to be excited and entertained safely.

Notions of living the wire became apparent to me one December night in 2010, when I attended a fundraiser for one of Shaw/U Street's civic associations. The event took place at Town, a local gay dance club that opened in 2007. The two-story, twenty-thousand-square-foot club sports large, wall-mounted, high-tech video installations and a disco ball. The fundraiser was held in the early evening, before the night crowd gets going. On the first dance floor, groups of people, mainly White, gathered around cocktail tables set at its center. I listened in and participated in several conversations as I ate finger food and walked around, bidding on several silent auction items. I noticed that some people were talking about area crime in an odd way. They described neighborhood carjackings, shootings, and purse snatchings with laughter and jokes. They talked about crime as if it were something to brag about. It was as if they were describing a movie as opposed to having a serious discussion. It was as if they were proud to live in an area that was unsafe and edgy. It seemed that the neighborhood violence gave some newcomers to the area bragging rights and something interesting to talk about at parties.

During the auction, one White newcomer who worked for a socially responsible investment firm in a nearby Maryland suburb described a shooting that took place on her block. She explained that an elderly man was trying to stop a teenager from selling drugs there. In retaliation, the teen shot him in the head. The woman said that her minority neighbors held a candlelight vigil for the man; afterward, many celebrated his life by lighting up blunts of marijuana. The woman said she could not understand: if the issue was getting drugs off the block, why were her neighbors using drugs in tribute to the elderly man?

The conversations I heard were of the type that urban scholar David Grazian references when he claims, "Thrill-seekers compete among their peers for the bragging rights that accompany the experience of authenticity."[83] For some people, living the wire seemingly helps them "become authentic" by experiencing poverty and Blackness firsthand.[84] It also relates to aspects of what sociologist Andrew Deener discovered during the gentrification of the rougher sections of Venice Beach, California, where elite bohemia collided with the Black ghetto. One of his participants reported, "People are down here on Abbot Kinney [the bohemian corridor] and they're having their tea and coffee, and just kicking it and having a grand ol'time, looking at the little boutiques, and meanwhile, there's murder going on around them. It's stupid, ya know? But it was happening."[85]

The concept of living the wire revealed itself to me on several occasions. For instance, a new White resident was explaining what made Shaw/U Street exciting and cool: "I just knew after, like, certain nights when it's, like, really hot out on a Friday night and noticed people hanging out on the street outside a shop or whatever. You could tell certain nights that it was, like, 'OK, I'm gonna wake up in the morning, I'm gonna get an email, and someone's going to have gotten shot.'"

The term *living the wire* can be juxtaposed to *Living the Drama*, the title of urban sociologist David Harding's excellent ethnographic account of how poor neighborhoods influence negative outcomes for minority youth.[86] In it, Harding describes the ways in which violence and the fear of violence among boys living in impoverished areas of Boston greatly determine their life-course trajectories. According to Harding, "Violence and strategies for avoiding victimization loomed large in the lives of boys in poor neighborhoods. Whether it was where to go to school and how to get there, whom to befriend and whom to avoid, or how to interpret the behavior of the adult they encountered, many decisions could not be made without reference to the violence that casts a constant shadow over their lives."[87] *Living the drama* means to carefully navigate and cope with extreme forms of urban violence.

During the 2000s, crime drastically decreased in Washington, DC. However, in certain sections of Shaw/U Street, major violence still occurs occasionally.[88] In 2015, diners seated at P14's outdoor patio dove under their tables for cover when gunfire erupted nearby. Those shots killed a twenty-nine-year-old African American man who had grown up in the neighborhood.[89] The community has some remnants from its days as an infamous drug market. Moreover, it has some "hot spots" for robberies despite the redevelopment that has taken place.[90]

For Novella, an African American resident of the Foster Homes, a subsidized development about six blocks from Town, living the drama is an everyday occurrence. She says that even though the neighborhood has changed, a lot of gang violence and drug dealing still go on. Young men involved in crews, DC gangs, continue to wage territorial battles, and these disputes sometimes escalate into violence. Novella explains that if someone has a "beef" with a guy who crossed a turf boundary, he shoots at him. She claims that her generation used fistfights, not bullets, to settle disputes. But today, she says, guys shoot. Novella talks about crime and neighborhood violence as something to be feared, not joked about.

For several long-term African American residents, living the drama has had tangible consequences, such as the loss of a loved one. I met Curtis Mozie, known as C-Webb, while playing basketball at the Kennedy Recreation Center. Though in his forties, C-Webb has the stamina of a twenty-year-old. He would always want to play one more game when I could barely breathe after playing with him for more than an hour.

C-Webb has been documenting the violence that has plagued Shaw/U Street for decades. He records videos of the area youth as they grow up in the community, particularly the ones involved in the crews. He attempts to serve as a mentor and show them that running the streets usually leads to jail and/or death. C-Webb has compiled numerous videographic tributes to the many young men who have lost their lives to the violent streets near the Kennedy Recreation Center.

David Robinson, known as Day-Day, was one of the area's youth who lived the drama.[91] He grew up in the Washington Apartments, a subsidized housing complex a few blocks south of the Kennedy Recreation Center, and was raised by a single mother, Evon Davis; his father was rarely around. Although Evon, and several mentors, tried to keep David out of trouble, he struggled in school and lived by the code of the street.[92] He felt that to protect himself from the area crews, he needed to join one of them; so he joined the Seventh and O Street crew and carried a gun. In the ninth grade, David was arrested after a hallway shoving match with another area crew made its way out into the streets after school. A few years later, in 2009, David was shot at age seventeen after a fight broke out at a concert.

This near-death experience made David change his ways. He got a job at Home Depot, made a commitment to finish his high school degree, and got serious about his pregnant girlfriend. His goal was to finish school and be the father to his son that his father never was. Just before the birth of his son, David was shot by a group of young men who wanted his new $220 Nike sneakers. Instead of giving up the shoes, David had pulled his gun and was killed. Like many of the youth of Shaw/U Street, David lived the drama with serious consequences, despite the redevelopment that has taken place in this community and along the 7th Street corridor.

The Grit and the Glamour

Certain new upscale and exclusive neighborhood establishments, such as the Gibson, play off the community's edginess and the stereotypical image

Figure 11. Outside the Gibson.

of the iconic ghetto. The Gibson is a contemporary, "hidden" speakeasy. It is located in a nondescript gray building that looks abandoned (fig. 11). There is no signage, and no street-facing windows on the first floor. All that can be seen from the street is a small, unassuming doorbell-like buzzer discreetly placed near a front door. When the buzzer is pressed, a stylishly dressed young greeter comes out. If it is early evening, you will likely get in; otherwise, you have to put your name and cell phone number on a waiting list. When a spot opens at the bar—this can take an hour or more, depending on the night—the hostess texts you. Once inside, the environment changes from the gritty exterior to a posh, retro 1920s-style speakeasy interior with a dark-wood-framed bar showcasing illuminated shelves of liquor, dim lighting, and mixologists serving signature cocktails for fifteen bucks apiece (fig. 12).[93] On any given night, it is not uncommon to see and hear political appointees talking over a few drinks.

Directly next door to the Gibson is a ghetto-style liquor store with Plexiglas separating the customers from the merchandise, much of which is fifths of liquor. On any given night, a group of older or middle-aged African American men hang out in front. Additionally, a nearby bus stop ensures frequent bursts of activity from people of color outside the Gibson.

Figure 12. Inside the Gibson.

The liquor store's grit provides the perfect contrast to the glamour of the speakeasy. The juxtaposition of the Gibson, an exclusive, upscale cocktail establishment, to the grimy liquor store and a group of African American men on the street gives the speakeasy an ethos of hipness and edge based in part on a Black ghetto stereotype. All that is needed next to the Gibson to complete the iconic ghetto stereotype would be a storefront church.

The bar's White owners, Eric and Ian Hilton, deploy the trope of the iconic ghetto to attract resident tourists.[94] In describing how he and his design team came up with the concept of the Gibson, Eric remarks, "Our process starts with an exploration of atmosphere: what else is on the block, who lives in the neighborhood."[95]

This proximity of grit and glamour plays off the notion of neighborhood newcomers' preference for living the wire while it relates to the community's Black brand. The stereotype that the Gibson works off is that somehow a certain type of Blackness equals the authentic ghetto experience that certain customers, mainly White, seek. The Hilton brothers in Shaw/U Street have located their business where "stereotyped images of the city" give the Gibson its coolness and edge.[96]

The bar is one of DC's hottest, and its coolness, to a certain extent, is associated with an almost fabricated crime "hot spot." The Gibson uses imagery of an iconic ghetto where, as Elijah Anderson indicates, people are "both curious and fearful of 'dangerous' black people."[97] The men congregating in front of the liquor store next door and the faux-abandoned building that houses the Gibson provide the image people expect to see in the ghetto. Except in *this* gilded ghetto, studios rent for $2,300 a month and row homes sell for over $1 million.

Other local commercial establishments cash in on elements of living the wire. Some incorporate the neighborhood's African American history in a variety of ways, to make their places stand out and appear cool and attractive to a diverse set of middle- and upper-income customers. One of them is Busboys and Poets, a trendy restaurant, bar, bookstore, coffee shop, and performance venue all in one. As owner Andy Shallal (fig. 13) proudly and sincerely explains, Busboys incorporates a variety of African American traditions into its "DNA."

Shallal, an Iraqi American, describes the relationship between the Shaw/U Street community's past and Busboys and Poets, which was established in 2005: "This is historically a Black community. It was called Black Broadway . . . and I wanted to be able to bring that back in a way that I felt was

Figure 13. Owner Andy Shallal (*left*) and the author in Busboys and Poets' Langston Hughes Room (©Jim Stroup).

getting covered up by much of the changes that were taking place in this area. . . . And so we named this place Busboys and Poets in honor of Langston Hughes, who worked as a busboy while writing poetry in Washington, DC."

Not only does the name of Shallal's restaurant incorporate aspects of African American history, but the menu and performance programming do as well. Shallal explains:

> I went out of my way to be . . . more inclusive of African Americans. . . . The menu clearly had to be representative of things that the community liked. . . . Things like having catfish on the menu . . . represent a certain [kind of] hospitality. It is traditionally an African American dish. It is something that we happily make to say to the indigenous community here, which is mostly African American, that this is a place that speaks to them. Another part was the programming, which is really eclectic in its variety and mix. We have open mic here on a regular basis. . . . open mic in this area had a real strong tradition, strong history, mostly African American.

Shallal is clearly drawing on stereotypical notions of Blackness: catfish and spoken word as a form of protest politics.

A strong link exists between Busboys and Poets and a certain African American heritage and culture, but it is not just this culture that is important; the culture is tied to a specific Washington, DC, geography. In explaining why he opened the first Busboys near 14th and U Streets, Shallal expresses the connection between the neighborhood and his establishment: "It had to start here, because I wanted to establish the brand. I wanted to establish the Busboys and Poets idea, what it was about."

Shallal describes what the neighborhood was like before Busboys and Poets came in: "When we first moved here, there was the relief recovery center, which was right across the street here on the corner to us, which was an A[lcoholics] A[nonymous] center for recovering addicts and alcoholics. It was mostly Black men that belonged to that program. So . . . the whole time before we opened, there was a congregation of men at that corner." He noted, "The perspective of many is that there's a bunch of Black men on the corner, and there's only trouble that will go on."

Shallal recounts the racial tensions that arose when some of the new White condo owners perceived a threat across the street:

> So, we invited the director of the [AA] program to come and speak to the community here. We had a meeting right here in this room, where a few of the workers were here as well as some of the people who were involved with

the program . . . talking about the program. They [the new condo owners] became the biggest advocates for the program because . . . it's better to have a bunch of Black men standing on the sidewalk trying to recover than a bunch of Black men that are drug addicts. You know, the people that used to be here.

Shallal and many DC residents know that the area where Busboys is located used to be one of the city's most notorious open-air drug and prostitution markets.[98] The community's difficult past, especially the area in the vicinity of Busboys that was the site of the DC riots of 1968, an open-air drug market, and then a recovery center, is part of what gives Busboys its edgy and hip brand while being associated with Blackness, poverty, and authenticity.

40s, MD 2020, and Lottery Tickets?

While both the Gibson and Busboys and Poets use traditional ghetto tropes along with other characteristics to fabricate their coolness, sometimes those living in or frequenting Shaw/U Street encounter more vividly ingrained ghetto stereotypes. Good Libations is a liquor store that some might describe as having a multiple personality disorder, but in fact it represents the neighborhood extremely well. It has some features of both a stereotypical inner-city liquor store and a high-end wine shop. A worn wooden counter and a large, three-inch-thick wall of Plexiglas separate most of the liquor and the sales clerk from the customers. The panel has a small revolving door that the clerk spins around to take your payment and give you your purchase. The merchandise behind the Plexiglas includes an array of vodkas, bourbons, and scotches. However, a variety of wines, from well-known regions like the Napa Valley, are not behind that wall. Near the unprotected wines are high-end beers such as a twenty-two-ounce of Chimay for $12.99. Refrigerators in the back of the store contain pricey microbrews in addition to twenty-two-ounce cans and bottles of Heineken, Miller Lite, Pabst Blue Ribbon, and other cheaper beers.

Ron is the store's African American owner. He tells me he keeps the Plexiglas because it signals to customers that they need to make their purchase and get out, not linger in the shop. He adds that it prevents some petty thefts.

Ron began the business in 2005, and says that as the neighborhood has changed, his customer base has also changed. When he began, his customers were 70% Black, 25% White, and 5% Asian and Hispanic. He says that now they are 60% White, 35% Black, and 5% Asian and Hispanic. Subdivided row houses once stood across the street, and their African American occupants were among Ron's regular customers. Now, he says, the row houses are either single-family homes or duplexes and are occupied by Whites. A set of his African American customers come from the Section 8–subsidized Washington Apartments nearby as well as low-income co-ops.

Ron's establishment caters to both lower- and upper-income alcohol preferences. He remarks that the new, higher-income White and Black populations are "buying more wine, more upscale spirits, and more of the craft beers. Whereas the Blacks who I guess were born here or who have been living here for a long time, the old-timers . . . still continue to buy the lower-level items." Ron explains that he likes variety, and so offers a wide selection of alcohol. He does note that his longtime Black customers occasionally call him a "sellout" for increasing the amount of "White people's wine." But it might not be the wine that upsets Ron's longtime Black customers so much as the fact that it is freestanding, while most of the other beverages are kept behind the Plexiglas barrier.

The city banned the sale of forty-ounce single-container liquor in 2008, but Ron stopped carrying "40s" before that. He got tired of how many younger White newcomers to Shaw/U Street were buying them:

> For some reason, I guess these kids have grown up watching videos or whatever, and now it's . . . This one White guy came in; he was just like, you know, straight White guy, glasses, everything. And he was, like, "Oh, you don't have any 40s?" And I thought he was trying to make a joke, because . . . he came in looking for forty-ounces, MD 2020, and lottery tickets. And I was, like, "Huh?" He goes, "Well, I'm going to a party." I said, "What type of party is this?" He told me, he said, "Oh, we're going to a 'hood party." And I'm just like, nah, nah, get out of here. I have no problem with 40s, but don't come in because you're trying to be stereotypical.

Ron explained that this incident occurred frequently enough that he just stopped selling 40s.

To a certain extent, the neighborhood's redevelopment thrives on the community remaining racially diverse or, more specifically, Black and edgy. It helps give the community its pulse, its vibe, its coolness—but this "construction of coolness" reinforces and perpetuates traditional stereotypes to some degree. Some Whites think it is cool to live in a racially transitioning, formerly low-income neighborhood and throw stereotypical ghetto-themed parties. The Gibson's edge is associated with its proximity to a stereotypical "inner-city" liquor store and the group of Black men that congregate outside it. Other newcomers talk about tragic neighborhood crime and violence as if they were describing a scene from HBO's *The Wire*. It seems that the sporadic violence is merely a community backdrop to some newcomers who move to Shaw/U Street, in part, for excitement, entertainment, and authenticity from living the wire.

In the neighborhood, a certain amount of poverty, blight, Blackness, and danger gives it its authentic, edgy brand, which in turn is associated with property demand and skyrocketing home prices. This is a mind-boggling turnaround from the times when these same characteristics would likely have been associated with substantial property decline. The concept of living the wire helps to explain part of this phenomenon, where certain iconic ghetto features provide the "authentic" neighborhood drama, a live reality show of sorts, sought by some White middle- and upper-income newcomers.

For some, this concept might conjure notions of 1920s urban slumming, yet something profoundly different is occurring.[99] Living the wire is just that. It's not simply visiting an area as a tourist or urban thrill-seeker; it is residing within a Black-identified space.[100] Where living the wire mirrors the slumming concept is in the fact that the thrill, the edge, the coolness, the Black brand, is based on preexisting Black ghetto stereotypes—Black men and women as entertainers, drug dealers, and lazy people hanging out on the corner. It also brings up images of Black people as the Other. The neighborhood is hip partly because it is perceived as a place to avoid because it was once dangerous.

Summing Up

The urban landscape is constantly shifting, and many African American iconic urban ghettos across the nation are being rebranded as hip, edgy, and historic areas for the consumption of Black culture. Some of these communities are experiencing Black gentrification, while others are becoming more racially diverse by attracting middle- and upper-income Whites. One common feature is that many of these low-income Black neighborhoods are using forms of Black branding to attract development.

There is no question that DC's Shaw/U Street neighborhood has an African American brand. Its streets are dotted with walking-tour signs describing the accomplishments of African Americans associated with the neighborhood's past. Several neighborhood roads are named after significant Black figures, and community murals depict important African Americans. Moreover, trendy new restaurants as well as luxury apartment and condominium buildings are named after African American literary and musical icons.

Link to other USA areas using Black branding.

For some people, Black branding, and its association with neighborhood redevelopment, signifies racial progress. We have witnessed a major transition in the acceptance of Blackness. Black branding provides some evidence that we as a country appreciate and value elements of Black history. It was not long ago that many Americans feared the Black ghetto, and the majority of urban neighborhoods deemed Black were avoided. Today, historic Black neighborhoods are attracting a much more diverse population, and in some instances Black branding is associated with neighborhood redevelopment.

While the Shaw/U Street area's Black Broadway brand was shaped by multiple forces, one was the desire to reduce the community's negative iconic ghetto image. Decisions about having the rebranded image not be too Black, too poor, or too controversial were influenced by both African Americans and Whites in order to present a positive community image to outsiders. Oftentimes this external audience focus reinforces Black stereotypes, such as the one of African Americans as musical entertainers, clearly represented in Shaw/U Street's Black Broadway image; but it also relates to elite Blacks and other community stakeholders wanting to minimize negative African American stereotypes. The sanitized racial uplift image attempts to distance the community from iconic ghetto stereotypes.

Many historic Black communities are spinning a similar uplift and entertainment narrative regardless of whether the storylines are spun by Black-controlled local governments, elite Black residents, or White external elites, as in the Shaw/U Street case with Cultural Tourism, DC.[101] Much like Starbucks has commodified and exported a certain small Seattle coffee shop experience and McDonald's has duplicated a version of the classic American hamburger and fries around the world, Black neighborhoods are attempting to commodify a certain nostalgic Black history experience in cities around the United States.[102] By branding Black culture and mainstreaming the ghetto, we reduce some African American stereotypes, but at the same time we lose some complexity about how institutional racism contributed to creating the Black ghetto in the first place.

While Black and White preservationists work to counteract negative stereotypes of the iconic ghetto, some neighborhood newcomers are looking for authentic experiences based on their expectation that inner-city Black areas are dangerous and exciting. This iconic Black ghetto stereotype is associated with contemporary and hip, urban and grit. Real estate developers and commercial businesses have tapped into this valued "edge living" commodity and are selling it for a premium to those who can afford it. It is hard to conceptualize exactly what they are selling or what customers are purchasing, but part of the amenity bundle can be explained by what I have called "living the wire," which is based on preexisting stereotypical images of the iconic ghetto.

Living the wire refers to a notion of residing in a community that has an energy and an edge that distinguishes people who live in the inner city from those living in the "boring" homogeneous suburban and central city areas. Living the wire helps newcomers carve out their urban niche in the metropolis. They flock to historic Black neighborhoods to experience the thrill of viewing elements of the iconic ghetto.

While the fact that Whites feel comfortable moving to Black spaces might seem like racial progress, to a certain extent it is based on stereotypical portrayals of African Americans. Some newcomers move into African American communities based on a perceived association between urban authenticity and Blackness. The relationship between authenticity and Blackness is related to the stereotypical association of Blackness with poverty, danger, and excitement, which in turn symbolizes contemporary subtle racism. I consider this a form of subtle racism, compared to the past, when people would not move into a Black community due to blatant racism.

Harvard University sociologist William Julius Wilson uses the HBO series *The Wire* as part of his course on urban inequality.[103] One of his students, Kellie O'Toole, states, "People in society attempt to distance themselves from the 'other.' . . . 'The Wire' works against this idea by depicting the connection between mainstream and street culture. It shows that, while people sometimes think they live in different worlds, we are more alike than we are different."[104]

However, some newcomers to redeveloping ghettos who might be inspired by and appreciate elements of Black culture do not truly engage in the ghettos' complexity. The younger newcomers, the tourists in place, seem more concerned with consuming ghetto-inspired culture than connecting and identifying with those struggling with the ills of racism and structural inequality. The relationships among discrimination, institutional racism, and intergenerational poverty are not part of a narrative told to them in the community's rebranded story, nor are these relationships often addressed by newcomers when they engage in community politics.

Andrew Hurley explains that festive cultural districts often "discouraged visitors from reflecting deeply."[105] Few Shaw/U Street newcomers seriously contemplate the community's past to understand how the neighborhood was structured and how it produced concentrated poverty. Rather, iconic ghetto elements of poverty, crime, and Blackness are seen as exciting community backdrops. This situation reinforces Elijah Anderson's observation that "as the urban environment becomes ever more pluralistic and the

veneer of racial civility spreads, a profound stigma persists, embodied ultimately in black skin and manifested in the iconic black ghetto."[106]

This is not the first study to highlight that certain people are drawn to urban
areas that contain poverty and posh amenities. In his detailed ethnographic
study of the redevelopment of LA's Skid Row, Bernard Harcourt states, "It is
precisely that juxtaposition of high-end lofts and homeless beggars that gives
L.A.'s Skid Row a trendy, urban, edgy, noir flavor that is so marketable."[107] In
Chicago's gentrifying Wicker Park, Richard Lloyd notes that for upper-income
newcomers, "sharing it with working class and non-white residents, even if
personal interaction remains superficial, is part of their image of an authentic urban experience."[108] Lloyd explains that the newcomers' understanding of
their neighborhood's rough past as infested with gangs, drugs and prostitutes
"coincided with the bohemian disposition to value the drama of living on
the edge."[109] Christopher Mele and Sharon Zukin claim that some middle-
and upper-income New Yorkers find the close proximity of grit and glamour
an "authentic" postindustrial aesthetic.[110] What all these scholars describe un-
doubtedly manifests itself in Shaw/U Street, and provides concrete evidence
that consumer culture and the search for authenticity shape neighborhood
development.

The influences of reducing and reinforcing racial stereotypes on Black
branding processes have implications for theories of urban development and
growth. Black branding and living the wire correspond to Terry Clark's entertainment machine theory.[111] Clearly, in Washington, DC, city officials are
backing efforts to merge Black culture, entertainment, and diversity to form
a commodity to attract twenty- and thirty-somethings to Shaw/U Street.[112]
While the commodification of Black culture is part of Shaw/U Street's revitalization story, aspects of the community process, particularly the marketing of elements of Black culture, are shaped by a racial framework: reducing
some iconic ghetto images while at the same time promoting and reinforcing others. Both Black and White understandings of the iconic ghetto and
its association with Blackness relate to the construction, commodification,
sale, and purchase of the community's Black brand. This finding supports
Michelle Boyd, who states that Black branding "does not imply that race is
insignificant: despite academic clamoring for its end, race remains important
in the political life of African Americans."[113] Race is critical to both Black political life and the understanding of White consumer preferences, which are
associated with neighborhood change in inner-city America.

Racial understandings are critical to making the gilded ghetto. What
we see in Shaw/U Street is not the typical gentrification pattern but rather
the past of the neighborhood fashioned as a "city within a city": its Black

Broadway heyday in the early part of the twentieth century and its more recent past as an iconic Black ghetto in the 1970s, '80s, and '90s are critical elements in marketing this community to newcomers. It is precisely the community's history as a Black ghetto that helps make it cool, hip, authentic, and attractive to upper-income, mainly White, newcomers.

My findings challenge the claim that Black branding can safeguard a minority community from gentrification and displacement.[114] In the case of Shaw/U Street, cultural preservation helped make the community "capital ready." Investments in rehabilitating buildings and constructing historic districts, murals, and signage are signals that the community is "tourist ready," but they are also signals to investors and "tourists" who desire to live the wire. Black branding does not ensure that the community can control its own destiny, nor does it predict Black control over a Black branded neighborhood. In Shaw/U Street, the rise of the Black brand correlated with significant decline in the number and percentage of Black residents, and an increase in property values. Some of the Black population decline was based on choice, and some on forced displacement caused by rising property values.[115] As Hurley claims, "It is one thing to assess a commitment to social diversity through preservation and public interpretation, quite another to prevent soaring property values from displacing existing residents or a least imposing hardship on those with meager financial resources."[116]

The concept of living the wire helps explain why mixed-income living is so difficult to implement or maintain, and why it is not producing the expected results in terms of racial and income mixing. Gentrification author Sarah Schulman states, "Mixed neighborhoods create public simultaneous thinking, many perspectives converging on the same moment at the same time, in front of each other. Many languages, many cultures, many racial and class experiences take place on the same block, in the same building."[117] However, if one population is living the wire and the other is living the drama, crime might be interpreted in very different ways, making it difficult to develop shared understandings and goals. As policy makers promote mixed-income living environments, we cannot assume that people moving into these environments understand community circumstances and events in the same way that long-term residents do. For instance, some newcomers might view the perception of crime as important to the neighborhood's hip identity, while others might view crime as detrimental to their life chances.

This chapter demonstrates the importance of race in the process of Black branding and presents a plausible explanation for the arrival of some Whites in traditionally low-income African American communities. While interrogating Black branding and the influx of Whites in Shaw/U Street, this chapter generates more questions than it answers. For instance, by what specific mechanisms do cultural preservation initiatives lead to community revitalization? Moreover, at what population tipping point does the Black brand begin to fade? As noted in 2010, the Shaw/U Street neighborhood is only 30 percent African American, and it seems as if this percentage will only decline as the community continues to redevelop.[118] Will Shaw/U Street still hold on to its Black "authentic" identity if African Americans are no longer a sizable resident population? Lastly, how do newcomers in historic Black neighborhoods relate to the original residents?

In the next chapter, I examine how low-income African Americans and new White residents interact within this mixed-income, mixed-race community. As can be anticipated, racial conflict emerges, but race alone is insufficient for understanding the internal dynamics of this complex community. The influence of multiple social categories must be acknowledged to better understand the tensions and discords materializing in Shaw/U Street.

FIVE

Race, Class, and Sexual Orientation

I bring diversity to the most diverse Ward. I don't take it away, because I'm an immigrant, I'm gay, and I've been gay, openly gay, years before I was a council member, [and] I'm now a senior, right? I wasn't when I was first elected, but I am now. And you know, those are three contributing diverse elements.

—Jim Graham, DC's Ward 1 city council member from 1998 to 2014

The social and political behaviors within burgeoning, racially diverse urban neighborhoods are an enigma. Some literature suggests that the twenty-first century brought a new racial order, one in which individuals of distinct social categories are more civil with one another than in the past.[1] For instance, sociologist Elijah Anderson argues that while discrimination still exists, several urban spaces have developed a "cosmopolitan canopy," where people engage with one another across social categories with a "spirit of civility" and "goodwill."[2] However, other scholarship indicates that when different racial and ethnic groups live together in multiracial neighborhoods, intense debates often emerge.[3] Urban Institute scholars Margery Turner and Lynette Rawlings suggest that "given America's history of prejudice, discrimination, inequality, and fear, it is not surprising that diversity within a neighborhood sometimes leads to misunderstanding and conflict."[4]

Some scholars recognize that other categories in addition to race, such as gender, class, or sexual orientation, shape behaviors, attitudes, and discord.[5] Research on intersectionality has explored how multiple categories work simultaneously to inform individual identity and drive behavior.[6] There are several excellent individual- and organizational-level studies on intersectionality, but few have thoroughly explored how race, class, and sexual orientation operate at the community level to influence political debates and neighborhood change processes within gentrifying neighborhoods.[7]

In this chapter, I employ the concept of intersectionality, "the relationships among multiple dimensions and modalities of social relations," to investigate how distinct social categories influence community-level processes related to community change.[8] I probe how race, class, and sexual orientation shape political interactions. Specifically, I deploy what Leslie McCall describes as the intercategorical complexity approach to intersectionality research by adopting the existing social categories of race, class, and sexual orientation in order to assess their utility in explaining political engagement and conditions in Shaw/U Street.[9]

These categories are not completely static or visible, because people can choose different racial and ethnic identifications, present themselves as part of different social-class groups, or conceal their sexual orientation. Nonetheless, the categories are both present and meaningful in Shaw/U Street.[10] In this neighborhood, much of the remaining African American population is moderate- or low-income and lives in areas where subsidized housing remains. These low-income Black residents also tend to socialize and connect at certain institutions, such as particular churches, recreation centers, and civic associations, where little racial integration occurs. Much of the disadvantaged Black population shares the common interest of wanting to remain in the neighborhood despite rising costs. Additionally, in certain neighborhood sections, such as Logan Circle, many of the upper-income newcomers are gay, and leaders of their civic institutions tend to advocate for particular amenities that do not always align with some of the community's long-term Black institutions. Furthermore, elite African American real estate developers attempt to make high rates of return off the community's redevelopment, and this interest conflicts at times with the concerns of low-income Black residents.[11] While there is variation within the groups described, particular group-level interests are distinct and collide as these different factions compete for control over Shaw/U Street's future.

This chapter contributes to the intersectionality and gentrification literatures in at least three important ways. First, I demonstrate that as communities become more diverse, racial tension is a significant but not dominant driver of neighborhood politics. Rather, multiple social categories are critical to understanding political interactions in diverse neighborhoods. Second, multiple social categories embed themselves within the community's organizational structure and influence important political decisions affecting the neighborhood landscape. These insights suggest that intersectionality functions not only at the individual level but is also critical at the organizational and community levels. Third, as will be demonstrated, the community as it transitions is filled with intense conflicts, offering little evidence that Anderson's concept of the cosmopolitan canopy widely applies to the gilded ghetto.

Gentrification and Intersectionality: The Lenses of Race, Sexual Orientation, and Class

Traditional US gentrification studies tend to focus on racial discord. In conventional gentrification, White artists move into a low-income community of color.[12] Eventually, White professionals follow, and their arrival is associated with rising property values. Increased home values and rents force long-term, low-income minority residents out of the neighborhood. Then a different community forms, with new residents and norms, and the old neighborhood is for the most part unrecognizable.

Yet while race is an important concept in community change studies, other important characteristics, such as sexual orientation, often influence conditions within economically transitioning communities.[13] For instance, Manuel Castells's study of San Francisco's Castro neighborhood posits that the establishment of a new gay urban community "transforms established cultural values and existing spatial forms."[14] Moreover, Japonica Brown-Saracino demonstrates that an influx of gay residents can alter the physical and social infrastructure and meaning of space.[15]

Sometimes the onset of gay-oriented infrastructure occurs with limited conflict. For instance, Alan Collins observes little community resistance associated with the establishment of the Soho Gay Village in Central London, giving some credence to the notion that we have attained a postgay society.[16] However, in other contexts the emergence of gay symbols and culture has been contested.[17] Michael Sibalis demonstrates that the transformation of Marais, Paris, into a gay district was met with political opposition from middle-class residents whose rhetoric contained an "explicit or implicit homophobic message."[18] While gay populations have catalyzed gentrification processes in marginal ethnic and minority neighborhoods such as San Francisco's Castro, New York's Hell's Kitchen, and Atlanta's Mid-City, few studies have thoroughly explored interactions between gay newcomers and long-term African Americans in a gentrifying community. Further, little attention has been given to how sexual orientation, along with other social categories, explains community conflict.

In the 1990s and 2000s, scholars witnessed the emergence of Black gentrification and highlighted class conflicts within Black urban America.[19] In her study of the redevelopment of Chicago's Black Belt, Mary Pattillo claims,

"In the snapshot that this research represents . . . the issues are decidedly intraracial."[20] Her ethnographic study centers on the differences, divisions, and conflicts among African Americans, and claims that these distinctions relate to "divergent class interests within black America."[21] While Black gentrification works like Pattillo's and others, including Michelle Boyd's, Lance Freeman's, and Monique Taylor's, are extremely insightful for understanding class relations within Black America, they do not address how race, class, and sexual orientation accumulate to explain conditions in heterogeneous gentrifying neighborhoods.[22]

Dialogues and Debates

The remainder of the chapter consists of three vignettes. The first vignette illustrates how intergroup racial tensions explain political debates over community parking. The second demonstrates how homophobia is important to understanding the community conflict associated with the establishment of a gay bar in the neighborhood. The last illuminates how class dynamics within the African American population are critical to understanding both Shaw/U Street's redevelopment processes and their consequences. Cumulatively, these three illustrative stories demonstrate that the concept of intersectionality provides the key to comprehensively understanding civic dialogues and debates stemming from the organizational structure of this diverse community. This chapter also provides evidence that Elijah Anderson's concept of the "cosmopolitan canopy" does not generalize well to the gilded ghetto, as conflict proliferates across several dimensions in this diverse community.

Where Would Jesus Park?[23]

Shaw/U Street still has many African American churches, even though the community's Black population has substantially decreased. Many parishioners drive in from the suburbs and double-park near their respective churches while they attend Sunday services. Often, the double-parkers prevent legally parked cars they've blocked in from moving for several hours. In historic Black communities throughout the United States, such as Harlem and Bronzeville, Sunday double-parking is common.[24] In those communities, the practice is officially illegal, but an established norm that local police and old and new residents accept and allow.[25]

That is not the case in Shaw/U Street. Between 1999 and 2006, newer and some longer-term White residents fought with city government officials, in both the Williams and the Fenty administrations, to get the police to ticket double-parked cars.[26] Charles Reed, a long-term White resident and former chair of Advisory Neighborhood Commission (ANC) 2F, talked with me in his living room about Shaw/U Street's parking situation, and how the police came to ticket cars on Sundays:

> Well, they [the police] wouldn't have done that, but for the pressure that we generated. . . . Washington has an interesting facet of the structure of government that other cities do not have, and that's the ANC system.[27] What they, ANCs, do is they provide a channel for pressure on government at all levels, which reflects the interests and attitude of the community. So when you've got people upset about the church parking, it was channeled through the ANC. The ANC was able to pull together the Department of Transportation, the churches themselves, and those people who were adversely impacted by the parking situation, and the police to come up with solutions. That process worked very well.

However, while some felt that the ANC 2F political process for handling the parking situation worked well, others had a different take. Representatives from the community's historic Metropolitan Baptist Church believed that the mounting political pressure of the ANC's growing White faction pushed them out of the community.

Established in 1864 by former slaves, Metropolitan has been led by Rev. H. Beecher Hicks since 1977. While most of the congregation used to live in Shaw/U Street, by 2004 less than 1 percent resided in the church's zip code.[28] In 2010, I interviewed Rev. Hicks in his suburban Maryland office, located across the street from the stalled construction of Metropolitan's new church facilities.

I asked Rev. Hicks when he began to notice changes in the racial demographics and property values in Shaw/U Street. He said, "The dramatic shift really began to occur around the turn of the [twenty-first] century. The dawn of 2000 we began to see some really significant landownership changes in the area, and that was both good and bad, I suppose." After some probing, he elaborated:

> Well, you know . . . positively, . . . it permitted many members of the congregation to move to a higher standard of living outside of Shaw. . . . On the other hand, it left the church in a very precarious position because . . . when I came [to the church in 1977] we were surrounded to a great extent by people who knew the church, who understood it, who were engaged in its programs.

I mean, even the alcoholics in the neighborhood. They knew they could come . . . Wednesday[s] for the AA meeting[s] and the NA meeting[s]. All of those kinds of things were centered in the church, so the church was really a part of the life of the community, not an appendage. Not the camel's nose in the tent. . . . With the changing of hands of property and others moving in, there was not the appreciation for the church, its mission, its values. . . . And so it set up a kind of, I don't how I'm supposed to say [*he paused and then continued*], an unnatural kind of tug-of-war between the church and these new neighbors, and that was unfortunate.

Rev. Hicks explained that the "new" versus "old" tug-of-war was based on a racial divide that centered on the use of a nearby schoolyard for church parking:

It would appear to a casual observer that this is just the ebb and flow of financial fortunes. . . . And in our culture, which wants to pretend to be beyond race now, we're finding very painfully sometimes that that notion is inaccurate, and in fact it does have a racial component. . . . Our particular conflict came about because of the community's interest in what they call preserving the school and its schoolyard. For years before I got there, *for years*, the church had been using that schoolyard for parking on Sunday. Garrison School. Not only had we been using it, we had been maintaining it, and we had been paying for the privilege. . . . But our new neighbors saw the parking in the area as somehow anti-whatever purposes they may have had. So we were even taken to court to prevent us from using it. They forced the parking that we had placed on the school back into the streets. The streets got jammed more than they were already. Then they went to the powers that be and said, "OK, enforce the law," which was really a strategy, a not-too-veiled strategy, to say to the church, "You're not wanted here. We have no intentions of making any conciliatory movements to make your life easier or your continuance in this community something that makes sense."

The double-parking debate was fought on two fronts at different periods. First, in 1999, a new White resident raised the legal issue with the DC Board of Education about the relationship between Garrison and the church. The School Board member who moderated that debate was also White.[29] The board and the courts determined that it was not legal for the church to use the space for parking, even though it had been doing so for decades. This decision moved the church parking onto the streets.

Then in December 2005, others, mainly White newcomers to Shaw/U Street, fought the on-street double parking debate at ANC 2F gatherings. At one such meeting, resident Todd Lovinger told DC police lieutenant Mike Smith that people attending the church on his block "park illegally, blocking fire hydrants, sidewalks, and forcing residents into precarious situations."[30] Lovinger strongly encouraged Lieutenant Smith to ticket illegally parked churchgoers.

At the following ANC 2F meeting, the area's major Black churches came to articulate their concerns. At this meeting, Rev. Hicks represented several of the Black churches in the surrounding area. He asked Lovinger to meet with area clergy to see if they could develop a mutually acceptable solution. To that end, the ANC 2F commissioners and the churches agreed to establish the ANC 2F Ad Hoc Parking Committee.

At the next ANC 2F meeting, four recommendations were made, "three of which were suggested by the ANC 2F Ad Hoc Parking Committee and the fourth by the residents."[31] The fourth recommendation was titled "Immediate, Full-Time Enforcement of Parking Regulations." The ministers were upset by the residents' recommendation, since the purpose of the committee was to develop collective solutions, and the immediate parking enforcement recommendation was not mutually agreed on. Nonetheless, after much debate, a resolution containing the immediate-enforcement language was passed unanimously by the commissioners, the majority of whom were White. The churches lost the political battle, which, according to Rev. Hicks, was racially motivated.

During my conversation with Rev. Hicks, he handed me a book he had published that highlights Shaw/U Street's ongoing parking debate and its relationship to the departure of his church from the neighborhood. In the book, he states that the parking conflict "involves a racial shift in the community that has been brought on by residents who seem determined to take control of a community we have inhabited for more than one hundred years. Our new neighbors don't seem to desire to collaborate, cooperate, or even converse."[32] According to Rev. Hicks, the new neighbors were "upper-middle class, upper class whites who . . . had no need for a drug program or literacy program," church-sponsored services that certain members of Shaw/U Street's Black community desired and needed.

Some observers of the parking situation claimed that the central issue was not race but whether Metropolitan Baptist church had the legal right to park in a public space designated for children. For instance, a few Shaw/U Street Black leaders sided with the White faction that wanted Metropolitan off the

Garrison playground. B. Warren Lane, an African American and a forty-year resident of the neighborhood, claimed that the playground situation "is not a story about race."[33] He felt that the issue centered on the church and the playground—both serving primarily African Americans. Furthermore, at one of the ANC meetings, Rev. A. C. Durant of the Tenth Street Baptist Church told the attendees that "congregants feel attacked by the residents," and that he believed that this wasn't solely a racial issue but one tied to both race and culture.[34] He explained that African Americans in Shaw/U Street go to church on Sundays, but many of the new White residents do not.

Although the Sunday parking issue might not have been entirely based on race, the power dynamics behind the enforcement of parking laws can be assessed in racial terms. As Rev. Hicks states, "The challenge we faced was not simply a parking problem. What was [at] stake here was a redefinition of community. . . . I knew this was a fight we would never win."[35] The "redefinition of community" that Rev. Hicks refers to is the shift of power to new White residents, trumping the priorities of long-standing African American institutions (more on this in chapter 6), which can be characterized as being *in* the community but not *of* it—the majority of their congregants no longer lived in Shaw/U Street.

Rev. Hicks explained to me that the church sought to stay in the community and had planned to build parking garages to mitigate the double-parking concerns, but it did not have the support of the neighborhood political leadership. Jackie Reed, wife of ANC 2F chair Charles Reed, said, "Of course they [Metropolitan] were furious. They had plans to tear down, like, eight or ten buildings that they owned [to build parking garages]. They wanted to build a bridge over our street to . . . properties on the other side. . . . They had huge plans, which were thwarted." When Metropolitan did not receive the backing of the local majority White political leaders, Rev. Hicks decided to sell the church building and nearby properties.

As Metropolitan Baptist Church left Shaw/U Street, the ANC 2F discussed new possibilities for the Garrison playground. New, mainly White, residents were advocating for a dog park. At the January 2008 ANC 2F meeting, the group Dog Owners of Logan Circle reported that members were working with the DC city staff to identify an appropriate field to be converted into a dog park. Four community sites were discussed, including the Garrison Elementary playground. Apparently, even though the city had not decided on the location of the dog park, some residents had been using the Garrison playground unofficially for that purpose. At the April 2008 ANC 2F meeting, the police reported receiving complaints from school parents, almost all African American and Hispanic, that sections of the field were covered with dog excrement.

Several explanations can be given for the parking debates. They could be viewed as a political battle between newcomers versus an institution comprising mainly those who lived outside the community; or rather, the narrative could have been a religious versus a secular battle. Alternatively, the debates could be understood as the intersection of race and community status. However, the battle itself was racial. And while race is an important factor in explicating political struggles over Sunday parking, additional social categories are critical for understanding other conflicts that arose in Shaw/U Street.

Gayborhood Meets the Ghetto

Mary, a White, lesbian professional in her late twenties who has recently moved into Shaw/U Street, shares her thoughts on the gay presence in the neighborhood:

> And so, I, I always wonder if. . . . First of all I—I have no way of knowing—but if I were African American, if I were the guy that lives across the street, how would I feel about all these White people moving in? Would I feel like they're pushing me out? Because that would be awful! Then I wonder, how would he feel about two lesbians living across the street from him? I mean, I don't know, I don't know how accepting [he'd be]. He's not going to say anything to me about it. But, you know I wonder, how they [African Americans] feel about it, especially the ones that are middle- and older-age. How [do] they feel about their neighborhood . . . being taken over—not taken over, but all these White people moving in—and a lot of them are gay, too. Hmm, that's like a whole other thing.

Mary's comments illustrate that to her, and possibly to her African American neighbors, White and gay are two distinct categories. She was curious about what her African American neighbors thought of her being "White" and "gay." The notion that sexual orientation is a meaningful, separate social category is also reflected in the comments of some of the community's longtime residents.

For instance, Tessie, an elderly African American resident in subsidized housing, says, "I heard awhile back that gay people were coming in and buying up all our property. And excuse my French, I said, 'Well, damn—I thought it was the White people.' Now it's the gay people. I said, 'Well, OK, so which is it gonna be?'" Mary's and Tessie's comments illustrate that to some, sexual orientation is a category distinct from race.

The social categories of gay and straight are central to understanding Shaw/U Street's political debates. One day, Ralph, a lawyer and an openly gay White male in his thirties, chats with me at one of the community's new coffeehouses. In response to my asking whether sexual orientation plays a role in neighborhood conflicts, Ralph says, "I don't think I have ever experienced conflict over orientation. Except I've observed it at the ANC meetings. . . . Yeah, I've certainly seen it at the ANC meetings." Shaw/U Street's ANC 2C was the site for much community debate and conflict between straight and gay populations over the proposed liquor license for Be Bar, a gay-oriented nightclub.

In December 2005, entrepreneurs Tom McGuire and Mike Watson, both White and openly gay, bought a $1.4-million, two-story building that once was a Salvation Army office to open Be Bar.[36] Two prominent African American churches, Shiloh Baptist Church, headed by the Reverend Dr. Charles Wallace Smith, and Scripture Cathedral Church, directed by Pastor C. L. Long, were located a few blocks north.[37] Both ministers were uncomfortable with Watson and McGuire's plan for a nearby bar, ostensibly because the club intended to serve liquor. However, there were also concerns that Be Bar would be a gay bar.

The Black church and the gay bar share some significant characteristics. The Black church is historically where African Americans escaped discrimination. It also grounded and gave birth to the civil rights movement. Similarly, the gay bar is a space free of discrimination in a heterocentric society, and where the gay civil rights movement was born.[38] While many African Americans and homosexuals face immense bigotry in the United States, they are often at odds with each other.[39] Political scientist Cathy Cohen notes that in the Black community, being openly gay "deflate[s] one's community standing."[40]

Be Bar's liquor license was discussed at an ANC 2C meeting in March 2006. Scripture's Pastor C. L. Long claimed that the club was too close to the church's day care center.[41] In DC, establishments serving liquor are required to be at least four hundred feet from schools, public libraries, recreation centers, and day care centers. However, there are loopholes, and several liquor-serving establishments are within the four-hundred-foot restriction.

After listening to Pastor Long, the ANC 2C voted 3 to 1 to protest Be Bar's liquor license application. At the time, Leroy Joseph Thorpe Jr., an African American long-term resident, was the ANC 2C chair. He, along with two other African American commissioners, voted to deny Be Bar its license. While other Black leaders might have couched or hid their ambivalence toward a gay establishment, Thorpe, on several occasions, displayed his disdain for homosexuality. In fact, at a 1999 public meeting he called David Catania, a White, openly gay city council member, a "faggot."[42] When asked to apologize for his comment by the Gay and Lesbian Activists Alliance, Thorpe refused.[43]

The sole ANC 2C vote in favor of supporting Be Bar's license came from Alex Padro. An elected member of ANC 2C, Padro represents Shaw/U Street's growing number of gay newcomers of diverse races/ethnicities. He has multiple identities. He's gay, Hispanic, a homeowner, a newcomer to some, and director of the Shaw Main Streets initiative, which advocates for economic improvements in the neighborhood. He is also an avid historian of Shaw/U Street's Black history. At times, some of these multiple identities put him at odds with the rest of the ANC 2C commissioners, who represent the long-term and, to a certain extent, lower-income Black faction of the community.

While much of the Be Bar protest originated from ANC 2C, the bar is actually located within ANC 2F, which has a large concentration of gay residents. At ANC 2F's February 2006 meeting, Be Bar co-owner Mike Watson, his lawyer, Andrew Kline, and Alex Padro sought support for the bar. At the time, the majority of ANC 2F's commissioners (four of six) were openly gay.[44] According to the meeting minutes, the commissioners reported that they "would be pleased to work further with Watson and Kline" to help them establish Be Bar's liquor license.

While ANC 2F supported Be Bar, its commissioners ultimately decided at their March 2006 meeting to unanimously protest the license. ANC 2F supported the business, but wanted leverage for a voluntary agreement with Be Bar. In DC, ANCs and businesses often enter into voluntary agreements to regulate business hours. As the commissioners' formal protest to the city's Alcohol Beverage Control Board stated, "The commission and the applicant are working cooperatively with the aim of entering into a mutually acceptable voluntary agreement." It noted that "upon acceptance of a mutually agreeable voluntary agreement . . . the protest shall be withdrawn."

Citywide organizations also became involved in political debates concerning Be Bar's liquor license. The DC Black Church Initiative, directed by Rev. Anthony Evans, was among those protesting the liquor license application. Rev. Evans stated, "Granting the permit will undermine the moral character of the Shaw community, stain its tradition and send the wrong message to children and families. . . . The pending application in question will only promote an alternative lifestyle that runs counter to the values of the Shaw community."[45] The DC Coalition of Black Lesbian, Gay, Bisexual and Transgender Men and Women, led by Brian Watson, supported Be Bar.

At the April 19 meeting of the Washington, DC, Alcoholic Beverages Regulation Administration (ABRA), the room was filled with seventy people representing the two factions: African American members of Scripture Cathedral Church and Be Bar supporters, mainly White, gay residents, except for Brian Watson from the DC Coalition of Black Lesbian, Gay, Bisexual and Transgender Men and Women. Also present were Rev. Evans from the DC Black Church Initiative, ANC 2C chair Leroy Thorpe, openly gay ANC 2F commissioner Christopher Dryer, and an attorney representing Scripture Cathedral Church.[46] At the meeting, Watson stated, "Evans and Long don't speak for the whole African-American community. They just speak for the churches' members. . . . I don't see it as a black-white issue. I see it more as a sexuality issue. It's not a race thing."[47]

Due to the political controversy, the ABRA board postponed its decision on whether to grant Be Bar's license to a future meeting. In the meantime, Be Bar co-owner Tom McGuire made his political rounds to city council members, and the Gay and Lesbian Activists Alliance sent letters of support for Be Bar to DC's Ward 2 council member Jack Evans. The letter urged Evans "to speak out against the homophobic opposition to the Be Bar in Shaw."[48] Evans oversaw the political ward in which the club is located.

At the May 3 ABRA meeting, many in attendance were against Be Bar. However, the ABRA board, based on legal technicalities, decided not to officially recognize ANC 2C's or Scripture's protests.[49] ANC 2F's symbolic protest got resolved, since a "voluntary agreement" had been completed. Thus, ABRA's decision to not recognize the other protests cleared the way for the approval of Be Bar's license. McGuire attended the ANC 2F meeting later that night and thanked the commissioners for their support. In emphasizing the focus of the bar, he stated, "We're hoping we raise the bar, specifically for venues targeting the gay community in D.C."[50] On Friday, September 1, 2006, Be Bar opened for business.

The tension between segments of Shaw/U Street's gay and Black communities, which are not mutually exclusive, did not diminish with Be Bar's opening. Around 11:30 p.m. on September 7, 2008, two gay men, Tony Randolph Hunter and Trevor Carter, parked their car near Be Bar to head to the nightclub. They were attacked by a group of four young men. After several blows, Hunter was unconscious. He was rushed to Howard University Hospital, where he died ten days later. One of the young men involved, Robert

Hanna, told police that he was acting in self-defense after Hunter allegedly made sexual advances. It appeared that homophobia, not race, was the main driver of this fatal assault, since both Hunter and his assailants were African American. In 2009, Hanna pleaded guilty to one count of simple assault, and served six months in jail for a beating that resulted in Hunter's death.[51]

The intense debate and conflict over Be Bar centered on homophobia. While the conflict did have aspects of White/Black tensions, as the owners of the bar were White and the church leadership and the chair of ANC 2C were Black, the importance of sexual orientation in explaining the community conflict is clear. Alex Padro recalls, "This is the first time the [LGBT] community has had to deal with flagrant bigotry of this type. Unfortunately, these churches are pretty much the definition of bad neighbors. There have only been a handful of times that the issues of gay businesses and gay residents being a part of the community have come up, but unfortunately when they have come up, they have not been the most positive experiences."[52]

Sexual orientation not only explains the debate leading up to the approval of Be Bar's liquor license, but also appeared to have motivated the lethal beating that took place near the club. This situation suggests that sometimes, distinctions other than race matter most.

The Increasing Significance of Class: Hair Salon or High Culture?

One of Shaw/U Street's prominent bloggers is a gay newcomer whose Internet site, *Fifth and Oh*, is named for the intersection of 5th and O Streets in the neighborhood. In one of his blog posts, he discusses how community issues frequently turn "into a racial thing." He adds, "But here's the thing: I don't think it's quite that (pardon the expression) black-and-white. There are quite a few white folks around here who stuck it out through the drug wars as well. By no means are all of the 'gentrifiers' (a term I really despise) white. Take my little condo development, for example: The developers were black, the realtor (and all his team) were black, the settlement attorneys were black, and half of the home owners are black."[53] In other words, in gentrifying Shaw/U Street, upper- and middle-income African Americans are taking part in guiding the community's redevelopment, and this can conflict with the interests of lower-income African Americans.

While race and sexual orientation are important for understanding Shaw/U Street's political debates, intraracial class difference, based on income, wealth, and educational distinctions, is also a significant factor in explaining divides and tensions in the community, as well as the trajectory of its redevelopment. E. Franklin Frazier's controversial book, *Black Bourgeoisie,* laid out the importance of class for the Black American experience in the twentieth century. He wrote, "The single factor that has dominated the mental outlook of the black bourgeoisie has been its obsession with the struggle for status."[54] Frazier's claim was mainly based on his observations of Black Washingtonians. Since the publication of this classic text, the Black middle class has tripled, and many African Americans have attained great wealth, while others remain part of the Black underclass.[55] The importance of intraracial class distinction in Shaw/U Street is illustrated by the relationship between two fourth-generation Black Washingtonians, Wanda Henderson and Roy "Chip" Ellis.

Henderson, who has long dreadlocks and a warm personality, comes from the lower-income segment of DC's Black community. Much of her childhood was spent in a public housing project located just north of Shaw/U Street. For the last twenty years, she has owned and managed a local hair salon.

Henderson's salon used to be at 1201 U Street; however, rising commercial rent prices forced her off the community's main business thoroughfare. She chose the intersection of 7th and T Streets for her next location because of its cheaper rent; it also had high foot traffic, owing to the nearby Shaw/Howard Metro stop. Moreover, Henderson knew the owner of the building, and thought that after she established herself she might be able to make an offer to buy it.

Many of Henderson's friends thought she was crazy to move her business to this particular location, as it had been an open-air drug market for decades.[56] When Henderson first moved there, the area was full of illicit activity, forcing her to push through crowds of drug customers and loiterers to get to her shop. Despite all this, she operated a successful business catering mainly to the area's moderate- and lower-income African American residents.

While Henderson grew up in the DC housing projects, Chip Ellis was part of DC's Black elite. He graduated from Howard University, served as a public relations political appointee in the Clinton White House, and in 2000 founded Ellis Development Group, which specializes in mixed-use luxury residential and commercial DC developments.[57] Since 2005, he had been trying to revitalize the block where Henderson's hair shop was located, as well the nearby Howard Theater.[58]

Ellis envisioned an upscale redevelopment for the area that would preserve its African American heritage.[59] In 2005, his original project called for Radio One, Inc., one of the country's largest Black-owned radio/media companies, to be the anchor commercial tenant. For a variety of reasons, including the decline in Radio One's stock price, the company backed out of the deal.[60] Ellis's development team then secured another leading African American tenant, the United Negro College Fund (UNCF), a college financial aid organization that supports African Americans attending historically Black colleges and universities.[61]

With UNCF on board as the lead tenant, in December 2010 construction began on Progression Place, a three-hundred-thousand-square-foot, transit-oriented, mixed-use development, including 180 luxury apartments, to be situated above the Shaw/Howard Metro stop. Progression Place would bring a major elite Black presence to the area; however, there was fear that the development might displace small Black-owned businesses. Referring to Ellis's development project, Wanda Henderson said, "As for the business owners, it doesn't give us much opportunity, because I doubt I'll be able to afford it later."[62]

Chip Ellis's upscale vision for Progression Place became clear to me after I attended a meeting that he and his development partner had scheduled with Organizing Neighborhood Equity (ONE DC) on January 28, 2010. I was invited to the meeting by Dominic Moulden, ONE DC's lead organizer, who had been working since 2005 on a community benefits agreement with Ellis. Ellis and his development partners had received over $23 million in city subsidies for Progression Place, and ONE DC wanted to ensure that low-income community members would benefit directly from this development.[63] In 2007, it negotiated an agreement with Ellis in which his development group would provide over $750,000 for a community fund as well as affordable housing units and discounted commercial space at the new development site.[64]

The meeting took place in ONE DC's conference room. Joining me there were Dominic Moulden; Pat, an African American ONE DC member and longtime subsidized housing resident in Shaw/U Street; Rosemary, a ONE DC organizer; Jessica, a ONE DC board member; Shari, another board member; and Meg, a Georgetown Law School student.

Ellis opened the conversation by saying, "We have the opportunity to make something great here that reflects the proud culture and history of this neighborhood." He explained how the UNCF had saved the Progression Place project by choosing to locate their headquarters within this development. He emphasized that the UNCF selected this particular location because of the "history of the neighborhood" and its proximity to Howard University. Another benefit was that the UNCF had secured $5 million in tax abatements and relocation support from the city.[65] Ellis next discussed how the UNCF planned to place a "College of Knowledge" in the base of the Progression Place building, which would likely be accessible to the community, "Black, White, or whoever."

Steve, a White male who represented development partner Four Points, LLC, continued the discussion. He said that after six months of negotiations, the UNCF agreed to buy fifty thousand square feet of commercial space for approximately $34 million. He explained that because of the amount of square footage the UNCF required, the number of affordable housing units in Progression Place needed to be reduced from 45 to 31.

As Chip and Steve presented this information, Dominic, who was sitting next to me, pointed to the handout that compared the former and the current project, indicating the decreased number of affordable units. The developers noticed Dominic's gesture, and stated that despite the reduction of affordable units, their "friends" at the DC planning office and in the deputy mayor's office were backing the plan. The developers told ONE DC that to change the specifications of the project, they needed to get their planned unit development amended, which must be approved by both the planning office and the zoning commission. The developers then asked ONE DC for a formal letter of support for the revised development plans to help get the altered planned unit development passed.

Following an awkward silence and looks of disgust from the ONE DC members, Chip Ellis said, "We need to keep a focus on the type of impact this will have on the community." He stressed that the youth of Shaw/U Street would see Progression Place's office employees as role models and would be able to receive financial aid for college from the UNCF. Jessica snapped, "We will have no youth left in this community." Ellis retorted, "I'm talking about the people going to school in this community. We have a lot of high schools in the area."

Shari then asked Chip and Steve what would happen to the businesses currently located on the soon-to-be-redeveloped site. Ten percent of the commercial space would be subsidized, renting at 50 percent under market rate for the first three years, at 25 percent under market for years four and five, and at the market rate thereafter. This subsidized space was part of the community benefits agreement signed by the developers and ONE DC, but which local business would be occupying it had not been determined. All that remained at the development site were a Chinese takeout, a bodega, and Wanda Henderson's hair salon.

Chip and Steve, along with the rest of us, knew that Wanda's shop could have qualified as the "local" business for the subsidized commercial space. But rather than addressing her shop, Steve declared, "We're not going to turn this block into the Gap [clothing store], and we don't want this to become Connecticut Avenue," a major commercial strip in the White part of town. Chip then interjected, "Let me be clear. I don't want this to be a pawnshop either, or even Radio Shack for that matter. I'd rather see an art gallery. I want this to be a signature destination spot. . . . I don't want the Chinese takeout. It's got bulletproof glass, and I don't want to see that." Shari understood that without a direct reference to incorporate Wanda's shop, it likely was not going to be part of the new development. After the meeting she said, "We are going to lose the fabric of our community."

While churches have significant meaning in the Black community, so too do Black-owned hair salons and barbershops. These spaces are critical arenas of African American identity and political dialogue. Melissa Harris-Lacewell, a leading Black politics scholar, states, "Black hair rituals contribute to the notion of a common African American experience. This notion of commonality allows barbershops and beauty salons to function as racialized public spaces with the potential to contribute to the development of black politics."[66] She argues that Black hair shops can be power spaces that solidify racial identity and political ideology in African American communities. However, it appeared that Chip Ellis's interests did not coincide with Wanda Henderson's. She served the low- and moderate-income residents of the area, and he wanted art galleries.

On June 2, 2010, I heard from a ONE DC representative that Henderson had been told by the Progression Place development team that she had to move out.[67] I immediately headed up the street from the ONE DC offices to talk with her. One of her employees said that she was meeting with someone in her office, a small room at the back of the salon. After a few minutes, Henderson called me into her back room. She knew why I was there. She said, "I haven't told my staff yet. It's hard to keep people together. I'm devastated."

Henderson told me that the developers needed to get her out because of an unsafe structural beam; someone from the development team told her that she did not have to pay rent anymore, and that they would find her another location. They were going to pay her five or six months' worth of rent to help her build out another shop. She claimed that this amount would not even come close to covering the cost of setting up her hair shop elsewhere, and she knew that once the developers got her out, she probably would not return to Progression Place. Henderson did not have any legal documentation, but knew that the developers had received a permit for construction that included plans to build around her establishment. She knew this was possible, because there were two buildings on the block that the developers did not own, and they were building around and over these spaces. Henderson's was one of the only Black-owned businesses left on the block, and she did not understand why the developers could not work out something better for her. She told me that her dream had been to own the building containing her salon and remain on 7th Street.

As Henderson and I continued to talk, she said she would get a lawyer from the DC Bar Association, and would try to drum up political support from some of the African American city council members and ANC 2C commissioner Alex Padro. She asked me to comment on her strategy. I told her to imply to the developers that she had strong legal counsel, and then to seek political support. I also told her to continue paying her rent but with a certified check, to document that she was lease compliant. I further suggested that she ask the developers for legal documentation that the building was structurally unsound. This strategy seemed like it would buy her some time.

On July 31, I saw Henderson standing outside her shop. She explained that the developers were trying another tactic to get her out: a few days earlier, someone associated with the development team came by and asked her to sign a letter waiving her right of first refusal, which extended until her lease ended in 2013. She handed me the waiver letter and told me that she had spoken with Padro. He advised her not to sign, and connected her with some lawyers. I told her that she would eventually need to decide whether she wanted to continue to fight to remain at her current location or take the biggest payment she could get from the developers to move elsewhere. This was the second time the developers had tried to get her out. At this point, I was certain that the development team was going to drive her out to make room for Ellis's upscale vision.

In November 2010, Wanda Henderson relocated her business further north up 7th Street to Georgia Avenue, a less desirable and less expensive location outside Shaw/U Street (fig. 14). The developers agreed to pay to build out a new space for her, but in exchange she likely gave up her right to return to Progression Place. The interactions between her and Chip Ellis illustrate that race is not the only important aspect driving community events and conditions. In this case, class interests—Ellis's desire for iconic Black business ventures instead of ones catering directly to lower-income African American residents—help explain why Henderson's beauty shop was displaced and will likely not be a part of Progression Place.

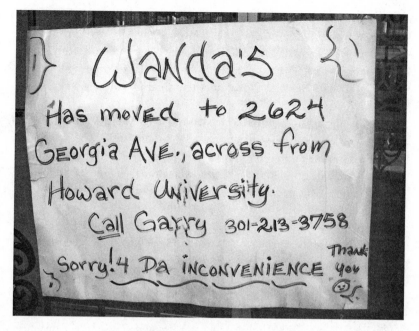

Figure 14. Wanda's hair salon—displaced.

Summing Up

In Shaw/U Street, the categories of race, sexual orientation, and class come together to explicate important community events and intense conflicts. In *Dream City*, prominent DC journalists Harry Jaffe and Tom Sherwood state, "No other city in America is as tormented or polarized by race, class, and power as the District of Columbia."[68] While Shaw/U Street is struggling with racial and class issues, sexual orientation is also a critical social category underpinning the neighborhood's political debates. As Rev. Hicks notes, community conflicts relate to the "shifting demographics" associated with race and class, and "changing lifestyles."[69]

In Shaw/U Street, distinct social categories, and their associated interests, manifest at the organizational level and explain important political decisions shaping the future of the community. Race, sexual orientation, and class influence critical decisions of churches, civic associations, and real estate development firms that affect the community's changing social and physical environment. The decision of the White-dominated ANC 2F to advocate for the ticketing of African American Sunday double-parkers was associated with the exodus of a Black institution that had served the community for over 150 years. The advocacy of gay residents through the ANC structure allowed the opening of a gay bar, despite church-led Black protests. Lastly, class-based interests explain why a large neighborhood redevelopment project favored elite Black businesses over ones that cater to lower-income African American residents.

This chapter advances the research on intersectionality by linking multiple groups' interests to organizational-level conflict and action and to important decisions shaping community conditions. By illustrating how race, sexual orientation, and class influence organizational and institutional decisions, this research extends the reach of intersectionality analysis from the individual to the community level. This study, along with other research, reinforces the fact that intersectionality functions at both micro and macro scales.[70] Furthermore, the Shaw/U Street findings suggest that gentrification processes can be fully understood only through assessing multiple social categories.

This chapter focuses on only three social categories: race, sexual orientation, and class. As alluded to throughout its pages, other social categories might help to explain Shaw/U Street's debates and conflicts. For instance, the parking and Be Bar controversies had a religious component, which might transcend race. As Alex Padro, the ANC commissioner who supported Be Bar from the start, states, "The faction that has had the most difficulty with the growing GLBT population are primarily African American Baptists." Further, age is another social category not thoroughly explored. As chapter 3 notes, many Shaw/Street newcomers are younger than the neighborhood's existing residents, and this difference might explain opposing preferences and political interactions surrounding the opening of new bars. Other social categories, such as birthplace and gender, also might explain contentious public debates. For instance, in sections of Shaw/U Street, particularly along 9th Street, tensions between African Americans and Ethiopian immigrants have been well documented.[71] The chapter's intent is not to investigate all meaningful social categories but to demonstrate that researchers must incorporate multiple categories in order to understand social interactions and political discourse in diverse communities.

Because this chapter takes an intercategorical complexity approach to study race, sexual orientation, and class, I describe how existing social categories relate to community conflict. An alternative approach would be to look at how these existing categories interact with one another.[72] In Shaw/U Street, race, sexual orientation, and class are not mutually exclusive. For example, one local African American preacher expressed to her congregation that the only people who can afford the community's properties are "rich homosexuals and lesbians."[73] This comment demonstrates that to some, homosexuality and class are intertwined in Shaw/U Street. Moreover, Chip Ellis's strong desire for elite Black institutions in Progression Place probably can be explained through an intersection of race and class. He did not desire just any elite businesses; he made a conscious effort to seek out powerful and prestigious Black-owned firms.

In the twenty-first century, one major crossnational challenge has been how nations, cities, and communities are to address increasing diversity.[74] Some urban scholars, such as Elijah Anderson, suggest that more than ever, diverse groups are interacting in certain settings with a "spirit of civility" and "goodwill." At the start of this century, Shaw/U Street contains racial, sexual, and economic diversity and is an excellent location for examining Anderson's claim. In this setting, several social categories have been associated with intense community debates and conflicts, suggesting that Anderson's cosmopolitan canopy concept does not generalize particularly well to the gilded ghetto. As policy makers intervene in the urban landscape to facilitate the creation of inclusive, diverse communities, they must also address multiple interests and conflicts that arise across several social categories. Just as individuals are complex actors with multiple identities that influence their behaviors, diverse communities must also be assessed from an array of social characteristics to understand the political conditions within them.

In addition to conflict, we must examine the assumption that low-income people who remain in Shaw/U Street benefit as the neighborhood transitions. This assumption is a central tenet of US urban housing policy of the 1990s and 2000s.[75] In the next chapter, I interrogate this assumption by more deeply investigating the political and cultural changes taking place in Shaw/U Street's civic fabric.

SIX

Linking Processes of Political
and Cultural Displacement

While the back-to-the-city movement and associated gentrification have been widely documented in several US cities, one unresolved puzzle is how this population influx will affect these cities and their low-income residents.[1] Some urban scholars, political figures, and real estate boosters celebrate this phenomenon, as it will likely increase property values and broaden municipal tax bases.[2] However, a controversial topic is whether the back-to-the-city movement and linked neighborhood redevelopment cause residential displacement.[3] Several quantitative studies claim that low-income residents in redeveloping neighborhoods have an exit rate similar to those in non-redeveloping neighborhoods.[4] Even so, other qualitative investigations have documented forced residential displacement in revitalizing neighborhoods of repopulating cities.[5] Rather than focusing on the displacement of long-time residents, this chapter addresses a gap in the gentrification literature by illustrating some of the social consequences for low-income residents able to remain in place as more affluent people settle into their community.

Shaw/U Street's redevelopment has several benefits for longtime residents who are able to stay in the community. The crime rate has dropped as the property values have skyrocketed.[6] New restaurants, grocery stores, and clothing and furniture outlets have opened. Also, community amenities, such as parks and libraries, have been upgraded. However, these improvements have come at a price for the longtime African American residents, as many have experienced political and cultural displacement.

The back-to-the-city movement, gentrification, and mixed-income development literatures have given residential displacement much greater attention than political and cultural displacement.[7] Political displacement occurs when a long-standing racial or ethnic group "become(s) outvoted or outnumbered by new residents," leading to the loss of decision-making power by the former group.[8] Political displacement might occur in redeveloping areas when low-income people remain but become overpowered by upper-income newcomers.[9]

There are at least four reasons why scholars and policy makers should be concerned with political displacement. First, evidence suggests that longstanding residents withdraw from public participation in gentrifying neighborhoods, and little is known about how and why this occurs.[10] Second, decreased civic engagement among existing residents may make it more difficult for them to form potentially economically beneficial relationships with newcomers.[11] Third, prior studies suggest that long-standing residents sometimes resent new neighborhood amenities, and an investigation of political displacement might help to explain the onset of resentment for amenities that, on the surface, seem to be community improvements.[12]

Fourth, political displacement might relate to cultural displacement. Cultural displacement occurs when the norms, behaviors, and values of the new resident cohort dominate and prevail over the tastes and preferences of the original residents.[13] While there may be points of common ground between old and new residents in redeveloping neighborhoods, often newcomers, as we have seen in the preceding chapter, seek to establish new norms, behaviors, and amenities that align with their desires.[14] If this occurs, long-term residents may find that their community no longer resembles the place they once knew, and they may no longer identify with their neighborhood.[15] With decreased attachment to place, low- and moderate-income residents might opt to leave economically transitioning neighborhoods, leading to their rapid conversion into homogeneous enclaves instead of integrated, mixed-income neighborhoods.[16]

This chapter details and explains the processes, and some consequences, of political and cultural displacement. I argue that Shaw/U Street's revitalization is connected with decreased political power among its existing residents. This process of political displacement is tied to cultural displacement, engendering feelings of alienation among some of these residents.

This chapter has two important implications. First, it suggests that political and cultural displacements are important interrelated community processes and outcomes associated with Shaw/U Street's redevelopment. Second, it highlights that maintaining political equity and power balances between long-standing and new residents in transitioning neighborhoods might be critical to ensuring that long-term residents benefit and thrive as their neighborhood revitalizes around them.

Benefits of Mixed-Income Living

Gentrification and neighborhood research suggests that when upper-income people move into a low-income community, poor people may ultimately benefit through a variety of mechanisms.[17] Through their cultural consumption patterns, more affluent newcomers will likely demand different types of neighborhood businesses and services than do the existing lower-income population.[18] For example, with more aggregate income in the community, local grocery stores are expected to upgrade and diversify their products and provide more purchasing options. In addition, newcomers will likely bolster the political infrastructure and demand greater levels of city funding for improved services and amenities, such as greater police presence, which might reduce crime.[19] Further, more middle-income people in a community may facilitate increased informal social interactions across racial and class divides, helping low-income people tap into the social capital within upper-income networks. By forming weak social ties with upper-income residents, low-income individuals might make employment contacts, increasing their job prospects and potential earnings.[20] Lastly, newcomers might help establish new neighborhood norms, such as the expectation that adults are employed.[21]

However, whether middle- and upper-income residents actually facilitate mechanisms of benefit for the poor is a debated topic. Several recent studies indicate that in mixed-income developments, meaningful interactions among middle- and low-income residents occur less frequently than expected.[22] And when such interactions do happen, they rarely seem to lead to greater economic opportunities for low-income people.[23] In terms of the political infrastructure, several studies demonstrate that the arrival of the middle class can bolster it within a community.[24] Yet evidence also suggests that upper- and middle-income people often have priorities that are different from their low-income neighbors, and advocate for amenities that are not a priority for many existing residents.[25] Finally, when new amenities and services such as upscale restaurants, organic grocery stores, and increased police presence appear, resentment among long-term residents can sometimes occur.[26] This chapter explains how and why resentment forms, even among existing residents who are able to stay as their community redevelops.

Processes of Political and Cultural Displacement

Staying in Place

While some forced residential displacement occurred in Shaw/U Street, a number of low-income residents were able to remain despite mounting gentrification pressures. Thousands of low- and moderate-income families live in the community's church-owned affordable housing projects, such as Foster House, Gibson Plaza, 1330, Lincoln Westmoreland I and II, and the Paul Lawrence Dunbar Apartments.[27]

In addition to the community's church-owned affordable housing stock, other privately owned, low-income housing remains in Shaw/U Street. DC has established a unique right-of-first-refusal law, meaning if a landlord wants to sell a rental property to someone interested in converting the property into luxury condos, the landlord must first give the tenants an opportunity to raise purchasing price funds.[28] This law has enabled some tenants to purchase their buildings and convert them into affordable condos or cooperatives. Shaw/U Street has several affordable housing cooperatives, including the Capital Manor Cooperative (converted in 2003), the Martin Luther King, Jr. Latino Cooperative (converted in 2006), the Second Northwest Cooperative Homes (converted in 1993), and the Northwest Cooperative (converted in 1977). Other properties, such as Frontiers East and West Condominiums, were preserved when the city converted these affordable rentals into moderately priced homeownership units. In 1998, these three- and four-bedroom rental units with parking were sold for between $100,000 and $150,000 each.[29] In 2009, some low-income housing units, such as the R Street Apartments, were preserved through housing tax credits, and city and foundation funds.[30] Moreover, tenants, working with local nonprofits, the DC government, and housing financial intermediaries such as MANA, Inc., the Local Initiatives Support Corporation, and the Enterprise Foundation, have preserved some of Shaw/U Street's affordable housing through tenant-owned cooperative conversions.

Theresa Sule, an affordable housing leader, explains:

> I think that people want a certain level of income in this community, but it's not gonna happen. And one of the reasons it's not gonna happen is that fortunately, the stable low-income buildings in this community, they're not owned by private owners. They're owned by institutions. Lincoln Westmoreland is owned by a church. Gibson Plaza is owned by a church. I mean, this building, we're owned by the tenants' association and nonprofits. So, I mean,

to maintain affordability, more than likely we'll renew our contracts, because I know the church has no interest in market finances. And our building, we have at least twenty more years on our HUD contract.

Jim Graham, one of Shaw/U Street's former city council representatives, states, "By and large, the gentrification impact was there, [but] not on the big apartment buildings." He stresses that the neighborhood's affordable housing was critical, because it kept "thousands of people who would have been put out. Thousands of people." Both Sule's and Graham's statements underscore the importance of affordable housing as a mechanism to prevent massive residential displacement.[31]

Distinct Tastes and Preferences

In Shaw/U Street, like many revitalizing communities, newcomers and long-term residents often have different tastes and preferences. Geovani Bonilla, a newly elected civic association president and neighborhood newcomer, explains how economic and age differences relate to distinct desires between newcomers and longtime residents:

> You had a lot of old neighbors that bought here years ago and lived here for thirty years who bought homes for $80,000, and now you've got the new neighbors that are coming in buying homes for $500,000 [and] $600,000. The older residents, and I guess primarily because much of them are mostly retired, they are looking more towards senior centers. They want arts and crafts. . . . The newer folks want more of the retail . . . the sit down restaurants. Uh, you know, more of the local nightlife, which is some of the things that older residents . . . don't necessarily want.

Many newcomers, like Geovani, advocate for amenities different from those desired by their long-term neighbors, a fact clearly recognized by Shaw/U Street's Black civic leaders. Rev. H. Beecher Hicks of the Metropolitan Baptist Church bluntly notes, "While the influx of well-off, mostly White urban pioneers and carpetbaggers into inner-city communities might improve their socioeconomic status and raise property values, there is a danger in the notion that these new residents share the values, interests, and concerns of their older, mostly African American neighbors."[32] Geovani's and Rev. Hicks's comments illustrate a perception that newcomers' tastes, values, and interests do not always align with those of existing residents. It has been well documented that often, gentrifiers and long-term residents have different opinions in redeveloping neighborhoods.[33] However, in Shaw/U Street White new-comers express their community preferences through political displacement, which engenders feelings of resentment among the long-term Black population and replicates, if not amplifies, prior social inequalities.

Political Displacement

From the mid-1970s through most of the '80s and '90s, African Americans held almost all of Shaw/U Street's formal and informal political positions. Then as more upper- and middle-income Whites, Blacks, and Hispanics, both straight and gay, moved into the neighborhood, the original Black population began to lose political power at multiple levels. A sketch of the city's political structure helps to explain how this political transition occurred.

As noted in chapter 2, since the enactment of home rule in 1973, DC residents have elected a mayor, eight city council ward representatives, four city-wide council members, and a city council chair, all for four-year terms.[34] Two city council seats (Wards 1 and 2) represent almost all of Shaw/U Street.[35] The home rule legislation, and a subsequent referendum, also set up thirty-seven political subdistricts known as Advisory Neighborhood Commissions (ANCs). ANCs make recommendations to the city council and city agencies on matters such as zoning, liquor licensing, and small grant making in their subdistrict area. The residents of each subdistrict elect ANC commissioners for two-year terms. Shaw/U Street has five ANCs.

Shaw/U Street's shifting political structure was exemplified by the changing representation in both Ward 1 and ANC 2C. David Clarke, who is White, was the first Ward 1 council member; Frank Smith, an African American, followed him when Clarke was elected city council chair.[36] Smith held the Ward 1 seat for sixteen years until Jim Graham, a White challenger, defeated him in 1998.

Smith and Graham represent the neighborhood's old guard and newcomers respectively. Smith was born in Georgia in 1942, attended Morehouse College, and was a founding member of the Student Non-Violent Coordinating Committee. He came to DC in 1968 to work at the Institute for Policy Studies, a leading 1960s antiwar and civil rights think tank.[37] Throughout his career, Smith was committed to Black political empowerment. In contrast, Jim Graham came to the United States from Scotland and spent most of his childhood in the DC suburbs. He received a BA from Michigan State and a JD from the University of Michigan, and came back to the DC area to work for the federal government. In 1979, he became a board member of Shaw/U Street's Whitman-Walker Clinic, and in 1984 he became the executive director. Under Graham's fourteen years of leadership, the clinic became one of the country's leading HIV/AIDS medical facilities. Graham, who is openly gay, has been a prominent gay rights and HIV/AIDS activist. As indicated earlier, Shaw/U Street's early gentrification involved gay men, and this constituency supported Graham's Ward 1 defeat of Smith.

With the back-to-the-city movement during the 2000s, Shaw/U Street's ANCs transitioned from domination by longtime African American residents to newcomer control.[38] One of the most contentious political transformations occurred in ANC 2C. As discussed in chapter 5, this ANC had been controlled by a controversial figure since the 1980s: "Mahdi" Leroy Joseph Thorpe Jr. is an incredibly outspoken African American leader who occasionally uses inflammatory language. For instance, he called the city's former interim police chief "a house Negro," and Jack Evans, the White Ward 2 city council member, "a pale-skinned, blond-haired cracker."[39] While some people disagree with Thorpe's views and governing tactics, he does, to a certain extent, represent the community's low-income African American population and their redevelopment concerns.

Alex Padro is one of Thorpe's biggest critics. Since moving to the community, Padro has been very engaged in local politics, and in 2001 he was elected to ANC 2C. Padro directs Shaw Main Streets, an initiative to stimulate local business development, and many residents see him as a growth proponent. Padro explains, "For decades our ANC unfortunately has been one of the most dysfunctional ones in the city, and we really just had folks that didn't have good qualifications, good backgrounds, weren't reasonable, and as a result . . . the neighborhood has lost out on a lot of [development] opportunities . . . that would definitely have benefited the community at large and those of low and moderate income—who some of these past elected officials claimed to be the focus of their interests."

Once elected to the ANC, Padro, along with other pro-development newcomers, began plotting Thorpe's ouster from it. In 2006, Padro and other recent Shaw/U Street arrivals encouraged Kevin Chapple, an African American newcomer, to run against Thorpe. In this fiercely contested election, Chapple defeated Thorpe by eighteen votes.

Thorpe, an eighteen-year veteran of the ANC system, did not easily give up his power and control.[40] First, as a lame duck ANC chair in December 2006, he resigned as chair and appointed Doris Brooks and Barbara Curtis, who both represent the long-term, African American resident faction, ANC chair and vice chair respectively. This move was very strategic. Thorpe understood that without him, the four-person ANC was split: two newcomers (Padro and Chapple) and two long-standing residents (Brooks and Curtis).

According to the ANC rules, if the ANC cannot elect a new chair, the former chair is retained. Thorpe's move helped ensure that Brooks would remain chair in 2007, since there would likely be a split vote for the new chair. Brooks, as ANC 2C chair, then named Thorpe her executive assistant and parliamentarian. Hence, those who wanted to do business with the ANC had to continue to contact Thorpe to get on the ANC agenda. As one community blogger noted at the time, "Laugh or cry about it, you gotta admit the man [Thorpe] has a pair."[41]

Despite these efforts, as more upper-income residents moved into the area, Thorpe's reign, and the low-income faction's political power, began slipping away. In the 2008 ANC 2C election, a long-term resident, affordable housing leader Theresa Sule, ran against Curtis. Sule had Padro's and the other newcomers' backing, because they thought she would support pro-growth development issues. When Sule defeated Curtis by fifty votes, Padro and his supporters believed they had broken the ANC 2–2 voting tie. However, during the first ANC meeting of 2009, when the commissioners voted on the new chair, Sule, an African American resident of subsidized housing, nominated Brooks, the long-term resident and previous ANC chair, instead of Padro. Padro was furious, and claimed that what Sule did was "a complete reversal and a stab in the back."[42] He and the newcomer faction waited patiently for the next election to retaliate. In the 2010 ANC 2C election, Sule lost overwhelmingly to newcomer Rachelle Nigro. With three newcomers among the four commissioners, the political takeover was complete, and Padro was finally appointed the ANC 2C chair.

The political transformation of ANC 2C represents various community changes as more upper-income residents arrive and become politically engaged. Geovani, the newly elected White president of a civic association that had been traditionally headed by African Americans, notes, "You look at the city that was historically [since the 1970s] a Black city run by Blacks. Now you look at the Black population, and the projections are that the District will look more like California by the end of ten years, where there will be more ethnicities [and] . . . it will be multiracial. So I think that they [Black Washingtonians] are like, 'Oh my God, we used to run the city.'" Geovani's population projections have in part already occurred in DC, and are clearly illustrated by Shaw/U Street's demographic changes and resulting political shifts.

Renowned sociologist William Julius Wilson predicted that an influx of upper- and middle-income residents would strengthen a low-income neighborhood's political infrastructure.[43] He hypothesized that newcomers would bolster the social structure of such communities, increasing the opportunity structure for disadvantaged residents. However, he did not predict that newcomers would take over critical political positions and advocate for new amenities, entirely transforming the cultural settings of urban African American neighborhoods.

Cultural Displacement: Catering to Newcomers' Tastes and Preferences

Shaw/U Street's changing political circumstances relate to the community's altering cultural landscape. In the late 1990s and 2000s, some newcomer-dominated ANCs and civic associations engaged in political actions to push out Black institutions symbolizing the old neighborhood, while advocating for new neighborhood amenities, such as bike lanes and dog parks. Some original residents perceived the changes as signs of gentrification and the manifestations of newcomer dominance.

Displacing a Black Church?

Both the neighborhood's changing resident population and the altering political landscape impacted some Black institutions, including the Metropolitan Baptist Church. Metropolitan, as was discussed in chapter 5, was founded in Shaw/U Street during the Civil War. It is important to briefly revisit that church's parking situation, because it highlights how the neighborhood's changing preferences and political structure relate to Metropolitan's departure.

When the church initially faced political pressure from new White residents regarding its use of a local school playground as a parking lot, its pastor, Rev. H. Beecher Hicks, had a plan. Rev. Hicks explains:

> Before Mr. Graham came to the council, Frank Smith and I had several meetings along with Walter Fauntroy [former minister of Shaw/U Street's New Bethel Baptist Church and DC congressional representative] . . . about ways to develop the Garrison Schoolyard. . . . We were offering to the city and the school board to actually take that schoolyard and put a two- or three-story parking garage on it, and included in it would have been a playground that would have been incorporated into the parking structure itself along with some opportunities, retail opportunities, along that corner. That's what Frank Smith and I were working on.

As for what happened to the plan: "Oh, it died!" Rev. Hicks exclaims. "I mean, you know Jim Graham came in and nobody wanted to hear that, because that would have solidified Metropolitan's place in the community. We submitted to the District plans to expand Metropolitan in its location, adding another story onto it and then going around 13th Street, which was property we already owned. And of course it was killed."

The church was prevented from using the schoolyard for parking, and some members started to double-park on Sundays, blocking in other cars. Newcomers to Shaw/U Street were furious and, working through one of community's ANCs, demanded that police ticket the double-parked cars. Rev. Hicks recalled that the majority of the church members would have preferred that the church remain in the neighborhood, but the lack of political support by the community's new political representative, Jim Graham, catalyzed the congregation's decision to move elsewhere.[44] A Black institution founded during the Civil War by former slaves is now absent from Shaw/U Street, in part due to the changing political power in the community and pressures stemming from the area's new population.

Go-Go, Gone

Black Washingtonians invented go-go music in the 1970s. Go-go combines jazz, funk, R&B, hip-hop, and Caribbean sounds, and is recognizable by its repetitive beat and improvisation. It was once quite popular on U Street as late as the 1990s; however, with the community's redevelopment and political shifts, many of U Street's go-go clubs have shut down.

Jim Graham, supported mainly by Shaw/U Street's new resident population, led the controversial political crusade to close local go-go clubs. Graham recalls, "There were people who said I was anti-go-go, and you know, actually I know nothing about go-go. . . . It's not about the music, it's about the people who are attracted and then acted out from being there, it was about people. So we worked very hard . . . to close . . . a good half dozen really bad businesses." Christine, a White newcomer and president of the U Street Neighborhood Association, says, "I remember one day getting off the Metro and walking down the street, and I saw a flyer . . . that had a White man hanging by a noose, and I was like, 'Oh my gosh, where am I living?' Until I saw it was about Jim Graham and the go-go [controversy]." Christine, who has been extremely active in local politics, understands that long-term residents were resentful of their diminished political power: "I can understand why people are upset. That you take an area that even though it had been completely depressed, but has a history of being African American, and then all of a sudden all these outsiders are running it."

With go-go gone, part of Shaw/U Street's and DC's Black history and culture has been erased from its streets. Author Natalie Hopkinson, a DC go-go historian, explains, "Go-go may be invisible to much of white Washington, but it's as much a part of the city as [the] pillars and monument[s] of its federal face. . . . Go-go is Washington."[45] Furthermore, Kip Lornell and Charles Stephenson Jr., authors of *The Beat! Go-Go Music from Washington, D.C.*, maintain that "go-go provides a voice for members of D.C.'s often overlooked, much maligned, and disenfranchised African American community."[46] With the political efforts to rid Shaw/U Street of go-go, aficionados of this musical genre must, for the most part, head to the DC suburbs to attend live performances of this District-conceived, African American form of cultural expression.

Ironically, some middle-income newcomers claim that they chose Shaw/U Street over other DC neighborhoods because of its racial diversity and Black history. Yet several recent arrivals engage in local politics to gain political power and advocate for changes that make it difficult for African American institutions. Dominic Moulden of Organizing Neighborhood Equity (ONE DC), expresses feelings that some longtime residents have when newcomers remark that their attraction to Shaw/U Street was based on its racial diversity and Black history: "Don't tell me that you moved to this neighborhood because you wanted diversity. No, you moved here because you realized you got the numbers to change the culture."

Biking for Whom?

In the 2000s, DC's mayors Anthony Williams and Adrian Fenty significantly improved the city's biking infrastructure. In 2000, the District had only three miles of bike lanes in its streets; by 2009 there were sixty miles.[47] This type of supplemental transport system has been greatly supported by DC's mayors, newcomers, real estate developers, and the urban planning field as both a sustainable mode of transportation and an economic development tool. However, it has been quite contentious in DC, since the city's biking infrastructure was disproportionately located in redeveloping low-income African American neighborhoods, primarily Shaw/U Street and Capitol Hill East (figs. 15, 16).

As urban planning scholar Ralph Buehler and colleagues note, "The construction of the bike lanes was not uncontroversial. In some neighborhoods bike lanes have become associated with redevelopment, rising property values, and resulting economic pressure on poorer households."[48] And Chris,

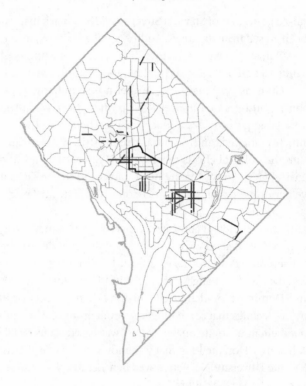

Washington, DC Bike Lanes, 2005

 Shaw/U Street Boundary ⌐————┬————⌐ 0   1   2 Miles

Figure 15. Washington, DC, bike lanes, 2005.

a former DC transportation planner in the Shaw/U Street area, says, "There seems to be this idea that . . . promoting biking is just one more form of gentrification." He mentions that he receives pushback from some long-term African American residents because they perceive that bike lanes will limit the amount of parking.

However, the biking infrastructure issue goes beyond parking availability. Some African Americans perceive it as an amenity being used to attract White gentrifiers and promote gentrification. In DC and its metropolitan area, Whites are much more likely than African Americans to bicycle.[49] In 2008, nearly 88 percent of the bike trips were taken by Whites, compared with only 6 percent by African Americans.

Furthermore, the Capital Bikeshare (CaBi) is a system of bike rentals accessed for a fee by DC residents and tourists (fig. 17). The CaBi system has been contracted by the DC Department of Transportation since 2010. However, although DC's Black population that year comprised 51 percent of the city's total population, only 5 percent of CaBi riders were African American.[50] Yet the city government spent ample resources to put this amenity and other bike-related infrastructure into economically and racially transitioning African American neighborhoods.

Some Shaw/U Street newcomers have relocated to the community because of its robust biking infrastructure. Paul, a recent arrival, explains, "A large part of the reason I moved to Shaw and pay D.C.'s higher taxes was because of the ability to bike or walk to work."[51] According to a *Washington Post* article, "Growth of cycling culture in the D.C. area and other cities has awakened the real estate industry to its potential as a fresh sales tool."[52] To that end, DC area real estate developers are designing condominium buildings with bike racks.

Washington, DC Bike Lanes, 2015

☐ Shaw/U Street Boundary ⊢ 0   1   2 Miles

Figure 16. Washington, DC, bike lanes, 2015.

Figure 17. Capital Bikeshare station.

While biking infrastructure is being constructed to attract new city residents, some existing African American residents resent it, because they view it as an amenity they did not request. In fact, some perceive it as a symbolic message that they are no longer wanted in the neighborhoods where it is being placed.[53]

Yappy Hour

Bike lanes are not the only Shaw/U Street amenity that has sparked debate. In November 2008, the community became the first in DC to have an official off-leash dog park (fig. 18).[54] The fifteen-thousand-square-foot fenced enclosure contains peagravel and smallstone surfaces where dogs can roam freely. It likely cost the city well over a half a million dollars to construct.[55]

Shaw/U Street's dog park came about after extensive advocacy by newcomers, mainly White middle- and upper-income residents. With political pressures from newly White dominated ANCs and civic associations, the city agreed to build the amenity, one that has become part of the changing landscape in gentrifying areas.[56] The Midcity Dog Park Committee helps provide funding for the park's upkeep and sets the park's rules, even though it is a publicly owned city space.[57] On any given evening, the dog park is filled with newcomers. Its arrival has been associated with other subsequent community changes, such as nearby bars and hotels hosting "yappy hours," where individuals show off their dogs while enjoying a drink.[58]

Very few longtime African American dog owners use the park, and there is a perception that this newcomer amenity has been preferred over other local recreational spaces.[59] The school playground, where the new dog park is located, also contains basketball courts and a soccer field. At the time of the dog park's construction, no resources were dedicated to other playground amenities, which were in desperate need of upgrading. The soccer goals were askew, and the field was mainly dirt. The basketball courts had not been renovated since at least 1997, when DC's professional basketball team changed its name from the Bullets, as indicated by the faded Bullets logo on the court's worn surface.[60] Yet while soccer fields and basketball courts, which are often used by Hispanics and African Americans, are neglected, newcomer amenities are developed and upgraded. The physical juxtaposition of these amenities symbolizes tensions, political power, and cultural shifts occurring in Shaw/U Street.

Figure 18. Shaw/U Street's dog park.

Alienation, Resentment, and Withdrawal

Some long-term DC residents resent new infrastructure, such as bike lanes, bike-sharing systems, and dog parks. Marshall Brown, a political strategist and father of former DC City Council chair Kwame Brown, states, "They [the new white residents] want doggie parks and bike lanes. The result is a lot of tension. The new people believe more in their dogs than they do in people. . . . This is not the District I knew. There's no relationship with the black community. They don't connect at the church, they don't go to the same cafes, they don't volunteer in the neighborhood school, and a lot of longtime black residents feel threatened."[61]

The feeling of being threatened is compounded by a sense of detachment and disillusionment that sets in when people do not feel comfortable in neighborhood spaces. For instance, Gloria Robinson, ONE DC's affordable housing community organizer who used to live in the area, comments, "I just feel like, and this could be my own paranoia . . . when I'm walking through there, especially when the street sidewalks are bustling, it's like folks are looking at me as if I don't belong there. I'm serious! It may be my paranoia, but . . . that's the feeling I get." This feeling of not belonging anymore can lead to greater civic participation, as in Robinson's case, but it can also lead to withdrawal.

One of the most noticeable and significant withdrawals from Shaw/U Street's civic life is Walter Fauntroy. A lifelong resident, former pastor of New Bethel Baptist Church, and former DC congressional representative, Fauntroy did more for Shaw/U Street and the city than any other African American political leader. In speaking about the recent redevelopment that has taken place, Fauntroy declares, "I can't be caught up in a fight where the cards are stacked against you. [Shaw/U Street] should be a place where . . . people can all live together, but I gave up, quite frankly."[62] When the person who has devoted his life's work to maintaining and preserving Shaw/U Street says "I gave up," something is clearly amiss. The political and cultural displacement in the community is severe, and current and former Black leaders as well as some low-income residents resent the changes that have taken place there in the last decade.

Summing Up

This chapter reveals important political and cultural consequences associated with Washington, DC's back-to-the-city movement. The new, mainly White, population moving into DC has helped to stimulate Shaw/U Street's redevelopment. For scholars such as William Julius Wilson and others, the movement of the middle class to disadvantaged Black neighborhoods had the promise of improving the life chances and circumstances of low-income people.[63] In fact, Shaw/U Street's redevelopment has been associated with less crime, greater aggregate community income, higher property values, increased social diversity, and signs of increased political strength.[64]

However, there appears to be significant social costs for low-income residents: political and cultural displacement and feelings of community loss. As new upper- and middle-income residents have come into Shaw/U Street, some have joined civic associations, seized political power, and advocated for policies that cater to their tastes and preferences. The combination of the political takeover and the development of new amenities is associated with fear, resentment, and civic withdrawal among some existing African American residents. These findings coincide with and extend the works of Gibbs Knotts and Moshe Haspel, who demonstrate that gentrification can lead to political destabilization through lower voter turnout among long-standing residents, and Lance Freeman, who highlights that long-term residents often resent new amenities in redeveloping communities.[65] This research elaborates on these studies' findings by linking feelings of resentment to the political destabilization process and the cultural changes brought on, in part, by newcomer political action.

The extent to which this situation might generalize to other cities and neighborhoods remains to be seen. To begin with, DC experienced a back-to-the-city movement comprising a large number of new White residents, fifty thousand between 2000 and 2010, which might relate to a particular type of neighborhood redevelopment and resulting social consequences. For instance, both New York and Chicago experienced the back-to-the-city movement in the 1990s, but some of their redeveloping neighborhoods, such as Harlem and Bronzeville, experienced Black gentrification.[66] And while some political displacement occurred at the level of the informal civic association in these neighborhoods, it rarely affected the formally elected city council positions. Furthermore, the resulting cultural displacement did not take place to the same extent. For example, many iconic Black churches remain in Harlem and Bronzeville, and these institutions did not face as much newcomer opposition as those in Shaw/U Street.[67]

Second, DC is unique as the home to the federal government. This function is related to the lack of political representation that DC residents, compared with other US cities, face. After almost a century without elected city representation, DC residents finally attained the privilege to vote locally after the enactment of home rule in 1973.[68] Since that time, many locally elected officials have been African American. This unique DC context might contribute to why the movement of middle- and upper-income Whites to low-income African American communities and the ensuing political shifts are so contentious.

Despite the political and cultural losses, what are the benefits to low-income people who are able to remain in Shaw/U Street while the neighborhood redevelops? With the revitalization, crime rates have dropped, there are more grocery stores, and public amenities, such as parks, have been upgraded. However, the local schools have not improved much, and the diverse racial demographics of the community are not reflected in the public school system. The racial makeup of the neighborhood itself has changed much more quickly than that of the public schools, a pattern experienced in other gentrifying neighborhoods.[69] Either the newcomers do not have children or they send their kids to private schools.[70] Even with the minimal demographic changes in the neighborhood schools, what is the social value of the new Shaw/U Street community environment for a generation of children growing up in this mixed-income, mixed-race milieu, and will this environment ultimately increase their life chances?[71] Only time will tell.

The back-to-the-city movement is occurring in urban America. The past two decades have seen a surge of people, particularly to the downtowns, to cities once depopulating. This recentralization is associated with the redevelopment of low-income, primarily African American neighborhoods. While some celebrate the back-to-the-city movement and its associated neighborhood revitalization, urban planners and federal and local policy makers have often overlooked important social consequences related to this population growth. Some low-income people in redeveloping neighborhoods are losing their political power and feelings of community attachment. This, in some circumstances, leads to resentment and alienation among long-standing residents, who feel powerless as their community improves economically. Understanding the processes of political and cultural displacement, and attempting to minimize their effects, is critical to ensuring a more inclusive gilded ghetto.

In the remaining chapters, I clarify what the circumstances in Washington, DC, and the Shaw/U Street neighborhood mean for urban theory and policy. DC's gilded ghetto is formed by an accumulating array of external and internal community forces, and I reinforce what these production and consumption development dynamics mean for contemporary theories of urbanism. I then turn to a practical policy discussion that centers on ways to address diversity segregation, and other policy interventions, that would make the gilded ghetto more equitable and just.

PART THREE

What Does It All Mean?

SEVEN

The Cappuccino City

Advancing Urban Theory

Over the last twenty years, a series of competing and interrelated urban paradigms has emerged that includes the global city, the neoliberal city, the dual city, and the entertainment city, many of which have been referenced throughout the book.[1] Each perspective claims that certain dynamics—technological advances, global interconnections, privatization, inequality,

Figure 19. The cappuccino.

and new amenity preferences—are critical to understanding urban growth and change. In this chapter, I suggest an alternative framework, *the cappuccino city*. The concept of the cappuccino city is based on my Washington, DC, findings and borrows certain aspects from prior urban theories in order to offer a more comprehensive, nuanced, and detailed perspective on contemporary urbanism. The cappuccino city framework describes and explains a wide-ranging set of interconnected characteristics, processes, and outcomes unfolding in DC that likely have implications for other US cities whose economies are increasingly dominated by the service sector.[2]

On several levels, the cappuccino is a metaphor for important social and spatial processes and their outcomes occurring in twenty-first-century Washington, DC. A cappuccino is nothing more than a refined, refurbished regular cup of coffee with milk. It essentially contains the same ingredients as a coffee with milk, but is upscale and more than double the price. A coffee is dark in color; a cappuccino is lighter in hue, because steamed milk foam is added to espresso, which is the result of boiling water pressed through finely ground coffee beans. In DC, the formerly low-income, Black working-class communities—the coffee—have begun to experience a White influx—the steamed milk—and these neighborhoods have become both lighter in hue and more expensive. In the 2000s, as Whites entered DC at a rapid pace, median home values increased from $212,000 to $445,000.[3]

Cappuccino cities feature upgraded amenities. Just as flipped properties in gentrifying communities have special perks, such as granite kitchen countertops and stainless steel appliances, so the cappuccino city boasts a newly built downtown sports arena, refurbished mixed-use apartment buildings, trendy restaurants, hip bars, dog parks, and walkable, bikable, and Metro-accessible neighborhoods close to downtown—enhancements preferred by educated twenty- and thirty-somethings—along with "third wave" coffee shops.[4]

Already part of the postindustrial "urban imaginary," coffee shops are important amenities in the cappuccino city and the gilded ghetto.[5] As sociologist Andrew Papachristos and his colleagues claim, "Coffee shops are integral to the leisure and lifestyle amenities package so attractive to urban gentrifiers."[6] The modern coffeehouse is where people blend leisure, work, and politics.[7] It is where the high-wage, postindustrial worker can be creative and free from the confines of the office, yet remain productive. Wi-fi has turned these places into efficient, globally connected workspaces that are redefining twenty-first-century American urbanism.[8] Thus, coffee shops and the lifestyle they both cater to and cultivate play a key role in the cappuccino city.[9]

Dynamics and Characteristics of the Cappuccino City

Although Millennials frequent coffeehouses, they do not come to DC or any other city only for this amenity and its related lifestyle; they come for the high-wage jobs that proliferate in the city's advanced service-sector economy. The increased number, or proportion, of high-wage employment opportunities is a result of intersecting global, federal, and local forces. Whether newcomers find work in government- or in private-sector consulting, technology, or finance, in the cappuccino city high-wage workers disproportionately concentrate in and near the central business district.

Downtown Expansion

Central business district expansion characterizes a cappuccino city. Because of a sufficient increase in downtown high-wage service-sector employment opportunities, this area expands as people come to live, work, eat, relax, and conduct business during their nonwork hours. Many US cities have experienced a downtown revival, a process I have previously labeled the new urban renewal.[10] Today, as downtown population returns, the central business districts are expanding.

The back-to-the-city movement, "the great inversion," is a defining cappuccino city feature.[11] In the early twentieth century, Chicago school sociologists Robert Park and Ernest Burgess theorized that as individuals experienced greater wealth, they would move outward from the city centers.[12] Indeed, this movement persisted throughout much of the twentieth century. However, in the last few decades, White affluent and middle-class individuals have been relocating to the city center.[13] The movement of upper-income Whites to the central city is associated with the downtown expansion and the subsequent gentrification of low-income minority neighborhoods just on the periphery of the central business district.[14] As that district expands, another defining feature of the cappuccino city is the formation of the gilded ghetto.

Gilded Ghetto Formation

In the cappuccino city, certain dark ghettos become gilded ghettos. Several forces, at multiple levels, relate to this circumstance. Peter Marcuse highlights some of these redevelopment production dynamics by noting that "where globalization, high technology, and financialization are well advanced, and where a ghetto, with a stock of readily convertible housing, is located within easy access to the central business district, gentrification has been a major factor and key component in dilution of the ghetto."[15] DC's Shaw/U Street neighborhood, once the quintessential dark ghetto, is today the prototypical gilded ghetto.

The gentrification production forces highlighted by Marcuse are ever present in DC, and have contributed to Shaw/U Street's redevelopment. DC's unique global economy, related to contracting and financial oversight from the federal government, has boomed in the last decade. And as its economy proliferated, its downtown has expanded with substantial federal and local government investments, which in turn led to greater housing demand in nearby low-income African American neighborhoods, including Shaw/U Street.

But these global, federal, and local production forces do not fully explain neighborhood gentrification in the former Black ghetto. The cultural consumption of what is perceived as an "authentic," hip, diverse community is also critical. Some upper-income newcomers are enticed to the gilded ghetto because it is still seen as an iconic Black ghetto. Thus, the gilded ghettos are driven by both production and consumption gentrification dynamics.

The cappuccino city features increasing racial and ethnic diversity. As Elijah Anderson notes, "The American city of today is more racially, ethnically, and socially diverse than ever."[16] He suggests that within such cities, people seek out the cosmopolitan canopy, public spaces "that offer a respite from the lingering tensions of urban life and an opportunity for diverse peoples to come together."[17] These neutral, pluralistic spaces are urban pockets where "people engage one another in a spirit of civility, or even comity and goodwill."[18] Shaw/U Street represents a kind of cosmopolitan canopy "where people of differing racial and cultural types not only share space but seek out each other's presence."[19]

However, the gilded ghetto of the cappuccino city does not reflect Anderson's cosmopolitan canopy all that closely. White newcomers express tolerance and a yearning for diversity, but some form exclusive networks and advocate for amenities that coincide with their preferences—even if these preferences do not always align with those of long-term minority residents. Such neighborhoods thus represent a form of inclusion and exclusion at the same time. As French urban scholar Sylvie Tissot claims, "Residents who move into mixed-income, inner-city neighborhoods generally express a taste for diversity while simultaneously attempting to distance themselves from 'undesirables.'"[20] The exclusionary processes show up in places like dog parks. "Although seemingly small, trivial public places, dog runs play a crucial role in the processes of inclusion and exclusion among the residents of gentrifying neighborhoods," Tissot explains.[21] To be sure, the processes she highlights are witnessed in dog parks and also in the associations that advocate for them in DC's gilded ghetto.

Racial Saliency

Race remains significant in the cappuccino city, although other social categories, such as class, sexual orientation, and age, are influential there as well. Race is critical to explaining political processes such as city and community elections, types of Black branding initiatives, amenity preferences, and redevelopment outcomes. While some scholars, such as Terry Clark, Jennifer Hochschild, Vesla Weaver, and Traci Burch, claim that race is becoming less significant, the cappuccino city provides a counter to this line of reasoning, suggesting the continued relevance and importance of race to twenty-first-century urban analysis. Race helps contextualize urban population movements, amenity preferences, and political processes and outcomes. While I agree with Clark that urban scholars need to better account for "amenities, lifestyles, and entertainment to capture key [urban] dynamics," I disagree with the notion that race is becoming less salient.[22]

While race remains significant, other social categories have become increasingly important, and intersectionality is a useful analytical tool in understanding the cappuccino city. Although characteristics such as race, class, and sexual orientation have become less predictive of individual behavior, as social categories these remain important for comprehending and explaining organizational and community conflicts and tensions within the civil societies of diverse, mixed-income, mixed-race neighborhoods of the cappuccino city.[23] Multiple traditional categories are vital for understanding the politics of Shaw/U Street, but they cannot be understood in isolation. A comprehensive understanding of urban politics in the cappuccino city and its gilded ghettos comes from assessing a variety of social categories simultaneously.

Service Sector Job Growth and Amenity Politics

Cappuccino city politics are the politics of delivering service-sector job growth and upgraded lifestyle amenities. Achieving both job growth and upgraded amenities calls for enticing mobile, educated workers and their employers to the city center by deploying resources for downtown improvements. During the 1990s and 2000s, DC invested ample city resources to redevelop its east downtown with a massive sports entertainment complex combined with retail space, restaurants, and luxury condominiums. In the cappuccino city, development politics is, as Terry Clark, Richard Florida, Edward Glaeser, and Sharon Zukin duly note, about providing lifestyle amenities to attract affluent populations back to the city.[24] The cappuccino city government will invest in infrastructure to further court the Millennials—luxury housing units, sports entertainment complexes, bike lanes, dog parks, streetcars—and will likely decrease its proportion of spending on the social safety net. While this might seem to replicate some of the patterns that exist in a neo-liberal city, it differs in that the city is not rolling back but rather redeploying public dollars.[25] Furthermore, the cappuccino city perspective differs from Clark's entertainment city in that job production is seen as just as important as amenity development in driving city policies.

Political shifts occur in cappuccino cities. As new populations enter the city, these groups put pressure on the existing political structure. In the late 1970s, '80s, and early '90s, as discussed in chapter 2, the DC political machine and its figurehead, Marion Barry, ruled the city. After Barry's second downfall, the city's politics under Mayors Williams and Fenty represented the new breed of Black politics, where fiscal concerns and the preferences of the mainly White back-to-the-city population trumped all other priorities. Even though Black political leaders remained in place after Barry, Chocolate City and its traditional machine politics declined. However, because the cappuccino city is so integrated, diverse, and contentious, the political winds can shift at any given moment, as demonstrated by Vincent Gray's mayoral defeat of Adrian Fenty, and then Muriel Bowser's defeat of Gray. Nevertheless, the overall trend in cappuccino cities will be a decline of African American, civil rights–oriented political power.[26] This political pattern is distinct from the dual city perspective, which suggests that growing urban inequality will inspire more politicians reminiscent of the civil rights era rather than the technocrats of today.[27]

Second Suburbs and Increasing Inequality

The geography of poverty also shifts in the cappuccino city. In DC, as in other urban areas, Whites are moving to the city center as low-income African Americans move further from the city's core.[28] With the movement of low-income African Americans to the suburbs, the "second suburbs" are created.[29] We are no longer a country of "chocolate cities and vanilla suburbs"; rather, certain cities have become "Oreo cities," with increasingly White inner-city cores and darker suburban exteriors, like the cappuccino. While this urban development pattern is new to the United States, it is a common metropolitan circumstance in many western European regions.[30]

Certain American inner-city cores are becoming affluent entertainment playgrounds as their inner suburbs emerge as concentrated poverty pockets.[31] DC is following this pattern of development as east downtown, and nearby surrounding African American neighborhoods such as Shaw/U Street, the H Street Corridor, east Capitol Hill, and sections of Southwest and Southeast DC, gentrify. In turn, its poverty is moving further from the central business district to inner-ring Prince George's County suburbs.[32] In DC, some areas of inner suburban Prince George's County have been nicknamed DC's "Ward 9" because of their recent increase in both poverty and former DC residents.[33]

Increasing inequality, and a greater disparity between the rich and the poor, is another characteristic of the cappuccino city. This shift occurs through several mechanisms. The cappuccino city is connected to the world by the foreign governments, corporations, and markets in its customer base. This international market potential helps increase the profitability of the city's corporations, and these companies pay a premium to attract talented employees. Then, as educated young professionals become a larger share of the city's population, low-wage service jobs are produced, such as the Uber driver and the Starbucks employee. But wages stagnate in these occupations, while property values rise and those with less means are forced to exit the city. Some low-income people will stay put due to their ability to remain in subsidized housing, but the poor will become a smaller percentage of the city's population. This situation is distinct from the dual city and the global city perspectives, both of which predict that the number and percentage of poor and rich will grow.[34] In cappuccino cities, income disparities will rise, but the total number of the poor will decrease, because they cannot afford to live in the city anymore. They will take on the low-wage social-service jobs in the city, but they will increasingly live in certain declining inner suburbs.

As American cities become more service sector dominated and attract Millennials, the features, dynamics, processes, and outcomes of DC's twenty-first-century cappuccino city will, to varying degrees, surface and reveal themselves in other urban areas around the country. How do we make the gilded ghettos within these cities more equitable?

EIGHT

Making Equitable Communities

We need a resident plan to get people to benefit from all this development coming into the neighborhood. . . . We're being played like pawns.

—Elderly African American Shaw/U Street resident

The gilded ghetto holds much promise and potential for racial integration and improved social equity. However, the meaningful social interactions we had hoped for among upper-, middle-, and low-income individuals in mixed-income neighborhoods do not occur with great frequency, and when they do they tend to be highly contentious. Racial integration scholar Michael Maly argues, "When a diverse population shares residential space, it is rare that groups share common values, norms, and even goals. Racially and ethnically heterogeneous neighborhoods thus produce a certain amount of conflict."[1] Furthermore, in her superb study of DC's racially transitioning Mount Pleasant neighborhood, Gabriella Modan claims, "Divergent attitudes about what constitutes commitment to, and ownership of, the neighborhood cause a lot of conflict, as each group resents the other for trying to promote their vision of the neighborhood without (in the eyes of the other group) having the legitimacy as a community insider."[2] Much of this book's findings about Washington, DC, support the social dynamics highlighted by Maly and Modan.

My goals for this concluding chapter are twofold: one, to demonstrate that resident interactions across racial and income divides in the gilded ghetto do not occur as frequently as we might have expected; and two, to outline a set of tentative policy recommendations to help achieve greater social connections in mixed-income communities. Hence, this chapter sketches out some potential avenues for promoting just, equitable neighborhood growth that could improve the life chances of low- and moderate-income residents in redeveloping communities.

Some well-intentioned urban planners, policy makers, scholars, and practitioners have focused on helping low-income people stay in gentrifying communities.[3] The thought is that minimizing displacement would maximize the potential positive spillover effects of growth and development for low-income and working-class families. However, in Shaw/U Street, many of these advantageous spillover influences, beyond lower crime rates, have not occurred for those who remain in the community's subsidized housing. A plausible reason for this is that few deep, meaningful interactions occur across racial and income divisions.

Many interactions between newcomers and existing residents typify the engagement that Richard, Michael, and Berin have on their block. One morning, I sat with Richard and his adult son Michael on the porch of their two-bedroom row home on 6th Street. Richard, an elderly African American, was born in Northern Virginia in 1932 and moved to DC in the 1950s to work in one of the city's hotels. Michael was born in 1954 and moved back in with his dad after finishing college and living in the DC suburbs for a time. Michael explains that in the last few years, his block has transformed from a drug-infested area into one where the vacant lot just north of his home was recently turned into $500,000 two-bedroom condos.

Berin and his partner, both White young professionals, own one of those $500,000 condos. Berin is a very environmentally conscious DC lawyer. One of his goals is to green the block with trees. He notes, "[One of the] things that most tell you about how the area changes are . . . the trees. . . . 'cause when you start getting new trees planted and cared for, it means that there are people who are engaged." Richard and Michael refer to Berin as "the tree guy." They tell me that they get along with him and their other White neighbors, but Michael says, "It's not like it goes any further than being neighborly. I don't go out and get drinks with them."

In response to my question about what Whites coming into the area has meant for the neighborhood, Richard and Michael both mention that the block has become quieter and crime has decreased. Then Michael says, pointing to the freshly blacktopped road, "The city just paved the road and redid the sidewalk," which he claims was likely related to Whites moving into the area. In fact, some of these improvements likely had to do with Berin's local government advocacy. Berin often speaks with city officials to request improvements on the block. While the interactions Richard and Michael have with their White neighbors are cordial, and they perceive that some improvements are related to these neighbors' arrival, their lives have not really changed as dramatically as their neighborhood and block have.

Few cross-race interactions occur within neighborhood organizations. One afternoon, over a glass of wine, Tim, the president of the Logan Circle Community Association, talks with me about the diversity of his association's membership. Although African Americans live in the Logan Circle area, he tells me that most of his membership meetings are quite racially homogeneous. He says, "I look around the room and there are thirty people, and only two of them are African American. You know, it's sort of a room full of White people."

Tim recalls that at his association meetings, he tells members that they need to find out what African Americans in the neighborhood wanted so as to attract them to meetings. But then he declares, "I don't practice what I preach in these meetings. What I preach . . . making sure you identify your target audience, find out what that audience cares about, what resonates with them, and then present very actionable items to them that they can act on. So, if I was actually practicing what I preach in . . . this community, I would be talking to the Black community to find out what they . . . care about, and then tailor my work to resonate with them on those specific issues . . . and I haven't."

Christine, the president of the U Street Neighborhood Association, also notes a lack of diversity at her organization's gatherings. Christine, who is White, speaks about the membership:

I think it's been a big challenge. We talk about reaching out to members. You know it's not just [that] we want more people who look the way we do, but I think, I know it's something that [a fellow member] and I talked about a lot when she was president. . . . You know there's clearly people that we're not reaching, and how do we get them involved with what's going on? I often will . . . sit at Ben's [Chili Bowl restaurant] or I'll sit out somewhere, and people will talk about the old days of the neighborhood and how the Blacks are getting pushed out, and it makes me so frustrated, because I just want to say, "Well, have them come to a meeting!" You know?

While White-dominated civic associations do not effectively reach out to the community's minority population, long-term African American residents are not always inclined to show up at these meetings either. Tessie, a fifty-eight-year-old African American woman and twenty-one-year Shaw/U Street resident, explains some of tension associated with the community's redevelopment:

In most neighborhoods or communities, you have folk . . . not ready for a change, you know. Or they ready for it, but they don't know exactly how they gonna deal with it or handle it. . . . But I'm looking here in my community and . . . [some were] saying, "Well, these people are coming in, and they're buying up my homes and what have you," but at the same time, my theory is that, well, why you letting them do it? What are you doing to keep them from doing it? Are you going out to meetings, are you doing workshops, are you doing a petition, what have you? What is it that you're doing to keep *what's going on* from happening?

Tessie claims that most of her African American neighbors do not attend important community meetings.

Race and class are important social categories that help explain the separation between newcomers and long-term residents. Novella, a subsidized housing resident, explains that many of her African American neighbors see gentrification as a White "conspiracy" to rid the city of Blacks. She says, "When we get together, we talk about this conspiracy."[4] If some African Americans view the redevelopment of the community as a White conspiracy, it is not difficult to understand why they have not participated in community meetings of associations that have become White dominated.

It is important to acknowledge, however, that perceptions of racism cut both ways. Some long-term, Black resident "gatekeepers" make attempts at newcomer integration difficult. One early evening, I attempted to join a group of men to play pickup basketball at the historic Shiloh Baptist Church. I entered the church and asked the front door attendant, an elderly African American man, "Where's the gym?" From behind the front desk, he gave me a scowl and retorted, "There's no games here." I then told him that I played with a group of guys over at the Kennedy Recreation Center, and they told me that there's a regular informal game upstairs. The man, with great emphasis, said, "There's no game here!" I understood the message: there is no game for a White man in his late thirties, a potential community gentrifier.

I left the church and walked a few blocks to the Kennedy "Rec" Center to see if the person who had told me about the Shiloh pickup games was there. I immediately saw my African American hoops informant and told him the story. He smiled and said, "OK, let's go over there." He brought me over to the older gentleman and exclaimed, "Hey, he can play. Let him in." With my escort vouching for me, I was allowed to pass the front desk. Upstairs, several men were lacing up their basketball shoes and setting up a score clock. When we began to play, I proceeded to hit three three-pointers in a row, and my team won the first game. Later that night as I left the gym and walked by the elderly doorman, we exchanged nods but did not say a word to each other.[5] After that evening, I had no trouble accessing Shiloh's gym.

For newcomers in transitioning African American neighborhoods, some institutions are initially closed off, and at times they experience intimidating behavior from existing residents. This unwelcoming behavior can feel like reverse racism. But once someone "proves" himself or gains the trust of a respected resident guide and *bridge maker*, the community opens up and becomes embracing. However, the newly arrived, like some members of the Logan Circle Community Association or the U Street Neighborhood Association, often do not engage sufficiently with longtime residents to understand initial resistance to newcomers. Without such engagement, misunderstandings frequently occur and persist between longtime residents and newcomers.

Some perceive that micro-level separation in Shaw/U Street is associated more with class than race. Community resident Ron, the African American owner of the liquor store Good Libations, sees interactions among his neighbors and customers occurring more along class lines:

> The interaction is more on the economic level. If you have Blacks who are, I don't want to say, well-to-do, but are working, making money, own their houses or whatever. They interact . . . a little bit more . . . with the newer Whites or Whites that have lived here longer than Blacks who are, like, struggling or subsidized through the government. They [the subsidized residents] looking at them [the newcomers and say], "OK, these newcomers are just pushing us out." . . . It's kind of, I feel bad about that. Because it's, like, it should be more. We're all in the same area. And maybe it's like I said, an economic thing. You have different conversations when you're on a different economic level than somebody who's not—music, wine, social issues.

Whether due to race, class, or a combination of the two, little bridging social capital is being developed as the neighborhood becomes more racially and economically mixed.[6] Instead of integration, organizations within the seemingly diverse community are segregated. I call this *diversity segregation*.[7] Diversity segregation is when the community, according to statistics, appears quite racially or economically diverse, but the neighborhood's social fabric remains segregated.[8] To make mixed-race, mixed-income communities more cohesive, social distance must be overcome to reach deeper understandings among traditionally separated populations.

Neutral "third spaces" may facilitate the development of bridging social capital. When I speak of neutral third spaces, I do not mean a Starbucks, where the customers might look diverse but fail to interact across divisions of race, class, and sexual orientation.[9] I refer to spaces where people feel comfortable speaking about difference and inequalities, and work through these challenging issues through shared activities that cut across differences. "Third places counter the tendency to be restrictive in the enjoyment of others by being open to all and by laying emphasis on qualities not confined to status distinctions current in the society."[10]

In urban communities, third spaces can arise in a variety of settings. These entities tend to be corner stores, coffee shops, bars, bookstores, and eating establishments.[11] They can also be recreation centers, day care facilities, community gardens, parks, libraries, schools, and civic organizations. The key is that the space must engender feelings of shared interests, as opposed to competition, and function with political equity.

While some of these entities are inclusive, they can also be exclusive establishments based on a variety of social categories. For instance, certain neighborhood associations exclude based on renting versus owning, which to a certain extent is based on class. Some civic associations include or exclude members based on geographic boundaries, which are often related to the racial composition of the designated area. Furthermore, some eating establishments are high priced and thus exclude low-income people to a certain extent, or they are informally designated for newcomers versus long-term residents.

While there is much micro-level segregation in Shaw/U Street, a few places function as spaces where people from all walks of life come together. Ben's Chili Bowl and Busboys and Poets are two of these spaces. In either place, one finds a diverse cross-section of the community eating, drinking, reading, listening, and learning from one another. These spaces reflect Elijah Anderson's cosmopolitan canopy.[12]

Ben's Chili Bowl symbolizes the best of mixed-race, mixed-income DC. As I walked into Ben's one afternoon for lunch, an Usher song, "That's What It's Made For," flowed from a speaker placed right above the front entrance. This song was followed by Laury Hill's "Everything Is Everything." I took a seat right next to the cash register at the counter, a perfect place to observe the action. I watched as the patrons ordered and the wait staff interacted with them.

After the R&B music finished, DC's famous "go-go" music came on; the wait staff, one wearing a black T-shirt that stated "I Am DC" and "I Demand the Vote" in red and white letters, started moving to the beat. The cashier, an African American man in his midtwenties, started tapping the beat on the countertop as he paused briefly from ringing up orders and taking customers' money. Another staff member caught the eye of an African American woman in her fifties who had just ordered and was standing to the left of the cash register; he started moving his shoulders back and forth, keeping time, and as he moved he dipped a little lower each time. The woman smiled and laughed as another customer called out to the dancing staff member, "Go ahead, go ahead." Ben's has energy, an unusually positive vibe, and the people who go here love it. It's truly a dining experience.

People from all different backgrounds, incomes, races, and ethnicities eat at Ben's and interact with civility. Next to me at the counter was an African American man in his fifties wearing a suit and tie. Directly behind me at one of the booths was a group of White men in their forties wearing suits. In line were DC landscape employees wearing their brightly colored orange-and-yellow reflective vests. One ordered "two smokes, fries, and two bottles of water." Individuals were very close to one another, but for whatever the reason—probably the good food—they were friendly and courteous. By sitting next to the cash register, I was about six inches from people who were ordering their food. Although this was extremely close, most people did not bump into me, and those who did apologized. Everyone mixes at Ben's regardless of race and class, and enjoys the restaurant's incredible chili with cheese and onions piled high.

Another Shaw/U Street mixed-race, mixed-income space is Busboys and Poets. Andy Shallal, the owner, talks about his unique restaurant:

> Places like this are very significant in the changes that have taken place, because they allow for the diffusion of tension. When people are sitting next to each other and eating next to each other, it certainly gives a sense of "I understand them a little better." There's an opportunity to intermingle, and once you start intermingling and eating together, you're much more likely to feel safe or comfortable with the other.
>
> So once they're in the same room, lots of stuff happens. You see relationship development. You see people reaching out to each other. The programs that we do are so significant, and the conversations. Black folks are sitting here and hear a White person get up and almost passionately support their sensibility. They see that, "Hey, you know, I can relate to these people. We can actually get along."

But the integrated space and cosmopolitan canopy of Busboys are not achieved without some effort.

The mixed-income literature distinguishes between those mixed-race and mixed-income communities that happen organically, "diversity by circumstance," and those that were socially planned, "diversity by direction."[13] The

Shaw/U Street area can be considered a "diversity by circumstance" community, since there was no planned action to make it diverse.[14] The process started to happen somewhat organically because of market forces as well the individual choices of new residents to move in and long-term residents to leave. No major urban renewal–like project kicked off the community's redevelopment or its racial and ethnic transition. However, a series of public investments, such as the Reeves Center and the completion of the Metro, cumulatively stimulated and sustained the neighborhood's twenty-year-plus redevelopment.[15]

The degree of micro-level racial integration achieved at Busboys and Poets is, in part, the result of conscious actions, and Shallal's own ambiguous racial profile. He explains, "When we first started opening Busboys and Poets, I knew U Street very, very well, and I did a lot of work, a lot of research, before I opened the place."

In responding to my asking him specifically what he did, Andy replies, "I went around and took in a lot of leaders in the community, and opened up and had lunch with them. . . . You know, people that were in power, people that run the ANC [Advisory Neighborhood Commission], people that run different organizations in the city. Then I talked to condo associations and things like that, where the newer residents were, because I did want to be inclusive. I went out of my way to be probably more inclusive of African Americans, because that's the historical content of the space."

Not only did Shallal reach out to the some of the community's Black leaders, but when the restaurant opened, a diversity norm proliferated: "I'd like to see the tables more mixed within themselves. Now we have a group of Black, a group of White, but they're at least next to each other. You get a lot of contact, but not as much as I want to see. I would come in sometimes [and see this] . . . natural sort of [segregated] selection. It's just like the bus ride, the Metro, or in high school. But you see that condition taking shape, and all of a sudden I'll come up and say, 'mix it up!'" It seems that even in a racially diverse restaurant environment within a racially diverse community, norms of race mixing are needed to establish micro-level integration.

Shallal also implemented programming to deal with the sensitive issues of race and diversity in the broader neighborhood. "Having program[s] simply helps . . . to having events that are programmed to deal with current issues that deal not only on a global level, but also on a local level. Dealing with gentrification, dealing with racial harmony, and so on. We started a program called ACTOR [A Continuing Talk on Race], which meets the first Sunday [of every month] that deals with race . . . changes that have taken place."

What is more, Shallal is a type of bridge maker. He explains the success of his restaurant:

> I am not Black, so it's hard to be able to immediately open the door and think that people are going to show up here who have lived here for years and years—Black people, White people. I'm not White either, so maybe that's the formula. The ownership and having a place, that is again, for lack of a better word, a bridge. That can combine all groups together. Because I do see myself as being an amalgam of many different groups. I'm of Arab descent, but I, when I came here to America, I was Black, you know, that was the only area that I could fit in. Over the years, you know, in the neighborhood, I was able to be in many different communities and feel comfortable.

Busboys and Poets, which now has six DC metro locations, has become a DC restaurant empire; however, even with Shallal's inclusive effort, not everyone is pleased with the way he has incorporated aspects of Black culture into the Busboys and Poets' brand. Stephen Crockett Jr., an African American writer, claims in a *Washington Post* article, "There is a certain cultural vulturalism, an African American historical 'swagger-jacking,' going on on U Street." He explains, "In a six-block stretch, we have Brixton, Busboys and Poets, Eatonville, Patty Boom Boom, Blackbyrd and Marvin. All are based on some facet of black history, some memory of blackness that feels artificially done and palatable. Does it matter that the owners aren't black? Maybe. Does it matter that these places slid in around the time that black folks slid out? Maybe."

Crockett's "swagger-jacking" notion struck a nerve in Shaw/U Street and in DC more generally, as others were upset with Busboys and Poets. Jessica, a lifelong DC resident, former Shaw/U Street community organizer, and Howard University graduate, says she resents Busboys and Poets because it markets Black culture and protest politics, but such values are not reflected in its employment practices. She feels that the wait staff is underpaid. She is also somewhat bitter about Shallal's success, and says that she can't understand why she or some other Black person could not have come up with the same concept. "Dammit, I had that idea," she says in a joking and sarcastic manner as we talk at the Organizing Neighborhood Equity (ONE DC) offices. She then says that a Howard University student was rumored to have had the idea for Busboys, but could not secure financing. Other than from Jessica, I never heard this rumor, but her tale indicates the intense dismay some original residents experience when they perceive an outsider making money from the community's redevelopment.

Before Crockett's article came out, Busboys was the victim of a minor but symbolically major form of protest. One night, someone stole a life-size poster of Langston Hughes that was stationed inside the restaurant to market a poetry conference. "I took it," said Thomas Sayer Ellis, a native Black Washingtonian poet and assistant professor of creative writing at Sarah Lawrence College. "You would think that an establishment that makes as much money as Busboys would have set in place a reading series with a respectful pay scale for writers."[16] Ellis was upset because he felt that Shallal greatly underpaid poets who performed at the restaurant. The week that this incident occurred, I was in Busboys writing up field notes and noticed that someone had carved on the back of the bathroom door, "Langston Hughes is not Ronald McDonald."

Regarding the incident and the graffiti in the bathroom, Shallal says, "It's hard not to take it personal[ly]." In responding to Crockett, Rucker, and Ellis, he remarks, "I think one thing that I've heard, although nobody says that to your face, naturally, is he's not Black, but he does all Black stuff. I hear that."

While Shallal has created a unique "third space" and cosmopolitan canopy, he and his restaurant face some racial resentment. However, he does not shy away from it, and his business confronts racial sentiments directly in its events and programs. In addition, he has engendered norms of integration and civic dialogue within Busboys and Poets. Shallal explains that his restaurant "is trying to hold on to a moment in time or history that transcends Black or White. It's American history, it's this area's history"—a Black history and a Black neighborhood that is helping Andy, who is not Black, make a lot of green.

Economic Justice

Some tension and resentment in mixed-income neighborhoods that were once "dark ghettos" is grounded in the reality and perceptions that community outsiders are making money off the neighborhood's redevelopment, while long-term, low-income African American residents and Black-owned businesses are getting pushed out. For instance, in Shaw/U Street some non-Black business newcomers, such as Andy Shallal and Ian and Eric Hilton, are making lots of money from their local restaurant investments.[17] Also, several White real estate developers, such as Jim Abdo and others, are making substantial profits from their Shaw/U Street residential developments.[18]

However, sometimes long-term Black businesses benefit. In Shaw/U Street, three of these family-owned enterprises are thriving today: Lee's

Flower Shop, Industrial Bank, and Ben's Chili Bowl. Rick Lee, the owner of the flower shop, grew up in the neighborhood in the '50s. He said that although he is not fond of the neighborhood's racial change, when the neighborhood become more White his flower business "started booming, you know . . . started really popping." While these three Black businesses are held up as symbols of racial uplift and equitable development, they are not the norm; many other small U Street businesses were displaced as the neighborhood revitalized.[19]

There are several ways that economic justice can be better achieved within mixed-income neighborhoods. One potential mechanism is to keep low-income housing in place while the neighborhood redevelops. Past practices and policies have allowed some of the poor to stay in place, but their continued residency is not always stable over the long term.[20] As the neighborhood continues to redevelop, a few of Shaw/U Street's church-owned subsidized buildings are opting out of their Section 8 contracts and now offer market-rate units.[21] Thus, a continued effort for affordable housing preservation will be critical to maintaining a mix of incomes in redeveloping communities.

Small-business preservation will also be important in mixed-income environments. ONE DC has been working for years to harness Shaw/U Street's redevelopment dynamics to better the lives of the community's remaining low-income residents. It has done this primarily through preserving affordable housing, but has also indirectly helped some long-term small businesses. As noted in chapter 5, in 2007 ONE DC established a community benefits agreement (CBA) with a major real estate development partnership, Ellis Enterprises and Four Points, which proposed to redevelop a section of 7th Street with a large, mixed-use, mixed-income development. The CBA established that two thousand square feet of retail space would be available at a below-market rate to a local business for five years.[22]

Wanda Henderson's hair shop, now the refurbished Wanda's on 7th, is the first tenant to benefit from this CBA.[23] Judging by the Black and White patrons displayed on her new website, it appears she is poised to serve the community's diverse clientele. To see a local Black-owned salon return to 7th Street in 2014 after it had been displaced from U Street in the 2000s and then displaced from 7th Street in 2010 represents not only an inspiring story of perseverance but also a form of equitable development.[24] ONE DC's nearly ten-year organizing effort, the CBA it established with the development partnership, and Henderson's tenacity are all important reasons behind Wanda's return to 7th Street.

However, the hair salon's long-term presence on 7th Street (fig. 20) is not

Figure 20. Wanda's—back on 7th Street.

guaranteed, as the CBA affords Henderson's below-market rent only for five years. It will be critical that she has access to investment capital for making the strategic investments that will prepare her when market-rate payments go into effect. Ensuring that a greater number of long-term, small Black-owned businesses have access to capital and are prepared to adapt their business models as the neighborhood around them redevelops is necessary for facilitating more equitable outcomes in gentrifying communities.[25]

Some of Shaw/U Street's economic justice solutions might be found outside the community. As noted in chapter 3, rising inequality has accompanied DC's expansion and growth. Ed Lazere, director of the DC Fiscal Policy Institute, states, "It's a classic story of a rising tide that is not lifting all boats. There are a lot of residents not able to connect with the city's economic engine. And the city's becoming more expensive around them."[26] Part of the Shaw/U Street redevelopment story has to do with the city's broader economic context. A key to solving economic justice concerns within that neighborhood is to link its low-income residents to the city's growing economic success.

One approach might be to create and maintain living-wage jobs for DC's existing low- and moderate-income residents. In 2011, the city's former mayor, Marion Barry, declared, "We're going to stop this trend of gentrification. We can't displace old-time Washingtonians. The key to keeping this city black is jobs, jobs, jobs for black people."[27] In 2016, the DC City Council unanimously endorsed a new minimum wage policy that could slightly reduce the city's growing income inequality gap and ensure that lower-wage DC jobs better enable people to stay in their community as it redevelops.[28]

Political Justice

If we, as a society, are concerned about stabilizing and maintaining diverse enclaves, political and cultural displacement must be addressed. As power shifts from a neighborhood's long-term residents to its newcomers, some residents feel that they no longer control their community. Furthermore, as local decisions are made to bring in new amenities, such as bike lanes, that do not align with most long-term residents' tastes and preferences, these residents begin to lose their attachment to place, making their eventual departure likely. These political and cultural losses perpetuate the transition of a neighborhood from one group, based on race or class, to another. As planners and policy makers of sustainable, inclusive urban communities, we need to minimize such losses and the related feelings of resentment when neighborhoods begin to change racially and economically.

One possible solution would be to slow down the political power shift. To accomplish this, we need appropriate ways to help long-term, low-income residents maintain a say in their local government. Ensuring that these citizens have some representation in local civic and neighborhood associations and other local governance bodies, such as the Advisory Neighborhood Commissions, might be one way to prevent their intense feelings of political loss.

Another plausible remedy would be to ensure that some of the original population's tastes and preferences are expressed in the built environment. While this is a viable option, efforts to accomplish it might fall short if the long-standing population does not feel part of the political process related to cultural preservation. In chapter 4, we saw how it was mainly Whites who had spearheaded Shaw/U Street's African American cultural preservation. When political decisions to promote preservation do not have the participation and engagement of the existing African American residents, these interventions can spawn resentment or be perceived as economic development and displacement engines rather than significant social markers.[29]

Still another option: create and promote neighborhood organizations that work to integrate new and existing populations in gentrifying neighborhoods. This recommendation coincides with Gibbs Knotts and Moshe Haspel, who state, "Our research . . . shows that the negative effects of gentrification can be ameliorated by neighborhood-level organizations that help preserve the sense of community in a neighborhood and integrate new residents into that community."[30] Redeveloping communities have few organizations whose mission it is to integrate diverse resident populations. Community organizations that bring people together for shared activities, such as neighborhood gardening efforts or other green infrastructure improvements, and build bridging social capital might be critical to reducing conflict in mixed-income areas. These "third space" organizations might also reduce micro-level segregation and bring forth more of the hypothesized benefits of mixed-income living for low-income residents. Community development block grants funds from the US Department of Housing and Urban Development, as well as private foundation funds, could be directed toward this purpose.

What's Going On?

Marvin Gaye's classic song addressing inner-city poverty conditions and the Vietnam War encapsulates the recent altering circumstances in the District. Many long-term African American residents in DC's redeveloping low-income communities are asking, "What's going on?" as they watch their city change from Chocolate City to Cappuccino City. DC's go-go clubs are gone, and doggie day cares, gastropubs, and faux speakeasies are emerging. The feel and pulse of the city and certain neighborhoods have changed; many areas are more posh, White, and expensive. New upscale restaurants, wine bars, cheese shops, and organic grocery markets are replacing the carryouts and pawnshops. The city once labeled "the murder capital" is now called "Capital Hip."[31] DC's nickname change is a symbolic shift, and helps to explain the twenty-first-century transformation of the dark ghetto into the gilded ghetto. "Woo ah, mercy mercy me. Ah things ain't what they used to be"—nor are things in the gilded ghetto what *they* seem to be.

Select Washington, DC, Old Downtown, and Shaw/U Street Demographics

Table A.1. Population Change.

	1980	1990	2000	2010	% Change 00–10
DC	638,328	606,900	572,059	601,723	5
Old DT	2,167	2,714	3,417	5,828	71
Shaw/U St.	28,723	29,567	29,741	34,750	17

Source: US Census Bureau.

Table A.2. Percentage Black.

	1980	1990	2000	2010	% Change 00–10
DC	70	66	60	51	-15
Old DT	54	64	56	20	-64
Shaw/U St.	81	67	53	30	-43

Source: US Census Bureau.

Table A.3. Percentage White.

	1980	1990	2000	2010	% Change 00–10
DC	27	30	31	39	26
Old DT	22	17	25	61	144
Shaw/U St.	16	20	23	53	130

Source: US Census Bureau.

Table A.4. Percentage with BA or Higher.

	1980	1990	2000	2010*	% Change 00–10
DC	27	33	39	49	26
Old DT	18	13	30	63	110
Shaw/U St.	19	29	36	61	69

Source: US Census Bureau.
*These estimates were based on the American Community Survey 2006–10.

Table A.5. Percentage Owner-Occupied Units.

	1980	1990	2000	2010	% Change 00–10
DC	32	35	39	41	5
Old DT	3	4	4	20	400
Shaw/U St.	14	22	26	35	35

Source: US Census Bureau.

Table A.6. Median Value for Owner-Occupied Units (in Thousands).

	1990	2000	2010	% Change 00–10
DC	170	212	445	110
Old DT	225	402	474	18
Shaw/U St.	173	240	587	145

Source: US Census Bureau.

Table A.7. Median Household Income.

	1980	1990	2000	2010	% Change 00–10
DC	42,959	51,314	50,961	64,267	26
Old DT	20,473	18,522	39,157	90,637	131
Shaw/U St.	27,450	40,044	40,336	83,302	107

Source: US Census Bureau.

Table A.8. Percentage Millennials (Age 20 to 34 Years).

	1980	1990	2000	2010	% Change 00–10
DC	30	30	27	31	15
Old DT	24	23	25	52	108
Shaw/U St.	30	36	34	45	32

Source: US Census Bureau.

Table A.9. Number of Millennials (Age 20 to 34 Years).

	1980	1990	2000	2010	% Change 00–10
DC	192,559	181,225	153,169	188,855	23
Old DT	523	611	851	3,011	254
Shaw/U St.	8,497	10,631	10,181	15,635	54

Source: US Census Bureau.

NOTES

CHAPTER ONE

1. Dash 1997, p. 11.
2. Robinson 2010, pp. 52–53.
3. "Farewell, AM.PM Carryout," post on *U Street Girl* blog, https://ustreetgirl.wordpress
   .com/2010/10/04/farewell-am-pm-carryout/ (accessed June 25, 2016).
4. See Martha's Table webpage, http://marthastable.org/about/ (accessed October 22,
   2015; content has since been altered).
5. In 2015, Martha's Table announced that it was leaving the neighborhood for a more
   impoverished DC community. See Steve Hendrix, "In a Changing D.C., Martha's
   Table Plans a $20 Million Move to Southeast," *Washington Post*, May 4, 2015.
6. See DC Condos Boutique's website, http://www.dccondoboutique.com/flats-at
   -union-row.php (accessed December 23, 2015; content has since been altered).
7. Langston Hughes lived in the Shaw/U Street community for a brief time in the 1920s.
8. Liebow 1967; Hannerz 1969.
9. Liebow 1967, p. 19.
10. I was introduced to *Tally's Corner* in 1996 as a predoctoral fellow at the National Insti-
    tute of Mental Health's Socio-Environmental Studies Laboratory. Carmi Schooler, the
    lab's director, insisted that I read Liebow's influential book. Schooler and Liebow had
    both worked for NIMH at the lab at different points in their careers. Little did Carmi
    or I know back then that I would return to Washington, DC, in 2009 to study the
    redevelopment of the same neighborhood that Liebow and Hannerz investigated.
11. Clark 1967; Hirsch 1998.
12. Jargowsky 1997; Massey and Denton 1993.
13. Clark 1967; Wilson 1987, 1996.
14. Clark 1967, p. 108.
15. Peter Marcuse (2012) also references gilded ghettos when he describes his classifica-
    tion of contemporary inner-city areas. He notes that the gilded ghettos are the low-
    income Black areas experiencing revitalization. For two excellent assessments of the
    term ghetto over time and space see Duneier 2016 and Hutchison and Haynes 2012.
16. Owens 2012.
17. It is important to note that a gentrification study of Chicago neighborhoods found
    that those with a high proportion of African Americans (40 percent or greater) were

associated with a slower rate of redevelopment between 2007 and 2009 compared with less segregated neighborhoods (Hwang and Sampson 2014). So even though, as pointed out by Owens (2012), a greater proportion of minority neighborhoods were redeveloping in the 2000s, they might be redeveloping at slower rates compared with other neighborhood types. While the specific gentrification rates among different neighborhood types might vary, there unquestionably exists a greater proportion of minority neighborhoods that experienced a White influx and redevelopment in the 2000s compared with the 1990s.

18. Maciag 2015.
19. Arena 2012; Boyd 2008; Freeman 2006; Fullilove and Wallace 2011; K. Gibson 2007; Inwood 2010; Jones and Jackson 2012; Lin 2011; Podagrosi and Vojnovic 2008; von Hoffman 2003.
20. *Iconic ghettos* is a term popularized by Elijah Anderson (2012), where he claims that inner-city African American neighborhoods are stereotypically considered places where Blackness is associated with poverty, crime, and chaos.
21. See the appendix, table 2.
22. See the appendix, table 3. The proportion of the Hispanic population in Shaw/U Street was a smaller, yet increasing presence, and its share grew from 6 percent to 13 percent between 2000 and 2010.
23. See the appendix, table 6, and Hyra and Rugh 2016.
24. Deener 2012; Lloyd 2010; Zukin 1982.
25. Grazian 2003; Lin 2011.
26. Massey and Denton 1993.
27. In 1968, during the riots that followed Martin Luther King Jr.'s assassination, storefronts along 14th Street, U Street, and 7th Street, Shaw/U Street's main business corridors, were set ablaze. In the years that followed, local African American churches, such as New Bethel Baptist Church, United House of Prayer, and Lincoln Temple United Church of Christ, built affordable housing to replace those destroyed structures (Gillette 1995; Ruble 2010).
28. Perry Stein, "Is Pricey Shaw a Model for Retaining Affordability amid Regentrification?," *Washington Post*, May 21, 2015.
29. Tach 2014.
30. *The Wire* is an award-winning cable TV series about the complexities of inner-city Baltimore's drug and law enforcement scene (Dreier and Atlas 2009).
31. See Eugene L. Meyer, "Washington's Shaw Neighborhood Is Remade for Young Urbanites," *New York Times*, December 1, 2015; and Perry Stein, "Is Pricey Shaw a Model for Retaining Affordability Amid Regentrification?," *Washington Post*, May 21, 2015.
32. For example, Boyd 2008; Freeman 2006; Hackworth 2007; Hyra 2008; Pattillo 2007; Smith 2000.
33. Brown-Saracino 2010; Lees, Slater, and Wyly 2008.
34. On the consumption side, see Lloyd 2010; Ocejo 2014; and Zukin 1982, 1995, 2010; and on the production side, see Arena 2012; Hackworth 2007; and Smith 2000.
35. Arena 2012; Goetz 2013; Hackworth 2007; Vale 2013.
36. Boyd 2008; Freeman 2006; Pattillo 2007.
37. Freeman and Cai 2015; Goetz 2013; Hyra 2012; Owens 2012.
38. Ellen and O'Regan 2011; Freeman 2005; Freeman and Braconi 2002, 2004; McKinnish, Walsh, and White 2010.
39. Arena 2012; Hyra 2008; Newman and Wyly 2006; Taylor 2002.
40. See Brown-Saracino 2010; Lees, Slater, and Wyly 2008.

41. There are some notable exceptions, including Ellen and O'Regan 2011 and Freeman 2006.
42. Quoted in WAMU radio news story, "Shaw's Roots: From 'Heart Of Chocolate City' To 'Little United Nations,'" by Rebecca Sheir, May 4, 2011, http://wamu.org/news /11/05/04/shaws_roots_from_heart_of_chocolate_city_to_little_united_nations.php (accessed June 25, 2016).
43. Yin 2014.
44. Emerson, Fretz, and Shaw 1995, p. 2.
45. A description of the vertical ethnographic approach appears in my earlier work (Hyra 2008). This data collection and assessment strategy borrows from the ethnographic methods advocated by Michael Burawoy and Loïc Wacquant (Burawoy 2009; Wacquant 2008).
46. Sampson 2012, p. 22.
47. Hyra 2008.
48. Ibid.
49. Hyra and Rugh 2016.
50. Massey and Denton 1993; Rugh and Massey 2014.
51. Greene 2014.
52. My ethnographic approach combined deductive and inductive forms of inquiry in that I had some questions and propositions that were formulated before I entered Shaw/U Street, but I remained open to important discoveries beyond my original questions.
53. For a more in-depth description of ONE DC, see Moulden and Squires 2012.
54. Archival records were also used as secondary data to complement my direct observations and interviews. Specifically, civic association meeting minutes were collected based on accessibility. Articles in DC newspapers that referenced the Shaw/U Street area were collected from the *Washington Post*, the *Washington City Paper*, the *InTowner*, and the *Washington Blade*, a gay-oriented newspaper. Additionally, I collected and assessed posts from six Internet blogs that extensively covered community issues. Some archival records dated back to 1999, but most covered between 2005 and 2012.
55. Abu-Lughod 2000, 2007; Davis 1998; Halle 2003; Mollenkopf and Castells 1991; Park and Burgess 1925; Soja 2010.
56. Fuller 2015.
57. Jackson 2015, p. 370.
58. Jackson 2016; Ruble 2010.
59. Gillette 1995.
60. Shaw/U Street is bounded by 15th Street, NW to the west, Florida Avenue to the north, North Capitol Street to the east, and M Street to the south. This is the community's designated area in the DC Shaw urban renewal plan of 1966. Within this area are several neighborhoods, such as Logan Circle, Greater U Street, Shaw, and Truxton Circle. Before the 1966 Shaw urban renewal plan, the area was known as Mid-City (Miller 2010; Ruble 2010; Schrag 2006).
61. Ruble 2010.
62. Crew 1996; Fitzpatrick and Goodwin 2001; Holloway 2002; Miller 2010; Moore 1999; Ruble 2010; Williams 2002.
63. Moore 1999.
64. Gilbert 1968.
65. Cashin 2004; Gale 1987; Lacy 2007.
66. Hannerz 1969; Liebow 1967.
67. Gillette 1995; Valk 2008.

68. Dash 1997; Robinson 2010.
69. I define *multiracial gentrification* as when upper-income individuals from different racial and ethnic backgrounds move to a low-income community. This is distinct from White-led or Black gentrification, where the newcomer population is largely from one racial group. In the 1990s, Shaw/U Street experienced multiracial gentrification; but in the 2000s it became White-led gentrification, and this study mostly covers the post-2000 redevelopment period.
70. As of July 2015, five-hundred-square-foot studios in the Louis are renting at $2,300 per month, and some of its one bedrooms are advertised for $5,000 per month.
71. See Annys Shin, "Gentrification in Overdrive on 14th Street," *Washington Post*, July 21, 2013; and Eugene L. Meyer, "Washington's Shaw Neighborhood Is Remade for Young Urbanites," *New York Times*, December 1, 2015.
72. Some scholarship suggesting that race has become less significant includes Clark 2011 and Hochschild, Weaver, and Burch 2012.
73. In 287 metropolitan areas, the average Black/White dissimilarity index fell from 78 to 60 between 1970 and 2010 (Rugh and Massey 2014).
74. Borchert 1980; Gale 1987; Gillette 1995; Green 1967; Hannerz 1969; Hopkinson 2012; Hyra and Prince 2016; Jaffe and Sherwood 2014; Kofie 1999; Liebow 1967; Modan 2007; Prince 2014; Ruble 2010; Williams 1988.
75. Others when referring to DC's recent demographic and social transformation explain it as "the new Latte City." See Petula Dvorak, "From Chocolate City to Latte City: Being Black in the New D.C.," *Washington Post*, October 15, 2015.
76. Center for Regional Analysis 2011.
77. Allard 2009; Kneebone and Berube 2014.
78. Baum-Snow and Hartley 2015; Ehrenhalt 2012.
79. In the 1990s and 2000s, these cities experienced inner-city gentrification and a decrease in the proportion of their African American population (Arena 2012; Furman Center for Real Estate and Urban Policy 2012; Inwood 2010; Owens and Brown 2014; Podagrosi and Vojnovic 2008).
80. For an analysis of foreclosure concentration variations in Chicago, New York, and Washington, DC, see Hyra and Rugh 2016.
81. For more on this, see Deener 2012; Freeman and Cai 2015; Hwang and Sampson 2014; and Owens 2012.
82. Anderson 2011.
83. Oldenburg 1999.

CHAPTER TWO

1. Fauntroy 2003; Gillette 1995.
2. McGovern 1998; Campbell 2003.
3. Barras 1998; Jaffe and Sherwood 2014.
4. Fauntroy 2003, p. 8.
5. Gandhi et al. 2009.
6. Modan 2007. It is important to note that while there are some unique constraints on the DC government due to federal oversight, other cities contend with certain limitations placed on them by their state capitals.
7. Gutheim and Lee 2006; Schrag 2006.
8. Dahl 1961; Erie 1988; Logan and Molotch 2007; Mills 1956; Stone 1989.
9. I assess and explain DC's political norms since they are critical for understanding city

elections, governance, and policy implementation (see Elazar 1966; Ferman 1996; Fuchs 1992; Hyra 2008).
10. Abbott 1999, p. 112.
11. Gillette 1995; Green 1967; Modan 2007; Williams 1988.
12. Ruble 2005.
13. Other parts of the District, the cities of Alexandria and Georgetown, continued to elect their local municipal representation, even though they were both initially within the District of Columbia borders (Gillette 1995).
14. Green 1967.
15. Fauntroy 2003.
16. This law also set the foundation for the creation of Advisory Neighborhood Commissions (ANCs), neighborhood-based planning bodies whose membership is elected locally. ANCs advise the city council and other citywide boards on neighborhood policy matters (Fauntroy 2003).
17. Harris 2010.
18. Gillette 1995.
19. One of Alexandria's main business sectors was the slave trade (Gillette 1995; Green 1967).
20. Horton 1996.
21. Green 1967, p. 33.
22. Fauntroy 2003.
23. Green 1967.
24. Ruble 2010.
25. Gillette 1995.
26. Abbott 1999; Gillette 1995; Horton 1996; Masur 2010.
27. Gillette 1995, p. 61.
28. Jacob 1996.
29. Gillette 1995.
30. Ruble 2010, p. 33.
31. Green 1967.
32. Schrag 2006.
33. Green 1967; Horton 1996; Ruble 2003, 2010.
34. Ruble 2010, p. 61.
35. Gillette 1995; Green 1967; Schrag 2006; Ruble 2010.
36. Cultural Tourism, DC 2003; Miller 2010; Ruble 2010.
37. Ruble 2010, p. 104.
38. Beauregard 2006; Jackson 1985.
39. Gale 1987; Gillette 1995.
40. Gale 1987; Lacy 2007.
41. Johnson 2002; Gale 1987.
42. Abu-Lughod 2007; Bean 2000; Katz 2012; Sugrue 1996.
43. Halpern 1995; Katz 2012; Reed 1999.
44. DC did have at least two prior race riots, in 1835 and 1919 (Green 1967).
45. Gilbert 1968; Gillette 1995.
46. Schrag 2006.
47. Greek 2009.
48. Gillette 1995.
49. Gilbert 1968.

50. Gilbert 1968; Gillette 1995; Jaffe and Sherwood 2014.
51. Schrag 2006.
52. Ibid., p. 137.
53. Fauntroy 2003; Gillette 1995; Jaffe and Sherwood 2014.
54. Holloway 2002; Ruble 2010.
55. Fitzpatrick and Goodwin 2001.
56. Gillette 1995; Ruble 2010.
57. Ruble 2010; Schrag 2006.
58. Fauntroy 2003; Harris 1995; McGovern 1998.
59. Gillette 1995; Ruble 2010.
60. Jaffe and Sherwood 2014; Leon 2010.
61. Jaffe and Sherwood 2014; Valk 2008.
62. Here I place "code of the street" within quotation marks because I am referencing Elijah Anderson's (2000) book *Code of the Street*, which was written long after Barry's time in Shaw/U Street. Even so, Anderson's work highlights the idea that in some inner-city African American communities, there are norms that are important to understand in order to develop trusting relations in ghetto areas.
63. Jaffe and Sherwood 2014.
64. Barras 1998; Gilbert 1968.
65. Siegel 1997, p. xii.
66. McGovern 1998, p. 42.
67. Gillette 1995; Jaffe and Sherwood 2014.
68. Ibid., p. 141.
69. Colburn and Adler 2001; Thompson 2006.
70. Fauntroy 2003.
71. Gillette 1995.
72. McGovern 1998, p. 197.
73. Gale 1987; McGovern 1998.
74. Jaffe and Sherwood 2014, p. 132.
75. Although several Black machines have existed throughout the country, Barry's was unique. An African American civil rights mayor, with the support of White elite actors and low-income African American voters, directed the machine. This circumstance is much different from Clarence Stone's description of Atlanta's political regime or Philip Thompson, Michael Owens, and Michael Rich's characterization of Atlanta's Black machine, which was perceived to be supported by White business elites and middle-income African Americans (Owens and Rich 2003; Stone 1989; Thompson 2006). And the DC case is distinct from Brad Tuttle's explanation of Newark's Black political machine under mayor Sharpe James, which was largely supported by campaign contributions from city employees (Tuttle 2009).
76. McGovern 1998, p. 201; Gillette 1995.
77. Jaffe and Sherwood 2014.
78. Fauntroy 2003, p. 16.
79. Barras 1998, p. 25.
80. Jaffe and Sherwood 2014, pp. 204–5.
81. Barras 1998, p. 25. The District had certain characteristics that made it ripe for the emergence of a Black political machine. It had a large population of low-income African Americans. In 1980, for instance, 46 percent of African American families earned less than $15,000 (Barras 1998). White and Black suburbanization in the first half of the twentieth century also increased the concentration of low- and moderate-income

African Americans in the city, and this population was susceptible to machine re-
wards, such as government jobs and symbolic racial representation.

82. Fauntroy 2003, p. 7.
83. Ibid., p. 5.
84. Barras 1998; Gillette 1995; Jaffe and Sherwood 2014.
85. Jaffe and Sherwood 2014, p. 120.
86. Ruble 2003.
87. Jaffe and Sherwood 2014, p. 100.
88. Barras 1998, p. 28.
89. Jaffe and Sherwood 2014.
90. Barry would also use this intraracial class strategy in the 1994 mayoral election to defeat the African American incumbent Sharon Pratt Kelly, a native Washingtonian who
graduated from Howard University's law school (Barras 1998; Jaffe and Sherwood
2014).
91. Barras 1998, p. 28.
92. Barras 1998; Green 1967; Hannerz 1969; Liebow 1967; Williams 1988.
93. Williams 1988, p. 51.
94. Hannerz 1969; Liebow 1967; Williams 1988.
95. Smith 1974, p. 246.
96. Barras 1998, p. 22.
97. Quoted in ibid., p. 23.
98. Fauntroy 2003, p. 16.
99. McGovern 1998, p. 41.
100. Jaffe and Sherwood 2014, p. xx.
101. Castaneda 2014; Dash 1997; Robinson 2010.
102. Fauntroy 2003; Gillette 1995; Jaffe and Sherwood 2014.
103. Barras 1998; Jaffe and Sherwood 2014; Ruble 2003.
104. Barras 1998, p. 13.
105. Barras 1998; Jaffe and Sherwood 2014.
106. Gillette 1995; Ruble 2003.
107. Fauntroy 2003.
108. Gandhi et al. 2009.
109. Ruble 2003.
110. Fauntroy 2003; Harris 2010.
111. Harris 2010; Ruble 2003; Thompson 2006.
112. Jaffe and Sherwood 2014, p. 400.
113. Harris 2010, p. 110.
114. Ruble 2010, p. 284.
115. Gandhi, Spaulding, and McDonald 2016; Jaffe and Sherwood 2014.
116. Schaller 2016.
117. Ibid., p. 146.
118. T. Gibson 2007.
119. Buehler and Stowe 2016; Jaffe and Sherwood 2014; Ruble 2010.
120. Harris 2010, p. 114.
121. Ruble 2010, p. 287; Harris 2010, p. 116.
122. Fenty's mother is White and his father is Black, and he is considered an African
American mayor. Ann E. Marimow and Jennifer Agiesta, "Blacks' Disillusionment
a Challenge for Fenty," Washington Post, March 1, 2010. Also see Harris 2012 for a
fantastic analysis of the "race-neutral" politics of leading Black politicians.

123. Jaffe and Sherwood 2014, p. 417.
124. Paul Schwartzman and Chris L. Jenkins, "Fenty Lost Black Vote, Then His Job," *Washington Post*, September 19, 2010; and Tim Craig and Nikita Stewart, "Gray Reverses Tack on Budget," *Washington Post*, May 27, 2010.
125. Robinson 2010.
126. Markman and Roman 2010.
127. Ruble 2010.
128. Erik Eckholm, "Capital's Onetime Political Star Now the Underdog," *New York Times*, September 10, 2010; and Robert McCartney, "Contradictions in Style Helping to Shape D.C. Mayoral Race," *Washington Post*, July 8, 2010.
129. Ryan Grim, "Brotherly Love," *Washington City Paper*, August 11, 2006.
130. Bernard Demczuk, "Dear French Street Neighbors," neighborhood flyer, September 12, 2010. Author's files.
131. Ann E. Marimow and Jennifer Agiesta, "Blacks' Disillusionment a Challenge for Fenty," *Washington Post*, March 1, 2010.
132. Nikita Stewart and Jon Cohen, "Fenty Lags in D.C. Race with Gray," *Washington Post*, August 29, 2010. Also see Tim Craig and Nikita Stewart, "D.C. Mayor's Race, Voters Appear to Embrace Conciliatory Style of Governing," *Washington Post*, September 15, 2010.
133. Marimow and Agiesta, "Blacks' Disillusionment a Challenge for Fenty." Also see Robert McCartney, "On His Home Turf, Signs of Discontent with Fenty," *Washington Post*, May 20, 2010; Robert McCartney, "First Task for the Winner of the Mayoral Race: Unite the City," *Washington Post*, September 15, 2010; and Tim Craig and Nikita Stewart, "Voter Mood Has Fenty Quickly Shifting Gears on Strategy," *Washington Post*, September 1, 2010.
134. Tamar Lewin, "School Chief Dismisses 241 Teachers in Washington," *New York Times*, July 23, 2010; and Bill Turque, "Rhee's Firing of 75 D.C. Teachers in 2008 Was Improper, Arbitrator Says," *Washington Post*, February 8, 2011.
135. Paul Schwartzman and Chris L. Jenkins, "Fenty Lost Black Vote, Then His Job," *Washington Post*, September 19, 2010.
136. Ibid.
137. Robert McCartney, "Gray Has Made the Most of the Right Moves," *Washington Post*, September 9, 2010.
138. Kojo Nnamdi, "D.C.'s Vote, a Bold Step into the Past," *Washington Post*, September 19, 2010.
139. Tim Craig, "Controversial Backers Steal Spotlight from Fenty and Gray," *Washington Post*, September 9, 2010.
140. Robert McCartney, "Contradictions in Style Helping to Shape D.C. Mayoral Race," *Washington Post*, July 8, 2010.
141. This conclusion was drawn based on my fieldwork in the neighborhood, where I noted the density of yard signs for each candidate and the sections of the neighborhood they were placed. I also viewed a precinct map displaying the vote percentage each candidate received by neighborhood geographic area. I compared this voting map with a map of the racial breakdown of census tracts. The tracts containing a larger percentage of African American residents yielded greater voting percentages for Gray. To view the voting map, see http://www.washingtonpost.com/wp-dyn/content/graphic/2010/09/15/GR2010091507402.html?sid=ST2010091500843 (accessed June 26, 2016).

142. See the DC Board of Elections and Ethics website, http://www.dcboee.org/election
     _info/election_results/results_2010.asp?prev=0&electionid=4&result_type=3 (ac-
     cessed October 23, 2012; content has since been altered).
143. Jaffe and Sherwood 2014.
144. Ted Mellnik and Emily Chow, "Bowser Wins Primary in Still-Divided City," *Washington Post*, April 2, 2014.
145. See table 2 of the appendix.
146. Ruble 2003; Gillette 1995; Fauntroy 2003.
147. Gillette 2003.
148. Barras 1998.
149. Gillette 2003, p. 208.
150. Barras 1998, p. 27.
151. Gale 1987; Lacy 2007.
152. The Fenty-Gray election suggests that postracial campaigns and governing strategies might, in some circumstances, make reelection in minority-dominated cities difficult. Recently, several cities have been run by a new generation of African American mayors, such as Newark's former mayor Cory Booker, Philadelphia's Michael Nutter, Detroit's former mayor Dave Bing, and New Orleans' former mayor Ray Nagin, who to varying extents are perceived as technocrats (Gillespie 2012; Thompson 2006). This new crop of Black mayors must walk a fine line between pushing for reforms and paying homage to the legacy of their city's urban Black political history. They must also understand the changing demographics of their cities and how racial, class, and cultural dynamics intersect and are important to their reelection and governing strategies.
153. Erie 1988.

CHAPTER THREE

1. DC, compared with other major US cities, had very little manufacturing. I use the phrase "postindustrial powerhouse" not to describe its transition from manufacturing to advanced service employment but rather to describe how this advanced service city rose to economic prominence as the US economy as a whole became increasingly service sector dominated. This said, DC did decrease its level of manufacturing employment in the 2000s (Cowell et al. 2012).
2. Deborah Nelson and Himanshu Ojha, "Redistributing Up," *Atlantic*, December 18, 2012, http://www.theatlantic.com/business/archive/2012/12/redistributing-up/266400/ (accessed June 26, 2016).
3. Carol Morrello and Ted Mellnik, "One in 7 Washington Households in the Top 5 Percent," *Washington Post*, February 11, 2013.
4. Taylor 1997; A. T. Kearney 2012; Marchio and Berube 2015.
5. Annie Gowen, "One of D.C.'s 'Stealth' Elite Remakes Hickory Hill," *Washington Post*, December 2, 2013.
6. Abbott 1999, p. 148.
7. Fuller 2009.
8. Abu-Lughod 2000; Castells 1991; Sassen 2012.
9. Sassen 2012, p. 18.
10. Knox and Taylor 1995; Sassen 2012; Taylor 2004; Taylor et al. 2011.
11. Castells 1991, p. 167.
12. Sassen 2012.
13. Castells 1991; Mollenkopf and Castells 1991; Knox 1991.

14. Fainstein 2001; Hyra 2008.
15. Glaeser 2011.
16. Clark 2011; Florida and Gates 2011; Glaeser, Kolko, and Saiz 2001; Gotham 2007; Knox 1991.
17. Abbott 1999; McGovern 1998; Knox 1991.
18. McGovern 1998, p. 193.
19. US Department of State 2011.
20. See the websites of US embassies, consulates, and diplomatic missions at http://www .usembassy.gov/ (accessed June 27, 2016).
21. Destination DC 2013.
22. Fuller 2002.
23. Chambers 2000; Chomsky 2004.
24. Versel et al. 2014.
25. Fuller 2009.
26. Sassen 2012.
27. Ibid., p. 16.
28. I gained this insight between 2007 and 2009, when I worked for one of DC's large national bank regulators, the Office of the Comptroller of the Currency. From its headquarters in the city, I investigated the causes and consequences of the subprime/ foreclosure crisis.
29. Of the $9 trillion in assets managed within the District's metropolitan region, DC-based institutions direct the vast majority of these funds.
30. Hyra et al. 2013; Levitin and Wachter 2013.
31. Gramlich 2007.
32. Squires and Hyra 2010.
33. Hyra et al. 2013.
34. Sassen 2009.
35. French 2009.
36. Abbott 1999; McGovern 1998.
37. Coates 1993; Frank 2008; Hira and Hira 2005.
38. Fuller 2009.
39. Ibid., p. 3.
40. Ibid., pp. 3–4.
41. See Deborah Nelson and Himanshu Ojha, "Redistributing Up," Atlantic, December 18, 2012, http://www.theatlantic.com/business/archive/2012/12/redistributing -up/266400/ (accessed June 26, 2016); Annie Gowen, "One of D.C.'s 'Stealth' Elite Remakes Hickory Hill," Washington Post, December 2, 2013; and Greg Jaffe and Jim Tankersley, "Capital Gains: Spending in Contracts and Lobbying Propels a Wave of New Wealth in D.C.," Washington Post, December 18, 2013.
42. Fuller 2009.
43. Nelson and Ojha, "Redistributing Up."
44. Cowell et al. 2012.
45. Ibid.
46. Ibid., p. 31.
47. Some of the increase in firm revenue is also due to mergers and acquisitions, not solely increases in federal government procurement.
48. The DC region also has several other important domestic and multinational firms that are critical to its metropolitan economy. In 2012, Sprint, which is headquartered

in Northern Virginia, serviced 56 million wireless customers and was the United States' third-largest long-distance phone provider. Mars, a leading food and candy producer, is also headquartered in a Northern Virginia DC suburb. Between 2005 and 2010, its revenue increased by $12 billion. Sodexo, a major, multinational, worldwide food and well-being service company, has its US headquarters in the Maryland suburbs. Between 2005 and 2012, its revenue grew by over $13 billion. Also, in the DC suburbs of Northern Virginia and Maryland are the headquarters of Marriott and Hilton, two of the world's leading hotel chains. These international giants increased their revenue by $13.8 billion between 2005 and 2011.

49. Nelson and Ojha, "Redistributing Up."
50. Rivers 2014.
51. Orr and Rivlin 2011.
52. For more on DC's growing income inequality, see Gandhi, Spaulding, and McDonald 2016.
53. Kerstetter, Reed, and Lazere 2009.
54. Biegler 2012.
55. DC Fiscal Policy Institute 2011.
56. Fuller 2009; Sturtevant and Champagne 2012.
57. Gale 1987, p. 26.
58. Frey 2013.
59. "March of the Millennials" is the title of a series of articles published in the *Washington Post* about the movement of young professionals to certain DC neighborhoods. See Elizabeth Chang, Neely Tucker, Jessica Goldstein, Clinton Yates, and Marcia Davis, "March of the Millennials: As Young People Flood into the City, the Only Constant Is Change," *Washington Post*, October 18, 2013.
60. Birch 2002, 2005, 2009; Simmons and Lang 2003.
61. Sturtevant and Jung 2011; Simmons and Lang 2003; Fishman 2005; Ehrenhalt 2012; Hyra 2012. While the phrase "back-to-the-city movement" is frequently used, there is no consensus on its definition. Some scholars define it as the movement of upper-income suburban populations to the city center (Laska and Spain 1980). Another camp of scholars defines the back-to-the-city movement as relative net migration flows (in-migration minus out-migration) among metropolitan subregions (Kasarda et al. 1997; Sanchez and Dawkins 2001; Sturtevant and Jung 2011). Others link it with population or investment increases in cities and their downtowns, regardless of where newcomers previously lived (Birch 2002, 2005, 2009; Glaeser and Shapiro 2003a, 2003b; Simmons and Lang 2003; Smith 1979; Wyly, Atia, and Hammel 2004). Still others regard it as merely "optimism about the possible residential resurgence of America's older cities" (Zavarella 1987, p. 376). The census of 2000 revealed that aggregate population levels in many urban areas increased during the 1990s (Birch 2002; Simmons and Lang 2003). To certain scholars, it appeared that the back-to-the-city movement was a valid and robust phenomenon. Proponents claimed that the 1990s urban repopulation pattern was a major demographic shift from the massive rates of suburbanization witnessed during the previous decades (Berube 2003; Sturtevant and Jung 2011).
62. See the appendix, table 1. It is important to note that this central city growth was outpaced by suburban population gains in the DC region (Sturtevant and Jung 2011).
63. Carol Morello and Dan Keating, "Asians, Hispanics Tip Urban Growth," *Washington Post*, April 6, 2011.

64. The Hispanic and Asian populations also increased, but by a much smaller amount: approximately 10,000 and 6,000 respectively (Center for Regional Analysis 2011).

65. See Carol Morello and Dan Keating, "Blacks' Majority Status Slips Away," *Washington Post*, March 25, 2011; Carol Morello and Dan Keating, "Census Confirms Skyrocketing Hispanic, Asian Growth in U.S.," *Washington Post*, March 25, 2011. In 1970, 70 percent of the city's population was African American. The decrease in the proportion of Black residents in the 2000s was due to not only the influx of Whites during that period but also the exodus of African Americans, a trend that had been occurring in DC since the 1970s (Center for Regional Analysis 2011; Gale 1987; Lacy 2007).

66. District of Columbia Office of Planning 2012; Frey 2013.

67. Elizabeth Chang, Neely Tucker, Jessica Goldstein, Clinton Yates, and Marcia Davis, "March of the Millennials: As Young People Flood into the City, the Only Constant Is Change," *Washington Post*, October 18, 2013.

68. Frey 2013.

69. Lachman and Brett 2015; Speck 2012; Talen 2013.

70. Gale 1987.

71. See the appendix, tables 2 and 7.

72. DowntownDC Business Improvement District 2011.

73. See the appendix, table 6.

74. Jacob Comenetz, "After Years of Revitalization, Penn Quarter's Personality Shines," *Washington Diplomat*, August 31, 2011.

75. Gale 1987.

76. Quotation is from Ann Cochran, "Positively Penn Quarter," *Renaissance*, Summer 2008, p. 20. Wachovia Wealth Management.

77. Quotation is from ibid., p. 19.

78. President Nixon created the Pennsylvania Avenue Development Corporation on April 17, 1973. Its focus was on redeveloping Pennsylvania Avenue, and many of the developments it initiated (with federal resources), such as Market Square, helped facilitate later development in the Penn Quarter neighborhood as well as other sections of downtown DC. For more on PADC, see Gale 1987; Gillette 1995; and Jacob Comenetz, "After Years of Revitalization, Penn Quarter's Personality Shines," *Washington Diplomat*, August 31, 2011.

79. See Justh 2009; Cochran, "Positively Penn Quarter"; and Comenetz, "After Years of Revitalization, Penn Quarter's Personality Shines."

80. Thomas Heath and David Montgomery, "Pollin: With Opening of MCI Center, 'I've Got Everything I've Ever Done in My Life on the Line,'" *Washington Post*, November 30, 1997.

81. David Montgomery, "MCI Center, Metro Station Stage Debut for Two," *Washington Post*, November 17, 1997.

82. David Montgomery, "MCI Center Promises More Construction Jobs for D.C. Residents," *Washington Post*, June 27, 1997.

83. According to their websites, Akridge and Western Development have a combined development portfolio of over $6 billion (see http://westdev.com/about-us/company-history/ and http://www.akridge.com/ [accessed June 27, 2016]).

84. Knox 1991.

85. See the Office of the Chief Financial Officer section of the dc.gov website at http://app.cfo.dc.gov/services/economic/tif_program/gallery_place.shtm (accessed June 27, 2016).

86. Schaller 2010.

87. Fannie Mae, a DC housing giant, was the major institutional purchaser of the bonds, nearly $37 million worth.
88. Justh 2009.
89. See the National Portrait Gallery website at http://www.npg.si.edu/inform/chronology .html (accessed June 27, 2016).
90. In 2010, over 1 million people visited the museum (DowntownDC Business Improvement District 2011). Also see Edward Epstein, "Portrait of a New Washington/ Penn Quarter: District of Columbia's Once-Derelict Neighborhood Welcomes Back Smithsonian Museums, Tourists with Rejuvenated Flair," *Chronicle Washington Bureau,* July 2, 2006, http://www.sfgate.com/travel/article/Portrait-of-a-new-Washington -Penn-Quarter-2532271.php (accessed June 27, 2016).
91. International Environmental Corporation 2009.
92. See US General Services Administration press release, "GSA Completes Sale of Penn Quarters Development Site," October 12, 2001, http://www.prnewswire.com/news -releases/gsa-completes-sale-of-penn-quarter-development-site-73627682.html (accessed June 27, 2016).
93. In 2005, my wife and I rented a one-bedroom condominium for $1,800 a month in this building.
94. See Amanda Abrams, "Penn Quarter/Chinatown: DC's Go-Go-Go Neighborhood," *Urban Turf* newsletter, February 10, 2011, http://dc.urbanturf.com/articles/blog/penn _quarter_chinatown_dcs_go-go-go_neighborhood/2971 (accessed June 27, 2016).
95. See real estate listings for this building at http://www.aidanduffy.com/myListings.php (accessed July 19, 2016).
96. Jaffe and Sherwood 2014.
97. See the appendix, table 6.
98. Jaffe and Sherwood 2014.
99. Ibid., p. 405. Also, see Annie Lowrey, "Washington's Economic Boom, Financed by You," *New York Times Magazine,* January 10, 2013, http://www.nytimes.com/2013/01 /13/magazine/washingtons-economic-boom-financed-by-you.html?_r=0 (accessed June 26, 2016).
100. McGovern 1998, p. 201.
101. Courtland Milloy, "D.C. to Poor: Take a Hike," *Washington Post Blog,* November 27, 2012, https://www.washingtonpost.com/local/dc-to-poor-take-a-hike/2012/11/27 /6b5b1670-38dc-11e2-b01f-5f55b193f58f_story.html. Work by Talen (2013) underscores how walkable urban neighborhoods have become increasingly expensive (accessed June 27, 2016).
102. District of Columbia Office of the Chief Financial Officer, Office of Revenue Analysis 2012.
103. See Galster and Tatian 2009; Jackson 2015; Modan 2007; Ruble 2010; and Carol Morello, Dan Keating, and Steve Hendrix, "Capital Hip: D.C. Is Getting Younger," *Washington Post,* May 5, 2011. The gentrification of DC's low-income Black neighborhoods has a long history that includes Georgetown, Foggy Bottom, and Southwest in the 1930s, '40s, and '50s (Asch and Musgrove 2016; Gale 1987; Gillette 1995); sections of Capitol Hill, Dupont Circle, and Logan Circle in the 1960s, '70s, and '80s (Asch and Musgrove 2016; Gale 1987; Lee, Spain, and Umberson 1985); and parts of downtown, Adams Morgan, and Mount Pleasant in the 1980s and '90s (Asch and Musgrove 2016; Gale 1987; Modan 2007; Williams 1988; McGovern 1998).
104. Greene 2014.
105. See the Black Cat's website at http://www.blackcatdc.com/history.html (accessed

June 28, 2016); Kenneth Jones, "DC's Off-Bway-Style Studio Theatre Plans $9.5 Million Expansion of Complex," *Playbill*, December 19, 2001; and Richard Harrington, "25 Years Later, It's Still 9:30," *Washington Post*, May 27, 2005.

106. See the website of housing developer Manna at http://www.mannadc.org/ (accessed June 28, 2016).

107. See the appendix, table 6.

108. Daniel J. Sermovitz, "TIAA-CREF's Latest D.C. Acquisition? U Street Apartments," *Washington Business Journal*, June 4, 2014; and Daniel J. Sermovitz, "The JBG Cos. Sells 14th Street Apartments for $76," *Washington Business Journal*, April 8, 2013.

109. See the appendix, table 1.

110. See the appendix, table 6.

111. Elizabeth Chang, Neely Tucker, Jessica Goldstein, Clinton Yates, and Marcia Davis, "March of the Millennials: As Young People Flood into the City, the Only Constant Is Change," *Washington Post*, October 18, 2013. Also see table 9 in the appendix, which presents my calculation using the Geolytics 1970–2010 neighborhood change dataset. I thank Meagan Snow for assisting me with this analysis.

112. Ralph, "Why Development Hasn't and Isn't Skipping Over Shaw," *Renew Shaw* blog post, February 6, 2007, http://remakingleslumhistorique.blogspot.com/2007_02_01_archive.html (accessed June 28, 2016).

113. Jura Koncius, "Destination Design: Where to Shop on 14th Street NW," *Washington Post*, June 19, 2013.

114. Sarah Halzack, "What a New Shopping Hub in D.C. Shows Us about the Future of Retail," *Washington Post*, August 14, 2015.

115. Castells 1991, 2000; Sassen 2012; Clark 2011.

116. Bell 1973.

117. Logan and Molotch 2007.

118. Castells 1991; Sassen 2012.

119. Neighborhood central business district proximity as one driver of low-income community redevelopment was also noted in Chicago by McMillen 2003 and in New York City by Hyra 2008. There is another study, by Guerrieri, Hartley, and Hurst 2013, which argues that low-income communities in close proximately to upper-income communities are more likely to gentrify. This study also lends credibility to my argument that the rise of the downtown is associated with the redevelopment of nearby low-income neighborhoods.

120. Abbott 1999; Knox 1991.

121. Acuto 2013.

122. Castells 1991; Sassen 2012; Taylor 2004.

123. Abbott 1999, p. 156.

124. McGovern 1998, p. 43.

125. Jennifer B. McKim, "For Some Empty Nesters, City Living Is Just Right," *Boston Globe*, August 19, 2012.

126. District of Columbia Office of Planning 2012.

127. Sturtevant and Champagne 2012, p. 3.

128. Arena 2012; Bennett, Smith, and Wright 2006; Ehrenhalt 2012; K. Gibson 2007; Goetz 2003; Gotham 2007; Grogan and Proscio 2000; Hackworth 2007; Hunter 2013; Hyra 2008; Lin 2011; Podagrosi and Vojnovic 2008; Tach 2014; Vale 2002; von Hoffman 2003.

129. Abu-Lughod 2000; Hyra 2008.

CHAPTER FOUR

1. Boyd 2008; Grams 2010; Pattillo 2007.
2. Boyd 2008, pp. xiv and 87.
3. Jackson 1985.
4. Massey and Denton 1993.
5. Boyd 2008, p. 75.
6. Gotham 2007; Hoffman 2003; Hurley 2010.
7. Boyd 2008; Grams 2010; Lin 2011.
8. Till 2003.
9. Wherry 2011, p. 94.
10. Boyd 2008; Grams 2010; Heck 2013; Hoffman 2003; Hurley 2010; Inwood 2010; Lin 2011.
11. Boyd 2008.
12. Pattillo 2007, pp. 301 and 297.
13. Hyra 2008.
14. Freeman and Cai 2015; Hyra 2008; Hyra and Rugh 2016.
15. Zukin 2012.
16. K. Gibson 2007; Podagrosi and Vojnovic 2008.
17. Hunter 2013.
18. Taylor 2008.
19. Taylor et al. 2010.
20. Glaeser and Vigdor 2012; Rugh and Massey 2014; Vigdor 2013. It is also important to note that while this level of metropolitan racial integration has occurred, poverty concentration in certain African American communities persists (Jargowsky 2014).
21. Hochschild, Weaver, and Burch 2012.
22. Anderson 2012; Carr and Kutty 2008; Hartman and Squires 2010; Marcuse 2012; Pearson, Dovidio, and Gaertner 2009.
23. Pearson, Dovidio, and Gaertner 2009, p. 4.
24. Anderson 2012, pp. 67–68.
25. Sassen 2012; Stiglitz 2012.
26. Knox 2008.
27. Brown-Saracino 2009; Florida 2014; Gotham 2005, 2007; Grazian 2003, 2008; Lloyd 2010; Mele 2000, Ocejo 2011; Wherry 2011; Zukin 2010.
28. Grazian 2003.
29. Ibid., p. 36.
30. Ibid., p. 20.
31. Clark 2011; Florida 2014; Glaeser, Kolko, and Saiz 2001.
32. Clark 2011, p. 1.
33. Ibid., p. 46.
34. Brumbaugh and Grier 2013; Clark 2011; Florida 2014.
35. Grams 2010; Lin 2011; Wherry 2011.
36. For instances of Black cultural preservation initiatives directed mainly by African Americans, see Boyd 2008; Grams 2010; and Hurley 2010.
37. Frank 2005; Heck 2013; Smith 2010.
38. Not all of those working to preserve Shaw/U Street's Black culture were White. Both African Americans and Hispanics were instrumental in that regard. For instance, a Black real estate developer, Roy "Chip" Ellis, spearheaded an eight-year effort to rehabilitate and restore the Howard Theater, a local performance venue that rivals

Harlem's Apollo Theater. Frank Smith, an African American and the area's former representative on the city council, oversaw the establishment of the community's African American Civil War Memorial and Museum. Moreover, Alex Padro, a local Hispanic civic leader who in 1999 partnered with Kathy Smith in launching one of the community's walking tours, worked for nearly a decade to promote historic preservation and economic revitalization along the community's 9th Street corridor. Yet although these important Shaw/U Street stakeholders, and others, such as Lawrence Guyot, John "Butch" Snipes, and Henry Whitehead, played an important role in local historic Black preservation, Kathy Smith was clearly the main driver preserving and promoting the community's Black history (Ruble 2010).

39. Smith and McQuirter 1996.
40. See Heck 2013. As of 2013, four community sections were recognized on the National Register of Historic Places.
41. This YMCA was the country's first Black Y, founded by Anthony Bowen, a former slave. Later in the early twentieth century, as noted, it became a gathering place for many Black intellects.
42. Frank 2005.
43. Cultural Tourism, DC 2003.
44. Frank 2005.
45. District of Columbia Office of Planning 2004.
46. Grossman 1989.
47. Massey and Denton 1993.
48. Drake and Cayton 1993.
49. Duneier 2016.
50. Hirsch 1998.
51. Myrdal 1944.
52. Abu-Lughod 2007; Katz 2012; Sugrue 1996.
53. Jargowsky 1997; Massey and Denton 1993; Wilson 1996.
54. Venkatesh 2000, 2006, 2008.
55. Small and McDermott 2006.
56. Newman 2000; Stack 1974.
57. Anderson 2012.
58. Williams and Smith 2001.
59. Frank 2005.
60. Dash 1997, p. 11.
61. Boyd 2008.
62. Ibid., p. 75.
63. Ibid., p. 71.
64. Ibid., p. 81.
65. Ibid., p. 156.
66. This quotation comes from my interview with Kathryn Smith, but it is also more formally documented in Smith and McQuirter 1996.
67. Quotation from Frank 2005, p. 37.
68. See Beemyn 2015 for an excellent history of sexual orientation and gay life in DC and Shaw/U Street.
69. Quotation from Frank 2005, p. 39.
70. Hurley 2010, p. 24.
71. Frank 2005, p. 72.
72. Boyd 2008; Grams 2010; Lin 2011.

73. Boyd 2008, pp. 81–82.
74. Alicia Ault, "U Street: The Corridor Is Cool Again," *New York Times*, April 14, 2006; Michael O'Sullivan, "14th Street," *Washington Post*, August 6, 2010; and Annys Shin, "An Unlikely Catalyst in D.C.: Recession-Fueled Boom Brings Investors and Development to 14th Street, NW," *Washington Post*, July 22, 2013.
75. Ruble 2010.
76. Lin 2011.
77. Clark 2011; Florida 2014.
78. Harcourt 2005.
79. Jagoda 2011; Williams 2011.
80. Venkatesh 2008.
81. Grazian 2003; Heap 2009; Hoffman 2003.
82. Anderson 2012.
83. Grazian 2003, pp. 21–22. David Grazian also elaborates on this notion of danger, excitement, and authenticity in his 2008 book, *On the Make: The Hustle of Urban Nightlife*.
84. Grazian 2003, p. 52.
85. Deener 2012, p. 214.
86. For other ethnographic depictions of "living the drama," see Sudhir Venkatesh's 2000 and 2006 books. For a more quantitative examination, see Patrick Sharkey's 2013 outstanding book, *Stuck in Place*.
87. Harding 2010, p. xi.
88. Markman and Roman 2010. In 1991, 482 murders occurred in Washington, DC, and in 2012 that figure dropped to 88; see http://www.disastercenter.com/crime/dccrime .htm (accessed June 30, 2016).
89. Peter Hermann, "Victim of U Street Shooting Was Trying to Bridge Two Worlds," *Washington Post*, December 6, 2015.
90. See Cahill and Roman 2010. For potential explanations of the persistence of crime in gentrifying neighborhoods, see Kirk and Laub 2010; Kirk and Papachristos 2011.
91. See Paul Duggan, "Guns in America: In D.C. Bullets Leave Another Fatherless Child," *Washington Post*, September 15, 2013.
92. Anderson 2000.
93. For an excellent analysis of the postindustrial city and mixology, see Ocejo 2010.
94. Melissa McCart, "Brothers Build a Restaurant Dynasty," *Washington Post*, May 5, 2010.
95. Ibid.
96. Gotham 2007, p. viii.
97. Anderson 2012, p. 69.
98. Dash 1997; Robinson 2010.
99. Heap 2009.
100. The concept of living the wire might also generalize to some extent to those visiting the Shaw/U Street neighborhood, but I am particularly interested in how living the wire is distinctive from 1920s-style urban slumming, where one visited but did not choose to live in inner-city environments. Furthermore, the concept might apply to those of other races and ethnicities. While I mainly illustrate the living-the-wire concept with the testimony of White residents, it is important to note that the attraction of the inner-city edge is not limited only to Whites.
101. Boyd 2008; Grams 2010; Inwood 2010.
102. Simon 2011; Ritzer 2013.
103. See Anmol Chaddha and William Julius Wilson, "Why We're Teaching 'The Wire'

at Harvard," *Washington Post*, September 12, 2010. At least twenty-one colleges and universities have a course that uses *The Wire* as part of the class's learning materials (see Taylor and Eidson 2012).

104. Quoted in Paul Massari, "Learning the Streets, Scene by Scene: HBO's 'The Wire' Is Entry Point for Course on Urban Life," *Harvard Gazette*, October 21, 2010.
105. Hurley 2010, p. 20.
106. Anderson 2012, p. 81.
107. Harcourt 2005, p. 8.
108. Lloyd 2010, p. 80.
109. Ibid.
110. Mele 2000; Zukin 2010.
111. Clark 2011.
112. For an important examination of the relationships among Blackness, diversity, and neighborhood development, see Summers's 2016 work on the revitalization of Washington, DC's H Street corridor.
113. Boyd 2008, p. 155.
114. Boyd 2008; Grams 2010; Lin 2011.
115. Jackson 2015.
116. Hurley 2010, p. 192.
117. Schulman 2012, p. 36.
118. Annys Shin, "An Unlikely Catalyst in D.C.: Recession-Fueled Boom Brings Investors and Development to 14th Street, NW," *Washington Post*, July 22, 2013; and Alexis Hauk, "Planned Eight-Story Development Threatens U Street Mural," *Washington City Paper Artsdesk Blog*, April 12, 2013, http://www.washingtoncitypaper.com/arts/museums-galleries/blog/13079108/planned-eight-story-development-threatens-u-street-mural (accessed June 30, 2016).

CHAPTER FIVE

1. Anderson 2011; Hochschild, Weaver, and Burch 2012.
2. Anderson 2011.
3. Maly 2005; Modan 2007; Sanchez-Jankowski 2008; Turner and Rawlings 2009; Williams 1988.
4. Turner and Rawlings 2009, p. 5.
5. Cohen 1999; Hunter 2010; Moore 2010.
6. Crenshaw 1991; Weber 2010.
7. Some individual analyses include Crenshaw 1991; McCall 2005; McQueeney 2009; Nash 2008; and Tester 2008. Organizational-level investigations include Moore 2010 and Watkins-Hays 2009, but none of these studies take place within a redeveloping community.
8. McCall 2005, p. 1771.
9. McCall 2005. Leslie McCall distinguishes three intersectionality research approaches: anticategorial, intracategorial, and intercategorical. Anticategorical research seeks to deconstruct traditional analytical categories, intracategorical studies focus on identities that overlap traditional boundaries, and intercategorical projects "adopt existing analytical categories to document relationships of inequality among social groups" (p. 1773). This chapter applies the intercategorical approach by understanding how the traditional social categories of race, sexual orientation, and class frame and explain civic political interactions.
10. One's race, ethnicity, gender, and sexual orientation contain a biological component,

but these categories, as well as interests stemming from them, are socially constructed. They are important explanatory factors in understanding behaviors and the reproduction of social inequalities (Lamont, Beljean, and Clair 2014; Massey 2007; Waters 1990).

11. These African American DC real estate developers include Roy "Chip" Ellis, Jair Lynch, and H. R. Crawford.
12. Goetz 2013; Lees, Slater, and Wyly 2008; Lloyd 2010; Smith 2000; Zukin 1982.
13. Brown-Saracino 2009; Castells 1983; Cohen 1999; Collins 2004; Collins 2005; Ghaziani 2014; Lees 2000; Lauria and Knopp 1985.
14. Castells 1983, p. 139.
15. Brown-Saracino 2009.
16. Collins 2004; Ghaziani 2011.
17. For an outstanding documentary film on this process, see *Flag Wars* (2003) by Laura Poitras and Linda Goode Bryant.
18. Sibalis 2004, p. 1751.
19. Boyd 2008; Freeman 2006; Hyra 2008; Jackson 2005; Moore 2009; Pattillo 2007.
20. Pattillo 2007, p. 12.
21. Ibid., p. 2.
22. Pattillo 2007; Boyd 2008; Freeman 2006; Taylor 2002.
23. The title of this section also appeared in Ruble 2010.
24. The dynamic of African Americans returning to the inner city to attend church on Sunday is common in other cities (Hyra 2008; McRoberts 2003).
25. This knowledge is based on my prior research from 1999 until 2004, when I spent five years living in and studying Harlem and Bronzeville (Hyra 2008).
26. Ruble 2010.
27. ANC commissioners are elected community representatives that communicate recommendations to DC's City Council and higher-level planning bodies. Although the ANCs have a purely advisory role, their support influences formal city-level decisions. The Shaw/U Street area has five ANCs, ANC 2F being one of them.
28. Hicks 2004.
29. This statement is supported from multiple sources, including David Car, "Black and White Coverage," *Washington City Paper*, December 17, 1999; my interview with Pat Penny, who was involved with the incident; and Patrice Gaines, "The Cast and Their Lot: Against a Backdrop of Gentrification, a Land Dispute Is Played Out among a Black Church, Its New White Neighbors and D.C. Officials," *Washington Post*, December 7, 1999.
30. ANC 2F Meeting Minutes, December 7, 2005, http://www.anc2f.org/files/minutes /2005/1205minutes.pdf (accessed June 30, 2016).
31. Ibid., January 2006.
32. Hicks 2004, p. 39.
33. Quoted in David Car, "Black and White Coverage," *Washington City Paper*, December 17, 1999.
34. ANC 2F Meeting Minutes, January 2006.
35. Hicks 2004, p. 16.
36. Will O'Bryan, "From A to Be Bar: An Exclusive Behind-the-Scenes Look at the Months-Long Creation of D.C.'s Newest Gay Bar," *Metro Weekly* (Washington, DC), August 24, 2006.
37. Shiloh is a historic African American church, much like Harlem's famed Abyssinian Baptist Church. In 2011, President Obama attended Shiloh's Easter services, and in

2010 the church held services for Dorothy Height, longtime president of the National Council of Negro Women, when she passed away.

38. June Thomas, "The Gay Bar: Is It Dying?," *Slate Magazine*, June 27, 2011; and see Chauncey 1994.

39. Cohen 1999; Harris-Lacewell 2004.

40. Cohen 1999, p. 14.

41. Will O'Bryan, "From A to Be Bar: An Exclusive Behind-the-Scenes Look at the Months-Long Creation of D.C.'s Newest Gay Bar," *Metro Weekly*, August 24, 2006.

42. James Jones, "Thorpe Thumped," *Washington City Paper*, November 10, 2006.

43. Jason Cherkis, Laura Lang, and Elissa Silverman, "Gunplay in Early April," *Washington City Paper*, April 23, 1999.

44. Will O'Bryan, "Gay-N-C," *Metro Weekly*, November 11, 2004.

45. Will O'Bryan, "From A to Be Bar: An Exclusive Behind-The-Scenes Look at the Months-Long Creation of D.C.'s Newest Gay Bar," *Metro Weekly*, August 24, 2006.

46. Will O'Bryan, "Be Bar Faces Off with Opponents," *Metro Weekly*, April 20, 2006.

47. Quoted in O'Bryan, "From A to Be Bar."

48. Letter to Evans from GLAA, May 1, 2006, http://www.glaa.org/archive/2006/glaa2 evansandgrahamonbebar0501.shtml (accessed July 11, 2016).

49. O'Bryan, "From A to Be Bar."

50. Quoted in ibid.

51. Keith L. Alexander, "Man Gets 6 Months in Assault near Gay Bar," *Washington Post*, October 15, 2009.

52. Quoted in Katherine Volin, "Gay Influx Brings Change to Shaw," *Washington Blade*, May 5, 2006.

53. *Fifth and Oh* blog post, "Reflections on the ANC Meeting," September 9, 2006, http://fifthandoh.blogspot.com/2006_09_01_archive.html (accessed July 11, 2016).

54. Frazier 1957, p. 194.

55. Gates 2004; Robinson 2010.

56. Castaneda 2014; Hannerz 1969.

57. Noted on the Ellis Development Group website: http://www.ellisdevelopmentgroup .com (accessed July 11, 2016).

58. Dana Hedgpeth, "From the Ground Up: Developer Has the Past in Mind for Shaw," *Washington Post*, May 22, 2006.

59. Anitia Huslin, "Jazzed Up about Reviving D.C. Landmarks," *Washington Post*, February 25, 2008.

60. Ovetta Wiggins and V. Dion Haynes, "Radio One Backs Out of Plan to Move Headquarters to D.C.," *Washington Post*, February 26, 2010.

61. Some have argued that the UNCF is an organization that attempts to cultivate the "talented tenth" of Black leadership (Thompson 1986; Wooten 2015).

62. Quoted in Dana Hedgpeth, "From the Ground Up: Developer Has the Past in Mind for Shaw," *Washington Post*, May 22, 2006.

63. Jonathan O'Connell, "D.C. Council OKs $23M for Radio One HQ," *Washington Business Journal*, January 9, 2008; and Jonathan O'Connell, "After Debates, Shaw Sees Progress on Developments," *Washington Business Journal*, November 16, 2007.

64. Moulden and Squires 2012.

65. Lydia DePillis, "Council Makes UNCF Deal Official, UNCF Gives Thanks," *Washington City Paper*, May 18, 2010.

66. Harris-Lacewell 2004, pp. 167–68.

67. Although Wanda Henderson had hoped that she would eventually be able to buy

the building in which her business operated, she was outbid by Chip Ellis and his development team, who, according to Henderson, purchased it for $1.2 million. However, she was able to negotiate leasing terms with them.

68. Jaffe and Sherwood 2014, p. xx.
69. Hicks 2004, p. 133.
70. Moore 2010; Tester 2008; Watkins-Hayes 2009.
71. Nieves 2008.
72. McCall 2005; Moore 2010.
73. Anne Hull, "A Boom Giveth, and It Taketh Away," *Washington Post*, November 14, 2005.
74. Anderson 2012; Berrey 2005; Vertovec 2007.
75. Chaskin and Joseph 2015.

CHAPTER SIX

1. Bennett, Smith, and Wright 2006; Fainstein 2001; Freeman 2006; K. Gibson 2007; Goetz 2013; Grogan and Proscio 2000; Hackworth 2007; Hyra 2008; Modan 2007; Podagrosi and Vojnovic 2008; Sassen 2012; Vale 2013; von Hoffman 2003.
2. Logan and Molotch 2007; Peterson 1981.
3. Davidson 2008; Jackson 2015; Newman and Wyly 2006; Slater 2009; Vigdor 2002.
4. Ellen and O'Regan 2011; Freeman 2005; Freeman and Braconi 2004; McKinnish, Walsh and White 2010.
5. Hyra 2008; Podagrosi and Vojnovic 2008; Taylor 2002.
6. In one section of the Shaw/U Street neighborhood, violent crime incidences per 1,000 residents dropped from 20 to 11 between 2001 and 2011 (see an Urban Institute website with demographics and statistics for DC neighborhoods, NeighborhoodInfoDC: http://www.neighborhoodinfodc.org/nclusters/Nbr_prof_clusb7.html#sec_2_violent (accessed July 12, 2016).
7. Fraser 2004; Knotts and Haspel 2006.
8. Martin 2007, p. 605.
9. Hyra 2008.
10. Michener and Wong 2015; Knotts and Haspel 2006.
11. Chaskin and Joseph 2011; Granovetter 1983; Putnam 2000; Tach 2009.
12. Curley 2010; Freeman 2006.
13. Taylor 2002; Zukin 1982, 2010.
14. Brown-Saracino 2009; Hyra 2008.
15. Abramson, Manzo, and Hou 2006.
16. Maly 2005.
17. Chaskin and Joseph 2015.
18. Lloyd 2006; Zukin 1982, 2010.
19. Freeman 2006; Joseph 2006.
20. Granovetter 1983; Sharkey 2013.
21. Wilson 1996.
22. Chaskin and Joseph 2015; Curley 2009, 2010; Davidson 2010; Tach 2014.
23. Chaskin and Joseph 2011; Tach 2009.
24. Hyra 2008; Martin 2007; Pattillo 2007.
25. Maly 2005; Modan 2007.
26. Freeman 2006.
27. Michelle Boorstein, "Putting Faith in Affordable Housing: Activists, Entrepreneurial Pastors Push Renewal of D.C. Churches' Efforts," *Washington Post*, June 23, 2007;

Jeff Clabaugh, "Jair Lynch Closes on Dunbar Apartments," *Washington Business Journal*, July 5, 2011; and First Rising Mount Zion Baptist Church Housing Corporation, Inc., "2010 Renovation: Gibson Plaza: Celebration & Groundbreaking July 28, 2010, Noon–2pm."

28. Bockman 2016; Gallaher 2016.

29. Lydia DePillis, "Monument Roll Dice on Logan Circle Redevelopment," *Washington City Paper*, June 17, 2011.

30. See Rob Richard and TeAnne Chennault, "Grand Re-opening: R Street Apartment Newly Rehabilitated, Resident Owned and Occupied," press release on April 13, 2009, by the National Housing Trust/Enterprise Preservation Corporation, http://www.prnewswire.com/news-releases/grand-re-opening-r-street-apartments-newly-rehabilitated-resident-owned-and-occupied-61799852.html (accessed July 12, 2016).

31. While public housing has been critical for keeping low- and moderate-income people in revitalizing New York City neighborhoods, in Shaw/U Street various federal programs, sustained Black church affordable housing participation, and the right-of-first-refusal law were all critical for preserving a mixed-income community.

32. Quoted in Patrice Gaines, "The Cast and Their Lot: Against a Backdrop of Gentrification, a Land Dispute Is Played Out among a Black Church, Its New White Neighbors and D.C. Officials," *Washington Post*, December 7, 1999 (also see *Washington Informer*, "Metropolitan Church Hosts Gentrification Roundtable," July 13, 2005).

33. Brown-Saracino 2009; Maly 2005; Modan 2007; Williams 1988.

34. Fauntroy 2003; Harris 1995; McGovern 1998.

35. The easternmost part of the community is in Ward 5, but it is a very small slice of the community.

36. Ruble 2003.

37. Jaffe and Sherwood 2014.

38. Shaw/U Street's formal political positions, such as city council posts, changed faster than the ANCs, since the boundaries of the city council districts, such as Ward 1, stretched into areas, such as Mount Pleasant, that had already gentrified.

39. Elissa Silverman, "Bad Company: Shaw Reformers Can't Cope with 'Mahdi' Leroy Joseph Thorpe," *Washington City Paper*, March 16, 2001.

40. James Jones, "Thorpe Thumped," *Washington City Paper*, November 10, 2006.

41. *Fifth and Oh* blog post, "Powerplays," December 13, 2006, http://fifthandoh.blogspot.com/2006_12_01_archive.html (accessed July 12, 2016).

42. Mike DeBonis, "Clinical Depression," *Washington City Paper*, January 30, 2009.

43. Wilson 1996.

44. Hicks 2004.

45. Natalie Hopkinson, "Missing a Beat," *Washington Post*, April 11, 2010. Also see Hopkinson 2012.

46. Lornell and Stephenson Jr. 2009, p. vii.

47. Buehler et al. 2012.

48. Ibid., p. 18.

49. Buehler and Stowe 2016.

50. Buehler 2011.

51. Quoted in Ashley Halsey III, "No Doubt about It—This Lane Is for Bike Traffic," *Washington Post*, November 14, 2009.

52. Deborah K. Dietsch, "Getting Home on Two Wheels," *Washington Post*, October 2, 2010.

53. Martin Di Caro, "Why the Fight over a Bike Lane in Shaw Isn't About Biking," WAMU radio story on November 13, 2015; see http://wamu.org/programs/metro_connection /15/11/13/when_a_bike_lane_debate_isnt_just_about_bicycling (accessed July 12, 2016).

54. Timothy Wilson, "Shaw Exercises Its Dog Park Rights: Neighborhood Area Is First in D.C.," *Washington Post*, November 20, 2008.

55. The cost of the Shaw dog park was estimated based on the fact that a similar but smaller, ten-thousand-square-foot dog park cost the city $400,000 to build (see Elizabeth Wiener, "Newark St. Dog Park Opens amid Protests," *Northwest Current* (Washington, DC), September 15, 2010).

56. Tissot 2011.

57. See the Shaw Dog Park website at www.shawdogs.org (accessed July 12, 2016).

58. See http://washingtondc.citysearch.com/list/196451 and http://diningindc.net/2011 /06/29/dog-friendly-happy-hours-for-the-dog-days-of-summer-in-washington-dc/ (accessed March 5, 2012; content has since been altered).

59. Yamiche Alcindor, "Parking Lot Plan for Shaw Surprises Neighbors," *Washington Post*, July 13, 2009; Martin Ricard, "In D.C., Kicking Inclusion Up a Notch," *Washington Post*, September 3, 2009; and the Friends of Bundy Dog Park website at www.friends ofbundy.wordpress.com (accessed July 12, 2016).

60. The name change from the Bullets to the Wizards occurred in 1995.

61. Quoted in Marc Fisher, "Does Culture Follow the Census?," *Washington Post*, April 11, 2011. Other scholars have noted how dog parks can be sites of tension and exclusion in gentrifying neighborhoods (e.g., see Drew 2011 and Tissot 2011).

62. Quoted in Amanda Abrams and Andrew Lightman, "The Changing Faces of Shaw," *IDCNORTH*, December 2008, p. 33; www.capitalcommunitynews.com. The name of this monthly magazine changed to *MidCityDC* in 2010.

63. Freeman 2006; Joseph 2006; Wilson 1996.

64. Cahill and Roman 2010.

65. Knotts and Haspel 2006; Freeman 2006; also see Michener and Wong 2015.

66. Boyd 2008; Freeman 2006; Hyra 2008; Pattillo 2007.

67. Hyra 2008.

68. Fauntroy 2003; Harris 1995; McGovern 1998.

69. Burdick-Will, Keels, and Schuble 2013; Lipman 2009; Martin 2008; Pattillo 2007; Davis and Oakley 2013.

70. Emma Brown, "For Many Young D.C. Parents, City Schools Remain a Sticking Point," *Washington Post*, October 21, 2013.

71. Two studies suggest that children living in lower neighborhood poverty environments, compared with high poverty concentrations, should have increased lifetime earning potentials (Chetty, Hendren, and Katz 2015; Sharkey 2013). However, a recent employment study suggests that in gentrifying communities, greater economic activity might not benefit long-term residents through increased access to local job opportunities (Meltzer and Ghorbani 2015).

CHAPTER SEVEN

1. Sassen 2012; Hackworth 2007; Mollenkopf and Castells 1991; Clark 2011.

2. As noted in the introduction, the cappuccino city framework is not expected to have implications for all cities. It is more likely to apply to cities that have an emerging service sector–dominated economy and a particular set of demographic shifts,

such as an increasing proportion of Whites and a decreasing proportion of African Americans. Some US cities that fit these criteria include New York City, Atlanta, New Orleans, and Houston.

3. See the appendix, table 6.
4. Clark 2011; Florida 2014; Pucher and Buehler 2012; Speck 2012; Talen 2013; Zukin 2010.
5. Glaeser 2011; Papachristos et al. 2011; Schulman 2012; Simon 2010, 2011.
6. Papachristos et al. 2011, p. 221.
7. Oldenburg 1999.
8. Graham 2013; Misra and Stokols 2012.
9. Florida 2014; Hyra 2008; Lloyd 2010; Papachristos et al. 2011; Wyly and Hammel 2005.
10. Hyra 2012.
11. Ehrenhalt 2012.
12. Park and Burgess 1925.
13. Baum-Snow and Hartley 2015; Birch 2009; Ehrenhalt 2012.
14. Hyra 2008, 2012.
15. Marcuse 2012, p. 57.
16. Anderson 2011, p. 1.
17. Ibid., p. xiv.
18. Ibid.
19. Ibid., p. 30.
20. Tissot 2011, p. 265.
21. Ibid.
22. Clark 2011, p. 12.
23. Clark (2011) presents empirical work suggesting that traditional social categories are less predictive of individual behavior than they once were.
24. Ibid.; Florida 2014; Glaeser, Kolko, and Saiz 2001; Zukin 2010. Here my urban theoretical framework borrows, to a certain extent, from others, such as Zukin (1995) and Atkinson (2003), who use the cappuccino as a metaphor for understanding the political regulation and redevelopment of public spaces. It is important to note that my cappuccino theory goes beyond urban politics and public space to describe and explain interrelated economic, political, and social dynamics that shape neighborhood development in the city and its metropolitan region.
25. From 2002 to 2008, the DC budget increased. While the city spent a great deal on social services for low-income people, its largest spending increases by percentage were in the areas of education and economic development policy priorities to attract Millennials (Gandhi, Spaulding, and McDonald 2016).
26. Arena 2012; Owens and Brown 2014; Thompson 2006.
27. Mollenkopf and Castells 1991.
28. Some low-income African Americans who once lived in the urban core have moved to neighborhoods a bit further from the center city, to the inner suburbs (Allard 2009; Kneebone and Berube 2013), or completely out of the metropolitan region, to distant southern centers (Frey 2010; Pendergrass 2013).
29. Allard 2009; Allard and Roth 2010; Kneebone and Berube 2013; Orfield 2002.
30. Hyra 2014.
31. Frey 2011, p. 1. Also see Allard 2009; Kneebone and Berube 2013.
32. Allard and Roth 2010; Asch and Musgrove 2016; Jackson 2015; Summers 2016; Williams 2016.

33. See Carol Morello and Dan Keating, "Number of Black D.C. Residents Plummets as Majority Status Slips Away," *Washington Post*, March 24, 2011; and Dan Malouff, "What's the Real Ward 9?," *Washington Post Blog*, March 25, 2011, https://www.washingtonpost.com/blogs/all-opinions-are-local/post/whats-the-real-ward-9/2011/03/09/AFdau8WB_blog.html (accessed July 12, 2016). DC has eight political districts known as wards, and each elects a city council representative.

34. My cappuccino hypothesis also runs counter to patterns articulated by Harvard University urban economist Edward Glaeser (2011), who states that economically growing, robust cities typically attract both the rich and the poor. I believe that growing cities that have service sector–dominated economies will attract the poor, but this population will likely live on the suburban fringe as central city areas become increasingly expensive. Between 2000 and 2010, DC's home values skyrocketed; median home sales prices went from $209,000 to $563,000, in constant 2015 dollars (NeighborhoodInfo DC 2016). In the 2000s, as home values rose, DC's supply of affordable rental housing declined, and the number of higher-rent units increased. Between 2002 and 2013, the number of rental units that served low-income households (rents under $800) declined from 60,000 to 33,000, while the number of units serving higher-income families (rents over $1,400) increased from 28,000 to 73,000 (DC Fiscal Policy Institute 2015). Also occurring in the 2000s were a decrease in the number of affordable homeownership opportunities and an increase in the number of high-cost homes. Between 2000 and 2007, the number of DC homes valued under $250,000 sharply declined from 58,400 to 19,100. During the same period, the number of higher-cost homes (over $500,000) rose sharply from 15,400 to 47,400 (DC Fiscal Policy Institute 2010). In cappuccino cities, it will become increasingly difficult for the poor to find affordable housing.

CHAPTER EIGHT

1. Maly 2005, p. 226.
2. Modan 2007, p. 105.
3. Freeman 2006; Godsil 2014; Moulden and Squires 2012; Slater 2009; Wyly and Newman 2006.
4. For more on the White conspiracy theory, see Gillette 2016.
5. For a description of the meaning of the nod, see Jones 2013.
6. Putnam 2000.
7. Anthropologist Jesse Mumm labels this phenomenon "intimate segregation," and sociologist Christopher Mele calls this "soft exclusion." Mumm and Mele presented these concepts at the American Anthropological Association 112th annual meeting in Chicago during a panel session on November 21, 2013; the session was organized by Mumm and titled "Gentrification and Race: Elements of the Elephant In the Room." Diversity segregation extends the concepts of intimate segregation and soft exclusion in that it highlights and explains how those seeking diverse communities socially segregate themselves within them.
8. DC was much like this during the nineteenth century, when most census tracts were integrated, though minorities and poverty were in the alleys while the more affluent people lived on the face blocks (Borchert 1980).
9. Simon 2010.
10. Oldenburg 1999, p. 24.
11. Anderson 2011; Oldenburg 1999.
12. Anderson 2011.

13. Maly 2005, p. 45. Also see Nyden, Maly, and Lukehart 1997.

14. As noted, there was a 2006 plan, "The Duke Plan," for Black branding the community, but no plan to racially diversify the area intentionally.

15. Ruble 2010.

16. Quoted in the Reliable Source, "Poet Says His Heist of Cardboard Langston Hughes Was a Literary Protest of Busboys & Poets," *Washington Post*, February 9, 2011.

17. Melissa McCart, "Brothers Build a Restaurant Dynasty," *Washington Post*, May 5, 2010.

18. Jonathan O'Connell, "Recession Tests Donatelli Development's Formula," *Washington Business Journal*, June 26, 2009; and Annie Lowrey, "Washington's Economic Boom, Financed by You," *New York Times Magazine*, January 10, 2013.

19. Hyra 2012; Ruble 2010.

20. Nor, as this book has argued, is this mechanism alone sufficient for achieving economic justice.

21. See the *EastShawDC* blog at http://eastshawdc.blogspot.com/2013/01/lincoln-westmoreland-ii-to-exit-section.html (accessed July 13, 2016).

22. Moulden and Squires 2012.

23. See http://www.wandasonseventh.com (accessed July 13, 2016).

24. While Wanda's story is an inspiration, it is not the norm. Other small businesses, such as Sister Space, have been displaced as the community redeveloped (Hyra 2012; Ruble 2010).

25. Hyra 2015.

26. Quoted in Sabrina Tavernise and Robert Gebeloff, "Economic Boom in Washington Leaves Gaping Income Disparities," *New York Times*, December 17, 2010.

27. Quoted in Carol Morello and Dan Keating, "Blacks' Majority Status Slips Away," *Washington Post*, March 25, 2011.

28. Aaron C. Davis, "D.C. Lawmakers Approve $15 Minimum Wage, Joining N.Y., Calif.," *Washington Post*, June 7, 2016.

29. Brown-Saracino 2009; Freeman 2006; Inwood 2010.

30. Knotts and Haspel 2006, p. 120.

31. Carol Morello, Dan Keating, and Steve Hendrix, "Capital Hip: D.C. Is Getting Younger," *Washington Post*, May, 5, 2011.

REFERENCES

Abbott, Carl. 1999. *Political Terrain: Washington, D.C., from Tidewater Town to Global Metropolis*. Chapel Hill: University of North Carolina Press.

Abramson, Dan, Lynne Manzo, and Jeffrey Hou. 2006. "From Ethnic Enclaves to Multi-Ethnic Translocal Community: Contested Identities and Urban Design in Seattle's Chinatown-International District." *Journal of Architectural and Planning Research* 23 (4): 341–60.

Abu-Lughod, Janet L. 2000. *New York, Chicago, Los Angeles: America's Global Cities*. Minneapolis: University of Minnesota Press.

———. 2007. *Race, Space, and Riots in Chicago, New York, and Los Angeles*. New York: Oxford University Press.

Acuto, Michele. 2013. "The Geopolitical Dimension." In *Global City Challenges: Debating a Concept, Improving the Practice*, edited by Michele Acuto and Wendy Steele, pp. 170–87. London: Palgrave-Macmillan.

Allard, Scott W. 2009. *Out of Reach: Place, Poverty, and the New American Welfare State*. New Haven, CT: Yale University Press.

Allard, Scott W., and Benjamin Roth. 2010. *Strained Suburbs: The Social Service Challenges of Rising Suburban Poverty*. Washington, DC: Brookings Institution.

Anderson, Elijah. 2000. *Code of the Street: Decency, Violence, and the Moral Life of the Inner City*. New York: W. W. Norton.

———. 2011. *The Cosmopolitan Canopy: Race and Civility in Everyday Life*. New York: W. W. Norton.

———. 2012. "Toward Knowing the Iconic Ghetto." In Hutchison and Haynes 2012, pp. 67–82.

Arena, John. 2012. *Driven from New Orleans: How Nonprofits Betray Public Housing and Promote Privatization*. Minneapolis: University of Minnesota Press.

Asch, Chris M., and George D. Musgrove. 2016. "'We Are Headed for Some Bad Trouble': Gentrification and Displacement in Washington, DC, 1920–2014." In Hyra and Prince 2016, pp. 107–35.

A. T. Kearney. 2012. *2012 Global Cities: Index and Emerging Cities Outlook*. Chicago: A. T. Kearney.

Atkinson, Rowland. 2003. "Domestication by *Cappuccino* or a Revenge on Urban Space? Control and Empowerment in the Management of Public Spaces." *Urban Studies* 40 (9): 1829–43.

Barras, Jonetta R. 1998. *The Last of the Black Emperors: The Hollow Comeback of Marion Barry in the New Age of Black Leaders*. Baltimore: Bancroft Press.

Baum-Snow, Nathaniel, and Daniel Hartley. 2015. "Demographic Changes in and Near US Downtowns." *Economic Trends*, June 5. Accessed July 14, 2016. https://www.clevelandfed.org/newsroom-and-events/publications/economic-trends/2015-economic-trends/et-20150605-demographic-changes-in-and-near-us-downtowns.aspx.

Bean, Jonathan J. 2000. "'Burn, Baby, Burn': Small Business in the Urban Riots of the 1960s." *Independent Review* 5 (2): 165–87.

Beauregard, Robert A. 2006. *When America Became Suburban*. Minneapolis: University of Minnesota Press.

Beemyn, Genny. 2015. *A Queer Capital: A History of Gay Life in Washington, D.C.* New York: Routledge.

Bell, Daniel. 1973. *The Coming of Post-Industrial Society*. New York: Basic Books.

Bennett, Larry, Janet L. Smith, and Patricia A. Wright, eds. 2006. *Where Are Poor People to Live? Transforming Public Housing Communities*. Armonk, NY: M. E. Sharpe.

Berrey, Ellen, C. 2005. "Divided over Diversity: Political Discourse in a Chicago Neighborhood." *City and Community* 4 (2): 143–70.

Berube, Alan. 2003. "Gaining but Losing Ground: Population Change in Large Cities and Their Suburbs." In *Redefining Urban and Suburban America: Evidence from Census 2000*, edited by Bruce Katz and Robert E. Lang, 1:33–61. Washington, DC: Brookings Institution Press.

Biegler, Caitlin. 2012. *Unemployment Still Rising in the District: 2011 Level Was Highest since Start of Recession*. Washington, DC: DC Fiscal Policy Institute.

Birch, Eugenie L. 2002. "Having a Longer View on Downtown Living." *Journal of the American Planning Association* 68 (1): 5–21.

———. 2005. *Who Lives Downtown*. Washington, DC: Brookings Institution.

———. 2009. "Downtown in the 'New American City.'" *Annals of the American Academy of Political and Social Science* 626 (1): 134–53.

Bockman, Johanna. 2016. "Home Rule from Below: The Cooperative Movement in Washington, DC." In Hyra and Prince 2016, pp. 66–85.

Borchert, James. 1980. *Alley Life in Washington: Family, Community, Religion, and Folklife in the City, 1850–1970*. Urbana: University of Illinois Press.

Boyd, Michelle R. 2008. *Jim Crow Nostalgia: Reconstructing Race in Bronzeville*. Minneapolis: University of Minnesota Press.

Brown-Saracino, Japonica, ed. 2009. *A Neighborhood That Never Changes: Gentrification, Social Preservation, and the Search for Authenticity*. Chicago: University of Chicago Press.

———, ed. 2010. *The Gentrification Debates: A Reader*. New York: Routledge.

Brumbaugh, Anne M., and Sonya A. Grier. 2013. "Agents of Change: A Scale to Identify Diversity Seekers." *Journal of Public Policy and Marketing* 32: 144–55.

Buehler, Ralph. 2011. *Capital Bikeshare Study: A Closer Look at Casual Users and Operations*. Alexandria: Virginia Tech Urban Affairs and Planning.

Buehler, Ralph, Andrea Hamre, Dan Sonenklar, and Paul Goger. 2012. "Cycling Trends and Policies in the Washington, DC Region." *World Transport Policy and Practice* 18 (2): 6–29.

Buehler, Ralph, and John Stowe. 2016. "Bicycling in the Washington, DC Region: Trends in Ridership and Policies since 1990." In Hyra and Prince 2016, pp. 180–206.

Burawoy, Michael. 2009. *The Extended Case Method: Four Countries, Four Decades, Great Transformations, and One Theoretical Tradition*. Berkeley: University of California Press.

Burdick-Will, Julia, Micere Keels, and Todd Schuble. 2013. "Closing and Opening Schools:

The Association between Neighborhood Characteristics and the Location of New Educational Opportunities in a Large Urban District." *Journal of Urban Affairs* 35 (1): 59–80.

Cahill, Meagan, and John Roman. 2010. *Robbery in the District of Columbia: Patterns and Trends, 2000–2009*. Washington, DC: District of Columbia Crime Policy Institute.

Campbell, Scott. 2003. *The Enduring Importance of National Capital Cities in the Global Era*. Urban and Regional Research Collaborative Working Paper Series #03–08. Ann Arbor: University of Michigan.

Carr, James H., and Nandinee K. Kutty. 2008. *Segregation: The Rising Costs for America*. New York: Routledge.

Cashin, Sheryll. 2004. *The Failures of Integration: How Race and Class Are Undermining the American Dream*. New York: Public Affairs.

Castaneda, Ruben. 2014. *S Street Rising: Crack, Murder, and Redemption*. New York: Bloomsbury USA.

Castells, Manuel. 1983. *The City and the Grassroots: A Cross-Cultural Theory of Urban Social Movements*. Berkeley: University of California Press.

———. 1991. *The Information City: Information Technology, Economic Restructuring and the Urban-Regional Process*. Malden, MA: Blackwell.

———. 2000. "Materials for an Exploratory Theory of the Network Society." *British Journal of Sociology* 51 (1): 5–24.

Center for Regional Analysis. 2011. *Update from the 2010 Census: Population Change in the District of Columbia*. Arlington, VA: Center for Regional Analysis, George Mason University.

Chambers, John W., ed. 2000. *The Oxford Companion to American Military History*. New York: Oxford University Press.

Chaskin, Robert J., and Mark L. Joseph. 2011. "Social Interaction in Mixed Income Developments: Relational Expectations and Emerging Reality." *Journal of Urban Affairs* 32 (2): 209–37.

———. 2015. *Integrating the Inner City: The Promise and Perils of Mixed-Income Public Housing Transformation*. Chicago: University of Chicago Press.

Chauncey, George. 1994. *Gay New York: Gender, Urban Culture, and the Making of the Gay Male World, 1890–1940*. New York: Basic Books.

Chetty, Raj, Nathaniel Hendren, and Lawrence F. Katz. 2015. *The Effects of Exposure to Better Neighborhoods on Children: New Evidence from the Moving to Opportunity Experiment*. Cambridge, MA: Harvard University Press.

Chomsky, Noam. 2004. *Hegemony or Survival: America's Quest for Global Dominance*. New York: Henry Holt.

Clark, Kenneth B. 1967. *Dark Ghetto: Dilemmas of Social Power*. New York: Harper and Row.

Clark, Terry H., and Vincent Hoffmann-Martinot, eds. 1998. *The New Political Culture*. Boulder, CO: Westview Press.

Clark, Terry N., ed. 2011. *The City as an Entertainment Machine*. Lanham, MD: Lexington Books.

Coates, Joseph F. 1993. "The Future of Federal City—Washington, DC." *Technological Forecasting and Social Change* 44 (2): 219–27.

Cohen, Cathy J. 1999. *The Boundaries of Blackness: AIDS and the Breakdown of Black Politics*. Chicago: University of Chicago Press.

Colburn, David R., and Jeffrey S. Adler, eds. 2001. *African-American Mayors: Race, Politics, and the American City*. Urbana: University of Illinois Press.

Collins, Alan. 2004. "Sexual Dissidence, Enterprise and Assimilation: Bedfellows in Urban Regeneration." *Urban Studies* 41 (9): 1789–1806.

Collins, Patricia H. 2005. *Black Sexual Politics*. New York: Routledge.

Cowell, Margaret, Christina Gabriel, Sakina Khan, Heike Mayer, and Patrick O'Brien. 2012. *DC Innovation Strategy for Saint Elizabeths: Final Report*. Washington, DC: District of Columbia Office of Planning.

Crenshaw, Kimberlé. 1991. "Mapping the Margins: Intersectionality, Identity Politics, and Violence against Women of Color." *Stanford Law Review* 43 (6): 1241–79.

Crew, Spencer R. 1996. "Melding the Old and the New: The Modern African American Community, 1930–1960." In *Washington Odyssey: A Multicultural History of the Nation's Capital*, edited by Francine C. Cary, pp. 208–27. Washington, DC: Smithsonian Books.

Cultural Tourism, DC. 2003. *African American Heritage Trail*. Washington, DC: Cultural Tourism, DC.

Curley, Alexandra M. 2009. "Draining or Gaining? The Social Networks of Public Housing Movers in Boston." *Journal of Social and Personal Relationships* 26 (2–3): 227–47.

———. 2010. "Relocating the Poor: Social Capital and Neighborhood Resources." *Journal of Urban Affairs* 32 (1): 79–103.

Dahl, Robert A. 1961. *Who Governs?: Democracy and Power in an American City*. New Haven, CT: Yale University Press.

Dash, Leon. 1997. *Rosa Lee: A Mother and Her Family in Urban America*. New York: Plume.

Davidson, Mark. 2008. "Spoiled Mixture: Where Does State-Led 'Positive' Gentrification End?" *Urban Studies* 45 (12): 2385–2405.

———. 2010. "Love Thy Neighbour? Social Mixing in London's Gentrification Frontiers." *Environment and Planning A* 42 (3): 524–44.

Davis, Mike. 1998. *Ecology of Fear: Los Angeles and the Imagination of Disaster*. New York: Metropolitan Books.

Davis, Tomeka, and Deirdre Oakley. 2013. "Linking Charter School Emergence to Urban Revitalization and Gentrification: A Socio-Spatial Analysis of Three Cities." *Journal of Urban Affairs* 35 (1): 81–102.

Deener, Andrew. 2012. *Venice: A Contested Bohemia in Los Angeles*. Chicago: University of Chicago Press.

Destination DC. 2013. *Washington, DC's 2013 Visitor Statistics*. Washington, DC: Destination DC.

DC Fiscal Policy Institute. 2010. *Nowhere to Go: As DC Housing Costs Rise, Residents Are Left with Fewer Affordable Housing Options*. Washington, DC: DC Fiscal Policy Institute.

———. 2011. *New Census Data Show That One in Five DC Residents Lived in Poverty in 2010*. Washington, DC: DC Fiscal Policy Institute.

———. 2015. *Going, Going, Done: DC's Vanishing Affordable Housing*. Washington, DC: DC Fiscal Policy Institute.

District of Columbia Office of the Chief Financial Officer, Office of Revenue Analysis. 2012. *D.C. Office of Revenue Analysis Briefing Document, Number 2012-6*. Washington, DC: District of Columbia Office of the Chief Financial Officer, Office of Revenue Analysis.

District of Columbia Office of Planning. 2004. *Duke: Draft Development Framework for a Cultural Destination District within Washington, DC's Greater Shaw/U Street*. Washington, DC: District of Columbia Office of Planning.

———. 2012. "Washington D.C. Housing and Neighborhoods: Setting the Context 2000 to 2012." Presentation on April 17 to the Comprehensive Housing Strategy Task Force, Washington, DC.

DowntownDC Business Improvement District. 2011. *State of Downtown 2010*. Washington, DC: DowntownDC Business Improvement District.

Drake, St. Clair, and Horace R. Cayton. 1993. *Black Metropolis: A Study of Negro Life in a Northern City*. Chicago: University of Chicago Press.

Dreier, Peter, and John Atlas. 2009. "The Wire—Bush-Era Fable about America's Urban Poor?" *City and Community* 8 (3): 329–40.

Drew, Emily M. 2011. "'Listening through White Ears': Cross-Racial Dialogues as a Strategy to Address the Racial Effects of Gentrification." *Journal of Urban Affairs* 34 (1): 99–115.

Duneier, Mitchell. 2016. *Ghetto: The Invention of a Place, the History of an Idea*. New York: Farrar, Straus and Giroux.

Ehrenhalt, Alan. 2012. *The Great Inversion and the Future of the American City*. New York: Knopf.

Elazar, Daniel J. 1966. *American Federalism: A View from the States*. New York: Thomas Y. Crowell.

Ellen, Ingrid G., and Katherine O'Regan. 2011. "How Neighborhoods Change: Entry, Exit, and Enhancement." *Regional Science and Urban Economics* 41 (2): 89–97.

Emerson, Robert M., Rachel I. Fretz, and Linda L. Shaw. 1995. *Writing Ethnographic Fieldnotes*. Chicago: University of Chicago Press.

Erie, Steven P. 1988. *Rainbow's End: Irish-Americans and the Dilemmas of Urban Machine Politics, 1840–1985*. Berkeley: University of California Press.

Fainstein, Susan S. 2001. *The City Builders: Property Development in New York and London, 1980–2000*. Lawrence: University Press of Kansas.

Fauntroy, Michael K. 2003. *Home Rule or House Rule? Congress and the Erosion of Local Governance in the District of Columbia*. New York: University Press of America.

Ferman, Barbara. 1996. *Challenging the Growth Machine: Neighborhood Politics in Chicago and Pittsburgh*. Lawrence: University Press of Kansas.

Fishman, Robert. 2005. "Longer View: The Fifth Migration." *Journal of the American Planning Association* 71 (4): 357–66.

Fitzpatrick, Sandra, and Maria R. Goodwin. 2001. *The Guide to Black Washington: Places and Events of Historical and Cultural Significance in the Nation's Capital*. New York: Hippocrene Books.

Florida, Richard. 2014. *The Rise of the Creative Class, Revisited*. New York: Basic Books.

Florida, Richard, and Gary Gates. 2011. "Technology and Tolerance: The Importance of Diversity to High-Technology Growth." In *The City as an Entertainment Machine*, edited by Terry N. Clark, pp. 157–77. Lanham, MD: Lexington Books.

Frank, Stephanie B. 2005. "'If We Own the Story, We Own the Place': Cultural Heritage, Historic Preservation, and Gentrification on U Street." Master's thesis, University of Maryland, College Park.

Frank, Thomas. 2008. *The Wrecking Crew: How Conservatives Rule*. New York: Metropolitan Books.

Fraser, James C. 2004. "Beyond Gentrification: Mobilizing Communities and Claiming Space." *Urban Geography* 24 (5): 437–57.

Frazier, E. Franklin. 1957. *Black Bourgeoisie*. New York: Macmillan.

Freeman, Lance. 2005. "Displacement or Succession? Residential Mobility in Gentrifying Neighborhoods." *Urban Affairs Review* 40 (4): 463–91.

———. 2006. *There Goes the 'Hood*. Philadelphia: Temple University Press.

Freeman, Lance, and Frank Braconi. 2002. "Gentrification and Displacement." *Urban Prospect* 8 (1): 1–4.

———. 2004. "Gentrification and Displacement." *Journal of the American Planning Association* 70 (1): 39–52.

Freeman, Lance, and Tiancheng Cai. 2015. "White Entry into Black Neighborhoods: Advent of a New Era?" *Annals of the American Academy of Political and Social Science* 660 (1): 302–18.

French, George. 2009. "A Year in Bank Supervision: 2008 and a Few of Its Lessons." *US Federal Deposit Insurance Corporation's Supervisory Insights* 6 (1): 3–18.

Frey, William H. 2010. *State of Metropolitan America: Race and Ethnicity.* Washington, DC: Brookings Institution.

———. 2011. *Melting Pot Cities and Suburbs: Racial and Ethnic Change in Metro America in the 2000s.* Washington, DC: Brookings Institution.

———. 2013. *Greatest Metropolitan Net Migration Gains, 2009–2012: Seniors and Millennials.* Washington, DC: Brookings Institution.

Fuchs, Ester R. 1992. *Mayors and Money: Fiscal Policy in New York and Chicago.* Chicago: University of Chicago Press.

Fuller, Stephen S. 2002. *The Economic and Fiscal Impact of Foreign Missions on the Nation's Capital.* Washington, DC: National Capital Planning Commission.

———. 2009. *Federal Procurement Spending Increased to $66.5 Billion in the Washington Area in FY 2008 for a Gain of $6.1 Billion over FY 2007.* Arlington, VA: Center for Regional Analysis, George Mason University.

———. 2012. "How Will Changing Federal Spending Patterns Impact the Washington Area Economy and Which Sectors Will Drive Future Economic Growth?" Presentation on March 14 to the Metropolitan Washington Council of Governments Board of Directors, Washington, DC.

———. 2015. *The Washington Area Economy: Repositioning for Renewed Growth.* Arlington, VA: Center for Regional Analysis, George Mason University.

Fullilove, Mindy T. 2004. *Root Shock: How Tearing Up City Neighborhoods Hurts America, and What We Can Do About It.* New York: Ballantine Books.

Fullilove, Mindy T., and Rodrick Wallace. 2011. "Serial Forced Displacement in American Cities, 1916–2010." *Journal of Urban Health: Bulletin of the New York Academy of Medicine* 88 (3): 381–89.

Furman Center for Real Estate and Urban Policy. 2012. *The Changing Racial and Ethnic Makeup of New York City Neighborhoods.* New York: Furman Center for Real Estate and Urban Policy.

Gale, Dennis E. 1987. *Washington, D.C.: Inner-City Revitalization and Minority Suburbanization.* Philadelphia: Temple University Press.

Gallaher, Carolyn. 2016. *The Politics of Staying Put: Tenant Right to Buy in Washington, DC.* Philadelphia: Temple University Press.

Galster, George, and Peter Tatian. 2009. "Modeling Housing Appreciation Dynamics in Disadvantaged Neighborhoods." *Journal of Planning Education and Research* 29 (1): 7–22.

Gandhi, Natwar M., James Spaulding, and Gordon McDonald. 2016. "Budget Growth, Spending, and Inequality in DC, 2002–2013." In Hyra and Prince 2016, pp. 159–79.

Gandhi, Natwar M., Yesim Yilmaz, Robert Zahradnik, and Marcy Edwards. 2009. "Washington, District of Columbia, United States of America." In *Finance and Governance of Capital Cities in Federal Systems,* edited by Enid Slack and Rupak Chattopadhyay, pp. 263–91. Montreal: McGill-Queen's University Press.

Gates, Henry L., Jr. 2004. *America behind the Color Line: Dialogues with African Americans.* New York: Warner Books.

Ghaziani, Amin. 2011. "Post-Gay Collective Identity Construction." *Social Problems* 58 (1): 99–125.

———. 2014. *There Goes the Gayborhood?* Princeton, NJ: Princeton University Press.

Gibson, Karen J. 2007. "Bleeding Albina: A History of Community Disinvestment, 1940–2000." *Transforming Anthropology* 15 (1): 3–25.

Gibson, Timothy A. 2007. "City Living, D.C. Style: The Political-Economic Limits of Urban Branding Campaigns." In *Urban Communication: Production, Text, Context,* edited by Timothy A. Gibson and Mark Lowes, pp. 83–107. New York: Rowman and Littlefield.

Gilbert, Ben W. 1968. *Ten Blocks from the White House: Anatomy of the Washington Riots of 1968.* New York: Frederick A. Praeger.

Gillespie, Andra. 2012. *The New Black Politician: Cory Booker, Newark, and Post-Racial America.* New York: New York University Press.

Gillette, Howard, Jr. 1995. *Between Justice and Beauty: Race, Planning, and the Failure of Urban Policy in Washington, D.C.* Philadelphia: University of Pennsylvania Press.

———. 2003. "Washington, D.C., in White and Black: The Social Construction of Race and Nationhood." In *Composing Urban History and the Constitution of Civic Identities,* edited by Blair Ruble, pp. 192–210. Washington, DC: Woodrow Wilson Center Press; Baltimore: Johns Hopkins University Press.

———. 2016. "Introduction: For a City in Transition, Questions of Social Justice and Economic Viability Remain." In Hyra and Prince, pp. 1–8.

Glaeser, Edward. 2011. *Triumph of the City: How Our Greatest Invention Makes Us Richer, Smarter, Greener, Healthier, and Happier.* New York: Penguin Press.

Glaeser, Edward L., Jed Kolko, and Albert Saiz. 2001. "Consumer City." *Journal of Economic Geography* 1 (1): 27–50.

Glaeser, Edward L., and Jesse M. Shapiro. 2003a. "City Growth: Which Places Grew and Why." In *Redefining Urban and Suburban America: Evidence from Census 2000,* edited by Bruce Katz and Robert E. Lang, vol. 1 (Washington, DC: Brookings Institution Press), 13–32.

———. 2003b. "Urban Growth in the 1990s: Is City Living Back?" *Journal of Regional Science* 43 (1): 139–65.

Glaeser, Edward L., and Jacob Vigdor. 2012. *The End of the Segregation Century: Race Separation in America's Neighborhoods, 1890–2010.* Civic Report no. 66. New York: Manhattan Institute.

Godsil, Rachel D. 2014. "Autonomy, Mobility, and Affirmatively Furthering Fair Housing in Gentrifying Neighborhoods." *Poverty and Race* 23 (1): 1–2, 8, 10–11.

Goetz, Edward. 2003. *Clearing the Way: Deconcentrating the Poor in Urban America.* Washington, DC: Urban Institute Press.

———. 2013. *New Deal Ruins: Race, Economic Justice, and Public Housing Policy.* Ithaca, NY: Cornell University Press.

Gotham, Kevin F. 2005. "Tourism Gentrification: The Case of New Orleans' Vieux Carre (French Quarter)." *Urban Studies* 42 (7): 1099–1121.

———. 2007. *Authentic New Orleans: Tourism, Culture, and Race in the Big Easy.* New York: New York University Press.

Graham, Mark. 2013. "The Virtual Dimension." In *Global City Challenges: Debating a Concept, Improving the Practice,* edited by Michele Acuto and Wendy Steele, pp. 117–39. London: Palgrave-Macmillan.

Gramlich, Edward M. 2007. *Subprime Mortgages: America's Latest Boom and Bust.* Washington, DC: Urban Institute Press.

Grams, Diane. 2010. *Producing Local Color: Arts Networks in Ethnic Chicago.* Chicago: University of Chicago Press.

Granovetter, Mark. 1983. "The Strength of Weak Ties: A Network Theory Revisited." *Sociological Theory* 1 (1): 201–33.

Grazian, David. 2003. *Blue Chicago: The Search for Authenticity in the Urban Blues Clubs.* Chicago: University of Chicago Press.

———. 2008. *On the Make: The Hustle of Urban Nightlife.* Chicago: University of Chicago Press.

Greek, Mark. 2009. *Washington, D.C. Protests: Scenes from Home Rule to the Civil Rights Movement.* Charleston, SC: History Press.

Green, Constance M. 1967. *The Secret City: A History of Race Relations in the Nation's Capital.* Princeton, NJ: Princeton University Press.

Greene, Theodore. 2014. "Gay Neighborhoods and the Rights of the Vicarious Citizen." *City and Community* 13 (2): 99–118.

Grogan, Paul, and Tony Proscio. 2000. *Comeback Cities: A Blueprint for Urban Neighborhood Revival.* New York: Basic Books.

Grossman, James. 1989. *Land of Hope: Chicago, Black Southerners, and the Great Migration.* Chicago: University of Chicago Press.

Guerrieri, Veronia, Daniel Hartley, and Erik Hurst. 2013. "Endogenous Gentrification and Housing Price Dynamics." *Journal of Public Economics* 100: 45–60.

Gutheim, Frederick, and Antoinette J. Lee. 2006. *Worthy of the Nation: Washington, DC, from L'Enfant to the National Capital Planning Commission.* Baltimore: Johns Hopkins University Press.

Hackworth, Jason. 2007. *The Neoliberal City: Governance, Ideology and Development in American Urbanism.* Ithaca, NY: Cornell University Press.

Halle, David, ed. 2003. *New York and Los Angeles: Politics, Society, and Culture—a Comparative View.* Chicago: University of Chicago Press.

Halpern, Robert. 1995. *Rebuilding the Inner City: A History of Neighborhood Initiatives to Address Poverty in the United States.* New York: Columbia University Press.

Hannerz, Ulf. 1969. *Soulside: Inquiries into Ghetto Culture and Community.* Chicago: University of Chicago Press.

Harcourt, Bernard E. 2005. "Policing L.A.'s Skid Row: Crime and Real Estate Development in Downtown Los Angeles [An Experiment in Real Time]." *University of Chicago Legal Forum* vol. 2005.

Harding, David J. 2010. *Living the Drama: Community, Conflict, and Culture among Inner-City Boys.* Chicago: University of Chicago Press.

Harris, Charles W. 1995. *Congress and the Governance of the Nation's Capital: The Conflict of Federal and Local Interests.* Washington, DC: Georgetown University Press.

Harris, Daryl B. 2010. "The High Tide of Pragmatic Black Politics: Mayor Anthony Williams and the Suppression of Black Interests." In *Democratic Density and the District of Columbia: Federal Politics and Public Policy*, ed. Ronald Walters and Toni-Michelle C. Travis, pp. 103–17. New York: Lexington Books.

Harris, Fredrick C. 2012. *The Price of the Ticket: Barack Obama and the Rise and Decline of Black Politics.* New York: Oxford University Press.

Harris-Lacewell, Melissa. 2004. *Barbershops, Bibles and BET: Everyday Talk and Black Political Thought.* Princeton, NJ: Princeton University Press.

Hartman, Chester, and Gregory Squires. 2010. *The Integration Debate: Competing Futures for American Cities.* New York: Routledge.

Heap, Chad. 2009. *Slumming: Sexual and Racial Encounters in American Nightlife, 1885–1940.* Chicago: University of Chicago Press.

Heck, Allison J. 2013. "Producing Authenticity: The Process, Politics, and Impacts of Cultural Preservation in Washington, DC." PhD diss., Virginia Tech, Blacksburg.

Hicks, H. Beecher, Jr. 2004. *On Jordan's Stormy Banks: Leading Your Congregation through the Wilderness of Change.* Grand Rapids, MI: Zondervan.

Hira, Ron, and Anil Hira. 2005. *Outsourcing America: What's behind Our National Crisis and How We Can Reclaim American Jobs.* New York: AMACOM.

Hirsch, Arnold R. 1998. *Making the Second Ghetto: Race and Housing in Chicago, 1940–1960.* Chicago: University of Chicago Press.

Hochschild, Jennifer, Vesla Weaver, and Traci Burch. 2012. *Creating a New Racial Order: How Immigration, Multiracialism, Genomics, and the Young Can Remake Race in America.* Princeton, NJ: Princeton University Press.

Hoffman, Alexander von. 2003. *House by House, Block by Block: The Rebirth of America's Urban Neighborhoods.* New York: Oxford University Press.

Hoffman, Lily M. 2003. "The Marketing of Diversity in the Inner City: Tourism and Regulation in Harlem." *International Journal of Urban and Regional Research* 27 (2): 286–99.

Holloway, Jonathan S. 2002. *Confronting the Veil: Abram Harris, Jr., E. Franklin Frazier, and Ralph Bunche, 1919–1941.* Chapel Hill: University of North Carolina Press.

Hopkinson, Natalie. 2012. *Go-Go Live: The Musical Life and Death of a Chocolate City.* Durham, NC: Duke University Press.

Horton, Lois E. 1996. "The Days of Jubilee: Black Migration during the Civil War and Reconstruction." In *Washington Odyssey: A Multicultural History of the Nation's Capital,* edited by Francine C. Cary, pp. 65–78. Washington, DC: Smithsonian Books.

Hunter, Marcus A. 2010. "The Nightly Round: Space, Social Capital and Urban Black Nightlife." *City and Community* 9 (2): 165–86.

———. 2013. *Black Citymakers: How the Philadelphia Negro Changed Urban America.* New York: Oxford University Press.

Hurley, Andrew. 2010. *Beyond Preservation: Using History to Revitalize Inner Cities.* Philadelphia: Temple University Press.

Hutchison, Ray, and Bruce D. Haynes, eds. 2012. *The Ghetto: Contemporary Global Issues and Controversies.* Boulder, CO: Westview Press.

Hwang, Jackelyn, and Robert J. Sampson. 2014. "Divergent Pathways of Gentrification: Racial Inequality and the Social Order of Renewal in Chicago Neighborhoods." *American Sociological Review* 79 (4): 726–51.

Hyra, Derek. 2008. *The New Urban Renewal: The Economic Transformation of Harlem and Bronzeville.* Chicago: University of Chicago Press.

———. 2012. "Conceptualizing the New Urban Renewal: Comparing the Past to the Present." *Urban Affairs Review* 48 (4): 498–527.

———. 2014. "Revisiting the US Black and the French Red Belts: Parallel Themes and a Shared Dilemma." In *Urban Ills: Twenty-First-Century Complexities of Urban Living in Global Contexts,* edited by Carol C. Yeakey, Vetta L. S. Thompson, and Anjanette Wells, 1:297–328. New York: Lexington Books.

———. 2015. "The Obama Administration's Place-Based Initiatives: Why Not Include Small Business Lending Components?" *Journal of Urban Affairs* 37 (1): 66–69.

Hyra, Derek, and Sabiyha Prince, eds. 2016. *Capital Dilemma: Growth and Inequality in Washington, DC.* New York: Routledge.

Hyra, Derek S., and Jacob Rugh. 2016. "The US Great Recession: Exploring Its Association with Black Neighborhood Rise, Decline and Recovery." *Urban Geography* 37 (5): 700–726.

Hyra, Derek S., Gregory D. Squires, Robert N. Renner, and David S. Kirk. 2013. "Metropolitan Segregation and the Subprime Lending Crisis." *Housing Policy Debate* 23 (1): 177–98.

International Environmental Corporation. 2009. *Hotel Monaco: Washington, D.C.* Oklahoma City: International Environmental Corporation.

Inwood, Joshua F. 2010. "Sweet Auburn: Constructing Atlanta's Auburn Avenue as a Heritage Tourist Destination." *Urban Geography* 31 (5): 573–94.

Jackson, John. 2015. "The Consequences of Gentrification for Racial Change in Washington, DC." *Housing Policy Debate* 25 (2): 353–73.

Jackson, John L. 2005. *Real Black: Adventures in Racial Sincerity.* Chicago: University of Chicago Press.

Jackson, Kenneth T. 1985. *Crabgrass Frontier: The Suburbanization of the United States.* New York: Oxford University Press.

Jackson, Maurice. 2016. "Music, Race, Desegregation, and the Fight for Equality in the Nation's Capital." In Hyra and Prince 2016, pp. 27–44.

Jacob, Kathryn A. 1996. "'Like Moths to a Candle': The Nouveaux Riches Flock to Washington, 1870–1900." In *Washington Odyssey: A Multicultural History of the Nation's Capital,* edited by Francine C. Cary, pp. 79–96. Washington, DC: Smithsonian Books.

Jaffe, Harry S., and Tom Sherwood. 2014. *Dream City: Race, Power, and the Decline of Washington, D.C.* New York: Simon and Schuster.

Jagoda, Patrick. 2011. "Critical Response I Wire." *Critical Inquiry* 38 (1): 189–99.

Jargowsky, Paul, A. 1997. *Poverty and Place: Ghettos, Barrios, and the American City.* New York: Russell Sage Foundation.

———. 2014. *Concentration of Poverty in the New Millennium: 2012 Update.* New York: Century Foundation.

Johnson, Valerie C. 2002. *Black Power in the Suburbs: The Myth or Reality of African-American Suburban Political Incorporation.* New York: State University of New York Press.

Jones, James. 2013. "Racing through the Halls of Congress: Understanding the Meaning of the 'Black Nod' among Congressional Employees." Paper presented on August 13 at the Annual Meeting of the American Sociological Association, New York City.

Jones, Nikki, and Christina Jackson. 2012. "'You Just Don't Go Down There': Learning to Avoid the Ghetto in San Francisco." In Hutchison and Haynes 2012, pp. 83–109.

Joseph, Mark L. 2006. "Is Mixed-Income Development an Antidote to Urban Poverty?" *Housing Policy Debate* 17 (2): 209–34.

Joseph, Mark L., and Robert Chaskin. 2010. "Living in a Mixed-Income Development: Resident Perceptions of the Benefits and Disadvantages of Two Developments in Chicago." *Urban Studies* 47 (11): 2347–66.

Justh, Kevin M. 2009. *Anatomy of a Successful Public Private Partnership: Gallery Place.* Master's Applied Research Project. Baltimore: Johns Hopkins University.

Kasarda, John D., Stephen J. Appold, Stuart H. Sweeney, and Elaine Sieff. 1997. "Central-City and Suburban Migration Patterns: Is a Turnaround on the Horizon?" *Housing Policy Debate* 8 (2): 307–58.

Katz, Michael B. 2012. *Why Don't American Cities Burn?* Philadelphia: University of Pennsylvania Press.

Kerstetter, Katie, Jenny Reed, and Ed Lazere. 2009. *New Census Data Reveal Growing Income Gaps in the District.* Washington, DC: DC Fiscal Policy Institute.

Kirk, David S., and John H. Laub. 2010. "Neighborhood Change and Crime in the Modern Metropolis." In *Crime and Justice,* edited by Michael Tonry, 39: 441–502. Chicago: University of Chicago Press.

Kirk, David S., and Andrew V. Papachristos. 2011. "Cultural Mechanisms and the Persistence of Neighborhood Violence." *American Journal of Sociology* 116 (4): 1190–233.

Kneebone, Elizabeth, and Alan Berube. 2013. *Confronting Suburban Poverty in America.* Washington, DC: Brookings Institution Press.

Knotts, H. Gibbs, and Moshe Haspel. 2006. "The Impact of Gentrification on Voter Turnout." *Social Science Quarterly* 87 (1): 110–21.

Knox, Paul L. 1991. "The Restless Urban Landscape: Economic and Sociocultural Change and the Transformation of Metropolitan Washington, DC." *Annals of the American Geographers* 81 (2): 181–209.

———. 2008. *Metroburbia, USA.* New Brunswick, NJ: Rutgers University Press.

Knox, Paul L., and Peter J. Taylor, eds. 1995. *World Cities in a World-System.* Cambridge: Cambridge University Press.

Kofie, Nelson F. 1999. *Race, Class, and the Struggle for Neighborhood in Washington, DC.* New York: Garland.

Lachman, M. Leanne, and Deborah L. Brett. 2015. *Millennials inside the Beltway: Optimistic Urbanists.* Washington, DC: Urban Land Institute.

Lacy, Karyn R. 2007. *Blue-Chip Black: Race, Class, and Status in the New Black Middle Class.* Berkeley: University of California Press.

Lamont, Michèle, Stefan Beljean, and Matthew Clair. 2014. "What Is Missing? Cultural Processes and Causal Pathways to Inequality." *Socio-Economic Review* 12 (3): 573–608.

Laska, Shirely B., and Daphne Spain, eds. 1980. *Back to the City: Issues in Neighborhood Renovation.* New York: Pergamon Press.

Lauria, Mickey, and Lawrence Knopp. 1985. "Toward an Analysis of the Role of Gay Communities in the Urban Renaissance." *Urban Geography* 6 (2): 152–69.

Lee, Barrett A., Daphne Spain, and Debra J. Umberson. 1985. "Neighborhood Revitalization and Racial Change: The Case of Washington, D.C." *Demography* 22 (4): 581–602.

Lees, Loretta. 2000. "A Reappraisal of Gentrification: Towards a 'Geography of Gentrification.'" *Progress in Human Geography* 24 (3): 389–408.

Lees, Loretta, Tom Slater, and Elvin Wyly. 2008. *Gentrification.* New York: Routledge.

Leon, Wilmer J. 2010. "Marion Barry, Jr.: A Politician for the Times." In *Democratic Density and the District of Columbia: Federal Politics and Public Policy,* edited by Ronald Walters and Toni-Michelle C. Travis, pp. 61–85. New York: Lexington Books.

Levitin, Adam J., and Susan M. Wachter. 2013. "Why Housing?" *Housing Policy Debate* 23 (1): 5–27.

Liebow, Elliot. 1967. *Tally's Corner.* Boston: Little, Brown.

Lin, Jan. 2011. *The Power of Urban Ethnic Places: Cultural Heritage and Community Life.* New York: Routledge.

Lipman, Pauline. 2009. "The Cultural Politics of Mixed-Income Schools and Housing: A Racialized Discourse of Displacement, Exclusion, and Control." *Anthropology and Education Quarterly* 40 (3): 215–36.

Lloyd, Richard. 2010. *Neo-Bohemia: Art and Commerce in the Postindustrial City.* New York: Routledge.

Logan, John R., and Harvey L. Molotch. 2007. *Urban Fortunes: The Political Economy of Place.* Berkeley: University of California Press.

Lornell, Kip, and Charles C. Stephenson Jr. 2009. *The Beat! Go-Go Music from Washington, D.C.* Jackson: University Press of Mississippi.

Maciag, Mike. 2015. "Gentrification in America Report." *Governing Magazine,* February. Accessed July 26, 2016. http://www.governing.com/gov-data/census/gentrification-in-cities-governing-report.html.

Maly, Michael T. 2005. *Beyond Segregation: Multiracial and Multiethnic Neighborhoods in the United States.* Philadelphia: Temple University Press.

Marchio, Nick, and Alan Berube. 2015. *Benchmarking Greater Washington's Global Reach: The National Capital Region in the World Economy.* Washington, DC: Brookings Institution.

Marcuse, Peter. 2012. "De-spatialization and Dilution of the Ghetto: Current Trends in the United States." In Hutchison and Haynes 2012, pp. 33–66.

Markman, Joshua A., and John K. Roman. 2010. *Homicides in the District of Columbia by Police District, 2001–2009.* Washington, DC: Urban Institute/Brookings Institution.

Martin, Leslie. 2007. "Fighting for Control: Political Displacement in Atlanta's Gentrifying Neighborhoods." *Urban Affairs Review* 42 (5): 603–28.

———. 2008. "Boredom, Drugs, and Schools: Protecting Children in Gentrifying Communities." *City and Community* 7 (4): 331–46.

Massey, Douglas S. 2007. *Categorically Unequal: The American Stratification System.* New York: Russell Sage Foundation.

Massey, Douglas S., and Nancy A. Denton. 1993. *American Apartheid: Segregation and the Making of the Underclass.* Cambridge, MA: Harvard University Press.

Masur, Kate. 2010. *An Example for All the Land: Emancipation and the Struggle over Equality in Washington, DC*: Chapel Hill: University of North Carolina Press.

McCall, Leslie. 2005. "The Complexity of Intersectionality." *Journal of Women in Culture and Society* 30 (3): 1771–1800.

McGovern, Stephen J. 1998. *The Politics of Downtown Development: Dynamic Political Cultures in San Francisco and Washington, D.C.* Lexington: University Press of Kentucky.

McKinnish, Terra, Randall Walsh, and Kirk White. 2010. "Who Gentrifies Low-Income Neighborhoods?" *Journal of Urban Economics* 67: 180–93.

McMillen, Daniel P. 2003. "The Return of Centralization to Chicago: Using Repeat Sales to Identify Changes in Housing Price Distance Gradients." *Regional Science and Urban Economics* 33 (3): 287–304.

McQueeney, Krista. 2009. "'We Are God's Children, Y'all': Race, Gender, and Sexuality in Lesbian- and Gay-Affirming Congregations." *Social Problems* 56 (1): 151–73.

McRoberts, Omar M. 2003. *Streets of Glory: Church and Community in a Black Urban Neighborhood.* Chicago: University of Chicago Press.

Mele, Christopher. 2000. *Selling the Lower East Side: Culture, Real Estate, and Resistance in New York City.* Minneapolis: University of Minnesota Press.

Meltzer, Rachel, and Pooya Ghorbani. 2015. "Does Gentrification Increase Employment Opportunities in Low-Income Neighborhoods?" Paper presented on November 13 at the Thirty-Seventh Annual Fall Conference of the Association for Public Policy and Management, Miami.

Michener, Jamila, and Diane Wong. 2015. "Gentrification and Political Destabilization: What, Where and How?" Paper presented on April 10 at the Forty-Fifth Urban Affairs Association Annual Conference, Miami.

Miller, James A. 2010. "Greater Shaw: A Gathering Pace for Black Washington." In *Washington at Home: An Illustrated History of Neighborhoods in the Nation's Capital*, edited by Kathryn S. Smith, pp. 196–212. Baltimore: Johns Hopkins University Press.

Mills, C. Wright. 1956. *The Power Elite.* New York: Oxford University Press.

Misra, Shalini, and Daniel Stokols. 2012. "A Typology of People-Environment Relationships in the Digital Age." *Technology in Society* 34 (4): 311–25.

Modan, Gabriella G. 2007. *Turf Wars: Discourse, Diversity, and the Politics of Place.* Malden, MA: Blackwell.

Mollenkopf, John H., and Manuel Castells, eds. 1991. *Dual City: Restructuring New York.* New York: Russell Sage Foundation.

Moore, Jacqueline M. 1999. *Leading the Race: The Transformation of the Black Elite in the Nation's Capital, 1880–1920.* Charlottesville: University of Virginia Press.

Moore, Kesha S. 2009. "Gentrification in Black Face? The Return of the Black Middle Class to Urban Neighborhoods." *Urban Geography* 30 (2): 118–42.

Moore, Mignon R. 2010. "Articulating a Politics of (Multiple) Identities: LGBT Sexuality and Inclusion in Black Community Life." *Du Bois Review* 7 (2): 1–20.

Moulden, Dominic T., and Gregory D. Squires. 2012. "Equitable Development Comes to DC." *Social Policy* 42 (3): 37–39.

Myrdal, Gunnar. 1944. *An American Dilemma: The Negro Problem and Modern Democracy.* New York: Harper and Brothers.

Nash, Jennifer C. 2008. "Re-thinking Intersectionality." *Feminist Review* 89 (1): 1–15.

NeighborhoodInfo DC. 2016. *DC City Profile—housing.* Accessed July 15, 2016. http://www.neighborhoodinfodc.org/city/Nbr_prof_cityc.html.

Newman, Katherine S. 2000. *No Shame in My Game: The Working Poor in the Inner City.* New York: Vintage.

Newman, Katherine, and Elvin K. Wyly. "The Right to Stay Put, Revisited: Gentrification and Resistance to Displacement in New York City." *Urban Studies* 43 (1): 23–57.

Nieves, Angel D. 2008. "Revaluing Places: Hidden Histories from the Margins." *Places* 20 (1): 21–25.

Nyden, Philip, Michael Maly, and John Lukehart. 1997. "The Emergence of Stable Racially and Ethnically Diverse Urban Communities: A Case Study of Nine U.S. Cities." *Housing Policy Debate* 8 (2): 491–534.

Ocejo, Richard E. 2010. "What'll It Be? Cocktail Bartenders and Redefinition of Service in the Creative Economy." *City, Culture and Society* 1 (4): 179–84.

———. 2011. "The Early Gentrifier: Weaving a Nostalgia Narrative on the Lower East Side." *City and Community* 10 (3): 285–310.

———. 2014. *Upscaling Downtown: From Bowery Saloons to Cocktail Bars in New York City.* Princeton, NJ: Princeton University Press.

Oldenburg, Ray. 1999. *The Great Good Place: Cafés, Coffee Shops, Bookstores, Bars, Hair Salons and Other Hangouts at the Heart of a Community.* New York: Marlowe.

Orfield, Myron. 2002. *American Metropolitics: The New Suburban Reality.* Washington, DC: Brookings Institution Press.

Orr, Benjamin, and Alice M Rivlin. 2011. "Affordable Housing in the District—where Are We Now?" Metropolitan Policy Program at the Brookings Institution. Washington, DC: Brookings Institution.

Owens, Ann. 2012. "Neighborhoods on the Rise: A Typology of Neighborhoods Experiencing Socioeconomic Ascent." *City and Community* 11 (4): 345–69.

Owens, Michael L., and Jacob R. Brown. 2014. "Weakening Strong Black Political Empowerment: Implications from Atlanta's 2009 Mayoral Election." *Journal of Urban Affairs* 36 (4): 663–81.

Owens, Michael L., and Michael J. Rich. 2003. "Is Strong Incorporation Enough? Black Empowerment and the Fate of Atlanta's Low-Income Blacks." In *Racial Politics in American Cities,* edited by Rufus P. Browning, Dale Rogers Marshall, and David H. Tabb, pp. 201–26. New York: Pearson

Papachristos, Andrew, Chris M. Smith, Mary L. Scherer, and Melissa A. Fugiero. 2011. "More Coffee, Less Crime? The Relationship between Gentrification and Neighborhood Crime Rates in Chicago, 1991 to 2005." *City and Community* 10 (3): 215–40.

Park, Robert E., and Ernest W. Burgess. 1925. *The City: Suggestions for Investigations of Human Behavior in the Urban Environment.* Chicago: University of Chicago Press.

Pattillo, Mary. 2007. *Black on the Block.* Chicago: University of Chicago Press.

Pearson, Adam R., John F. Dovidio, and Samuel L. Gaertner. 2009. "The Nature of Contemporary Prejudice: Insights from Aversive Racism." *Social and Personality Psychology Compass* 3 (3): 1–25.

Pendergrass, Sabrina. 2013. "Perceptions of Race and Region in the Black Reverse Migration to the South." *Du Bois Review* 10 (1): 155–78.

Peterson, Paul E. 1981. *City Limits.* Chicago: University of Chicago Press.

Phillips, Joy, Robert Beasley, and Art Rodgers. 2005. *District of Columbia Population and Housing Trends.* Washington, DC: DC Office of Planning, State Data Center.

Podagrosi, Angelo, and Igor Vojnovic. 2008. "Tearing Down Freedmen's Town and African American Displacement in Houston: The Good, the Bad, and the Ugly of Urban Revival." *Urban Geography* 29: 371–401.

Prince, Sabiyha. 2014. *African Americans and Gentrification in Washington, D.C.: Race, Class and Social Justice in the Nation's Capital.* New York: Routledge.

Pucher, John, and Ralph Buehler, eds. 2012. *City Cycling.* Cambridge, MA: MIT Press.

Putnam, Robert D. 2000. *Bowling Alone: The Collapse and Revival of American Community.* New York: Simon and Schuster.

Reed, Adolph, Jr. 1999. *Stirrings in the Jug: Black Politics in the Post-Segregation Era.* Minneapolis: University of Minnesota Press.

Ritzer, George. 2013. *The McDonaldization of Society: 20th Anniversary Edition.* Thousand Oaks, CA: Sage Publications.

Rivers, Wes. 2014. *High and Wide: Income Inequality Gap in the District One of Biggest in the U.S.* Washington, DC: DC Fiscal Policy Institute.

Robinson, Eugene. 2010. *Disintegration: The Splintering of Black America.* New York: Doubleday.

Ruble, Blair A. 2003. "Living Apart Together: The City, Contested Identity, and Democratic Transitions." In *Composing Urban History and the Constitution of Civic Identities,* ed. Blair Ruble, pp. 1–21. Washington, DC: Woodrow Wilson Center Press; Baltimore: Johns Hopkins University Press.

———. 2005. *Creating Diversity Capital: Transnational Migrants in Montreal, Washington, and Kyiv.* Baltimore: Johns Hopkins University Press.

———. 2010. *Washington's U Street: A Biography.* Washington, DC: Woodrow Wilson Center Press; Baltimore: Johns Hopkins University Press.

Rugh, Jacob S., and Douglas S. Massey. 2014. "Segregation in Post–Civil Rights America: Stalled Integration or End of the Segregated Century?" *Du Bois Review* 11 (2): 189–93.

Sampson, Robert J. 2012. *Great American City: Chicago and the Enduring Neighborhood Effect.* Chicago: University of Chicago Press.

Sanchez, Thomas W., and Casey J. Dawkins. 2001. "Distinguishing City and Suburban Movers: Evidence from the American Housing Survey." *Housing Policy Debate* 12 (3): 607–31.

Sanchez-Jankowski, Martin. 2008. *Cracks in the Pavement.* Berkeley: University of California Press.

Sassen, Saskia. 2009. "When Local Housing Becomes an Electronic Instrument: The Global Circulation of Mortgages—a Research Note." *International Journal of Urban and Regional Research* 33 (2): 411–26.

———. 2012. *Cities in a World Economy.* Thousand Oaks, CA: Sage Publications.

Schaller, Susanna F. 2010. "Situating Entrepreneurial Place-Making through Business Improvement Districts in Relation to Urban Development in Washington, D.C." PhD diss., Cornell University.

———. 2016. "Situating Entrepreneurial Place Making in DC: Business Improvement Districts and Urban (Re)Development in Washington, DC." In Hyra and Prince 2016, pp. 139–58.

Schrag, Zachary M. 2006. *The Great Society Subway: A History of the Washington Metro.* Baltimore: Johns Hopkins University Press.

Schulman, Sarah. 2012. *The Gentrification of the Mind: Witness to a Lost Imagination.* Berkeley: University of California Press.

Sharkey, Patrick. 2013. *Stuck in Place: Urban Neighborhoods and the End of Progress toward Equality.* Chicago: University of Chicago Press.

Sibalis, Michael. 2004. "Urban Space and Homosexuality: The Example of the Marais, Paris' 'Gay Ghetto.'" *Urban Studies* 41 (9): 1739–58.

Siegel, Fred. 1997. *The Future Once Happened Here: New York, D.C., L.A., and the Fate of America's Big Cities.* San Francisco: Encounter Books.

Simmons, Patrick A., and Robert E. Lang. 2003. "The Urban Turnaround." In *Redefining Urban and Suburban America: Evidence from Census 2000*, edited by Bruce Katz and Robert E. Lang, vol. 1 (Washington, DC: Brookings Institution Press), 51–61.

Simon, Bryant. 2010. "Race Doesn't Matter, Race Matters: Starbucks, Consumption and the Appeal of the Performance of Colorblindness." *Du Bois Review* 7 (2): 271–92.

———. 2011. *Everything but the Coffee: Learning about America from Starbucks.* Berkeley: University of California Press.

Slack, Enid, and Rupak Chattopadhyay, eds. 2009. *Finance and Governance of Capital Cities in Federal Systems.* Montreal: McGill-Queen's University Press.

Slater, Tom. 2009. "Missing Marcuse: On Gentrification and Displacement." *City* 13 (2–3): 293–311.

Small, Mario L., and Monica McDermott. 2006. "The Presence of Organizational Resources in Poor Urban Neighborhoods: An Analysis of Average and Contextual Effects." *Social Forces* 84 (3): 1697–1724.

Smith, Kathryn S., ed. 2010. *Washington at Home: An Illustrated History of Neighborhoods in the Nation's Capital.* Baltimore: Johns Hopkins University Press.

Smith, Kathryn S., and Marya McQuirter. 1996. *A Guide to the Historical Resources of Shaw.* Washington, DC: Thurgood Marshall Center for Service and Heritage.

Smith, Neil. 1979. "Toward a Theory of Gentrification: A Back to the City Movement by Capital, Not People." *Journal of the American Planning Association* 45 (4): 538–48.

———. 2000. *The New Urban Frontier: Gentrification and the Revanchist City.* New York: Routledge.

Smith, Sam. 1974. *Captive Capital: Colonial Life in Modern Washington.* Bloomington: Indiana University Press.

Soja, Edward W. *Seeking Spatial Justice.* Minneapolis: University of Minnesota Press.

Speck, Jeff. 2012. *Walkable City: How Downtown Can Save America, One Step at a Time.* New York: North Point Press.

Squires, Gregory D., and Derek S. Hyra. 2010. "Foreclosures—yesterday, Today and Tomorrow." *City and Community* 9 (1): 50–60.

Stack, Carol B. 1974. *All Our Kin: Strategies for Survival in a Black Community.* New York: Harper and Row.

Stiglitz, Joseph E. 2012. *The Price of Inequality: How Today's Divided Society Endangers Our Future.* New York: W. W. Norton.

Stone, Clarence N. 1989. *Regime Politics: Governing Atlanta, 1946–1988*. Lawrence: University Press of Kansas.

Sturtevant, Lisa A., and Maurice B. Champagne. 2012. "Domestic Migration to and from the Washington DC Metropolitan Area, 1985–2010." Working Paper no. 2012-01. Fairfax, VA: Center for Regional Analysis, George Mason University.

Sturtevant, Lisa A., and Yu Jin Jung. 2011. "Are We Moving Back to the City? Examining Residential Mobility in the Washington, DC Metropolitan Area." *Growth and Change* 42 (1): 48–71.

Sugrue, Thomas J. 1996. *The Origins of the Urban Crisis: Race and Inequality in Postwar Detroit*. Princeton, NJ: Princeton University Press.

Summers, Brandi T. 2016. "H Street, Main Street, and the Neoliberal Aesthetics of Cool." In Hyra and Prince 2016, pp. 299–314.

Tach, Laura. 2009. "More Than Bricks and Mortar: Neighborhood Frames, Social Processes, and the Mixed-Income Redevelopment of a Public Housing Project." *City and Community* 8 (3): 269–99.

———. 2014. "Diversity, Inequality, and Microsegregation: Dynamics of Inclusion and Exclusion in a Racially and Economically Diverse Community." *Cityscape* 16 (3): 13–45.

Talen, Emily. 2013. "Prospects for Walkable, Mixed-Income Neighborhoods: Insights from U.S. Developers." *Journal of Housing and the Built Environment* 28 (1): 79–94.

Taylor, Monique M. 2002. *Harlem: Between Heaven and Hell*. Minneapolis: University of Minnesota Press.

Taylor, Paul. 2008. *Race, Ethnicity and Campaign '08*. Washington, DC: Pew Research Center.

Taylor, Paul, Jeffrey S. Passel, Wendy Wang, Jocelyn Kiley, Gabriel Velasco, and Daniel Dockterman. 2010. *Marrying Out: One-in-Seven New U.S. Marriages Is Interracial or Interethnic*. Washington, DC: Pew Research Center.

Taylor, Peter J. 1997. "Hierarchical Tendencies among World Cities: A Global Research Proposal." *Cities* 14 (6): 323–32.

———. 2004. *World City Network: A Global Urban Analysis*. New York: Routledge.

Taylor, Peter J., Pengfei Ni, Ben Derudder, Michael Hoyler, Jin Huang, and Frank F. Witlox, eds. 2011. *Global Urban Analysis: A Survey of Cities in Globalization*. London: Earthscan.

Taylor, Ralph B., and Jillian L. Eidson. 2012. "'The Wire,' William Julius Wilson, and the Three Sobotkas: Conceptually Integrating 'Season 2: The Port' into a Macro-Level Undergraduate Communities and Crime Course." *Journal of Criminal Justice Education* 23 (3): 257–82.

Tester, Griff. 2008. "An Intersectional Analysis of Sexual Harassment in Housing." *Gender and Society* 22 (3): 349–66.

Thompson, Daniel C. 1986. *A Black Elite: A Profile of Graduates of UNCF Colleges*. Westport, CT: Greenwood Press.

Thompson, J. Phillip. 2006. *Double Trouble: Black Mayors, Black Communities, and the Call for a Deep Democracy*. New York: Oxford University Press.

Till, Karen E. 2003. "Places of Memory." In *A Companion to Political Geography*, edited by John Agnew, Katharyne Mitchell, and Gerard Toal, pp. 289–301. Malden, MA: Blackwell.

Tissot, Sylvie. 2011. "Of Dogs and Men: The Making of Spatial Boundaries in a Gentrifying Neighborhood." *City and Community* 10 (3): 265–84.

Turner, Margery A., and Lynette Rawlings. 2009. *Promoting Neighborhood Diversity: Benefits, Barriers and Strategies*. Washington, DC: Urban Institute.

Tuttle, Brad R. 2009. *How Newark Became Newark: The Rise, Fall, and Rebirth of an American City*. New Brunswick, NJ: Rutgers University Press.

US Department of State. 2011. *Foreign Consular Offices in the United States*. Washington, DC: US Department of State.

Vale, Lawrence J. 2002. *Reclaiming Public Housing: A Half Century of Struggle in Three Public Neighborhoods*. Cambridge, MA: Harvard University Press.

———. 2013. *Purging the Poorest: Public Housing and the Design Politics of Twice-Cleared Communities*. Chicago: University of Chicago Press.

Valk, Anne M. 2008. *Radical Sisters: Second-Wave Feminism and Black Liberation in Washington, D.C.* Urbana: University of Illinois Press.

Venkatesh, Sudhir, A. 2000. *American Project: The Rise and Fall of a Modern Ghetto*. Cambridge, MA: Harvard University Press.

———. 2006. *Off the Books: The Underground Economy of the Urban Poor*. Cambridge, MA: Harvard University Press.

———. 2008. *Gang Leader for a Day: A Rogue Sociologist Takes to the Streets*. New York: Penguin Press.

Versel, David, Jeannette Chapman, Lokesh Dani, and Lauren McCarthy. 2014. *Improving the Washington Region's Global Competitiveness*. Arlington, VA: Center for Regional Analysis, George Mason University.

Vertovec, Steven. 2007. "Super-Diversity and Its Implications." *Ethnic and Racial Studies* 30 (6): 1024–54.

Vigdor, Jacob L. 2002. "Does Gentrification Harm the Poor?" *Brookings-Wharton Papers on Urban Affairs*, 134–73.

———. 2013. "Weighing and Measuring the Decline in Residential Segregation." *City and Community* 12 (2): 169–77.

Wacquant, Loïc. 2008. *Urban Outcasts: A Comparative Sociology of Advanced Marginality*. Malden, MA: Polity Press.

Waters, Mary C. 1990. *Ethnic Options: Choosing Identities in America*. Berkeley: University of California Press.

Watkins-Hayes, Celeste. 2009. "Race-ing the Bootstrap Climb: Black and Latino Bureaucrats in Post-Reform Welfare Offices." *Social Problems* 56 (2): 285–310.

Weber, Lynn. 2010. *Understanding Race, Class, Gender, and Sexuality: A Conceptual Framework*. New York: Oxford University Press.

Wherry, Frederick F. 2011. *The Philadelphia Barrio: The Arts, Branding, and Neighborhood Transformation*. Chicago: University of Chicago Press.

Williams, Brett. 1988. *Upscaling Downtown: Stalled Gentrification in Washington, D.C.* Ithaca, NY: Cornell University Press.

———. 2016. "Beyond Gentrification: Investment and Abandonment on the Waterfront." In Hyra and Prince 2016, pp. 227–38.

Williams, Linda. 2011. *Critical Response III Ethnographic Imaginary: The Genesis and Genius of "The Wire."* *Critical Inquiry* 38 (1): 208–26.

Williams, Paul K. 2002. *Greater U Street*. Chicago: Arcadia.

Williams, Paul K., and Kathryn S. Smith. 2001. *City within a City: Greater U Street Heritage Trail*. Washington, DC: Cultural Tourism, DC.

Wilson, William J. 1987. *The Truly Disadvantaged: The Inner City, the Underclass, and Public Policy*. Chicago: University of Chicago Press.

———. 1996. *When Work Disappears: The World of the New Urban Poverty*. New York: Alfred A. Knopf.

Wooten, Melissa E. 2015. *In the Face of Inequality: How Black Colleges Adapt*. New York: State University of New York Press.

Wyly, Elvin K., Mona Atia, and Daniel J. Hammel. 2004. "Has Mortgage Capital Found an Inner- City Spatial Fix?" *Housing Policy Debate* 15 (3): 623–85.

Wyly, Elvin K., and Daniel J. Hammel. 2005. "Mapping Neo-liberal American Urbanism." In *Gentrification in a Global Context: The New Urban Colonialism*, edited by Rowland Atkinson and Gary Bridge, pp. 18–38. New York: Routledge.

Wyly, Elvin K., and Kathe Newman. 2006. "The Right to Stay Put, Revisited: Gentrification and Resistance to Displacement in New York City." *Urban Studies* 43 (1): 23–57.

Yin, Robert K. 2014. *Case Study Research*. Thousand Oaks, CA: Sage Publications.

Zavarella, Mario D. 1987. "The Back-to-the-City Movement Revisited." *Journal of Urban Affairs* 9 (4): 375–90.

Zukin, Sharon. 1982. *Loft Living: Culture and Capital in Urban Change*. Baltimore: Johns Hopkins University Press.

———. 1995. *The Cultures of Cities*. Malden, MA: Blackwell.

———. 2010. *Naked City: The Death and Life of Authentic Urban Places*. New York: Oxford University Press.

———. 2012. "The Spike Lee Effect: Reimagining the Ghetto." In Hutchison and Haynes 2012, pp. 137–57.